D1508245

Rethinking Liberal Education

Rethinking Liberal Education

Edited by

Nicholas H. Farnham
and
Adam Yarmolinsky

New York   Oxford
OXFORD UNIVERSITY PRESS
1996

Oxford University Press

Oxford New York
Athens Auckland Bangkok Bombay
Calcutta Cape Town Dar es Salaam Delhi
Florence Hong Kong Istanbul Karachi
Kuala Lumpur Madras Madrid Melbourne
Mexico City Nairobi Paris Singapore
Taipei Tokyo Toronto

and associated companies in
Berlin Ibadan

Copyright © 1996 by Oxford University Press, Inc.

Published by Oxford University Press, Inc.
198 Madison Avenue, New York, New York 10016

Oxford is a registered trademark of Oxford University Press

All rights reserved. No part of this publication may be reproduced,
stored in a retrieval system, or transmitted, in any form or by any means,
electronic, mechanical, photocopying, recording, or otherwise,
without the prior permission of Oxford University Press.

Library of Congress Cataloging-in-Publication Data
Rethinking liberal education / [edited by] Nicholas H. Farnham, Adam Yarmolinsky.
p.   cm.
Papers presented at a symposium held at the American Academy of
Arts and Sciences in Cambridge, Mass., in Apr. 1994.
ISBN 0-19-509772-6
1. Education, Humanistic—United States—Congresses.
2. Education, Higher—United States—Aims and objectives—
Congresses. 3. Education, Higher—United States—Curricula—
Congresses. I. Farnham, Nicholas H. II. Yarmolinsky, Adam.
LC1011.R45 1996
370.11'3'0973—dc20   95-3263

2 4 6 8 9 7 5 3 1

Printed in the United States of America
on acid-free paper

Contents

Contributors

Leon Botstein is president of Bard College, Annandale-on-Hudson, New York.

Ernest L. Boyer is president of the Carnegie Foundation for the Advancement of Teaching, Princeton, New Jersey.

Nicholas H. Farnham is director of the Educational Leadership Program of the Christian A. Johnson Endeavor Foundation, New York.

Howard Gardner is a professor at the Harvard Graduate School of Education, Cambridge, Massachusetts.

Stanley N. Katz is president of the American Council of Learned Societies. He is also a professor at Princeton University.

Bruce A. Kimball is a professor at the Warner Graduate School of Education, University of Rochester, New York.

Peter Lyman is university librarian at the University of California at Berkeley.

Susan Resneck Pierce is president of the University of Puget Sound, Washington.

Frank F. Wong was, until his death in April 1995, vice president of academic affairs at Redlands University, California.

Adam Yarmolinsky, until 1993 provost of its Baltimore campus, is a professor in the University of Maryland system. He serves as chief moderator of the Educational Leadership Program's seminars.

Rethinking Liberal Education

1

Introduction

Nicholas H. Farnham

Liberal education has always had its full share of theorists, believers, and detractors, both inside and outside the academy. The best of these have been responsible for the evolutionary development of the concept of liberal education, for its changing tradition, and for the resultant adaptation of educational institutions to serve the needs of society.

This book is the result of a meeting, primarily of believers, held at the American Academy of Arts and Sciences in Cambridge, Massachusetts, in April 1994. The reason for calling it was not simply to consider the unpleasant omens for liberal education that have been appearing as the end of a millennium is reached. A pessimist would include among them the end of the long period of economic growth for colleges, the decline of public support, the discovery that financial aid for tuition can be an Achilles' heel in times of rising costs, and the increasingly uncritical dependence of the public on the mass media and information technology, as well as a host of other external pressures and internal confusions. The meeting was called primarily to inspire further reflection on how liberal education can best continue to serve the healthy functioning of democratic society despite these apparent obstacles, for this concept still deserves a central pedestal in the educational pantheon.

Presidents and chief academic officers of eighty liberal arts undergraduate institutions participated in the meeting, along with a dozen scholars and a few leaders of educational associations. Nine of the presentations from the symposium are included in this volume, accompanied by a statement prepared by all of the participants representing their general agreement about liberal education.

The four-day symposium was sponsored by the Educational Leadership Program of the Christian A. Johnson Foundation and the American Council of Learned Societies. The Educational Leadership Program conducts research and seminars for college and school administrators. The American Council of Learned Societies supports scholarly research in the humanities.

Most of those invited to the Cambridge meeting had been through the experience of a Troutbeck seminar and therefore could come with at least some continuity of perspective as to what they believe liberal education to be about. Troutbeck is an intellectual retreat Adam Yarmolinsky and I founded ten years ago as an activity of the Educational Leadership Program. At Troutbeck, college and university leaders are invited to come in small groups to reenergize their connection with liberal education—to talk informally together about philosophy, history, and the meaning of education. Our plan was to combine a number of presidents who had been to Troutbeck with a few respected scholars and teachers who would provide intellectual cross-fertilization and to get this group to talk about where liberal education is heading in the next century.

The response was enthusiastic. "That's great," exclaimed the first college president polled about the idea over lunch. "We need to strategize about the future." "That's grand," said a professor similarly tested on another occasion, "but do you think the presidents can agree philosophically?"

Clearly, rethinking liberal education does not mean the same thing to every educator. To one it may mean primarily a strategic shift in requirements, to another the reformulation of the underlying philosophy to meet changing times. Any significant reform in education needs careful thought about both.

Consider two great episodes in educational reform in America. Charles Eliot introduced the elective principle and distribution requirements into the Harvard curriculum at the end of the last century in response to changes in educational philosophy imported from Europe. The plan was a brilliant strategic move that brought undergraduate education into line with the then-current direction for research and knowledge. Another historic change took place in the early twentieth century with the introduction of the Western civilization course requirement at Columbia College. The strategy of connecting the curriculum to culture rather than to specific disciplines represented an effort to adapt the curriculum to a different line of philosophical thinking about citizenship and knowledge. It has since had numerous imitators in other liberal arts colleges. Both these reforms represent successful strategies for bringing the institutional focus into balance with a prevailing philosophy about the nature and conditions of education.

Regrettably, education has not always been so lucky. Consider two episodes in educational reform that occurred more recently and were not successful. One was the attempt by Robert Hutchins to create a model for higher learning at the University of Chicago. Like Cardinal Newman seventy-five years earlier in Dublin, Hutchins was doomed to fail in his attempt to found a new model because he was more a philosopher than a strategist. His ideas about the curriculum did not survive to enter the mainstream of education. On the opposite side of the philosophical spectrum, the Commission on Education that President Truman created failed to bring into existence the radically democratic vision of its report, *Higher Education for American Democracy* (1947). This report called for federal and state funding to ensure that all financial barriers were removed for any American wanting a college education. Hutchins called the report "a Fourth of July oration in pedaguese." There was little support for it, either in the academy or in legislatures asked to fund it.

Successful reforms require a grounding in philosophy around which there is general agreement among teachers, scholars, and policymakers, as well as an operable strategy for enabling the institution to make that philosophy work. As the essays in this volume show, rethinking liberal education requires coming to grips with both elements. None of the essays is concerned about one element alone. Yet for the purposes of this introduction, it seems useful to separate some of the philosophical concepts explored in the papers from the strategies they propound.

An idea that may rise to the dignity of a philosophical concept—that the nature of liberal education requires exceptional flexibility in its implementation—is put forward in the first essay and is reinforced in several of them. In the next chapter, Bruce Kimball suggests that innovation is in the nature of liberal education and has been since the beginning. We cannot stand in the way of gay and lesbian studies, women's studies, African American studies, or other ethnic and area studies pushing for full-fledged academic status merely on the basis of a conflict with tradition or a discontinuity in content. Liberal education has always been a conflicted tradition involving variety and discontinuity in content.

In contrast to the emphasis on flexibility, Susan Resneck Pierce focuses on the extraordinary difficulty of maintaining integrity in liberal education. Variety and discontinuity in content do not mean that liberal education can tolerate a state of balkanization, in which content or students are separated by race, ethnicity, gender, or sexual orientation for no educationally sound reason. Nor does it mean that every social demand can be met.

Liberal education demands a curriculum oriented toward a political and social perspective, contends Leon Botstein. In the past that perspective has been human progress, he says. However, we no longer are in agreement about that view as an outcome of an educated citizenry. Botstein offers no answers but stresses the "desperate need" to forge a new understanding.

Frank Wong's essay suggests one such understanding. If liberal education is to fulfill its democratic purpose, it must cast off its links to a concept of high culture handed down from nineteenth-century Oxford. Even though the American version of high culture is nonaristocratic, it borrows from its British counterpart the vices of being "self-contained, self-perpetuating, and comfortably insulated from the rapid changes occurring in other parts of the society." American high culture, Wong argues, tends to be defined by the professoriate in place of the British aristocracy. This phenomenon has prevented a truly American tradition, based on the features of our society's cultural pluralism, from evolving.

In place of a nostalgic notion of high culture, liberal education requires a common learning experience, Stanley Katz's essay suggests. He outlines the importance of providing such an experience in a comprehensive and interrelated fashion. Traditional categories of disciplinary knowledge are no longer adequate for the curriculum, he points out. In research, "we have invented new disciplines and altered old ones." The curriculum needs to be reformulated to match these developments. At the same time he exposes some of the frustrations one encounters in trying to develop reforms among institutions that are by nature diverse and among faculties that are no longer sure about their goals.

Howard Gardner sees a goal for liberal education that is essentially the same for college as for the precollegiate years. Precollegiate reforms of recent vintage have been deficient in getting at what the author argues is the real purpose of education. They have been grounded in either a romantic desire to "get back to basics" or a progressive impulse to develop students' interests in ways that are personally and socially meaningful. While each of these approaches has its strengths and limitations, both fail to deal with the central mission of education, which Gardner posits as the "cultivation of understanding: the capacity to apply facts, concepts, skills and knowledge appropriately in new situations."

Peter Lyman finds a new requirement for liberal education in the information age: the need to come to terms with the significance of its technology. Liberal education today requires treating information technology as a culture in the broad sense. As the new communications technology transforms the production and consumption of information, liberal education must offer the educated person the ability to interpret these new texts. He suggests the need to develop critical skills that facilitate distinguishing between reality and appearances in electronic media and computer environments.

Liberal education requires teachers—lots of them, argues Adam Yarmolinsky: it "cannot be doled out to students in measured doses like vitamin supplements." There must be enough teachers to facilitate learning and to explore ideas with students. Because this goal cannot be accomplished without relatively high ratios of teachers, tutors, and mentors, it is particularly prone to financial difficulties in times of economic constraint.

Finally, Ernest Boyer explores the dimensions of a new paradigm for liberal education in an old-fashioned synonym for knowledge: scholarship. The scholarship of liberal education is broader than the scholarship of the research university; it means not just the scholarship of discovering knowledge but also the scholarship of integrating knowledge, applying knowledge, and sharing knowledge through teaching.

Taken together, these principles appear to describe an ideal model that would be almost impossible to fulfill. There are too many contrasting and even contradictory values involved. This suggests that there is no one shift in institutional or curricular focus, however dramatic, that can bring liberal education into harmony with the prevailing vision of what it ought to be. The operable strategy for bringing the institution into line must therefore work on multiple levels.

The strategies proffered in these essays do indeed come in various shapes and sizes. One method of regaining flexibility without losing integrity is outlined by Kimball in his proposal that the academic major be made less intrusive in the curriculum if not abandoned altogether. Both Katz and Yarmolinsky argue for increasing the flexibility of departmental organization in the institution, allowing the organization of the institution to approximate the subject matter of liberal education more closely. Pierce warns against the pressures for casual innovation that surround colleges and tend toward activities destructive to the institution. She suggests always weighing an innovation against the institution's explicit mission.

The essays contain several proposals to help make an orderly curriculum reflect the murky social and political reality of our time. All the authors share a sense of urgency about doing so. Wong would integrate the liberal education component of the institution with the research, vocational, and professional parts, thereby restoring what he sees as the early New England approach of combining intellectual and practical knowledge. Katz would integrate the first two years of college and the last two of high school into a single liberal arts unit. In calling for this change, he points out that liberal education is the logical focus for all of these years. He surmises that in commingling with schools to produce the combined curriculum, colleges would gain a stronger focus on pedagogy than they now have.

Botstein surmounts his considerable pessimism about being able to do very much to propose what might be termed an existential strategy. If we can know who we are, we might be able to conceive who someone else is, partially, and to move on from there to understand a little about political and social reality. Botstein suggests a curriculum that begins with questions about our identity.

Personal identity is also the jumping-off place for a curricular strategy proposed by Gardner—a scheme that uses seven essential issues to implement his goal of cultivating our understanding. Both Botstein and Gardner seem to be postulating that personal identity today is more knowable and less disputable than anything else—that it constitutes the bedrock of contemporary reality. This idea suggests that the one thing we surely will not be prone to dismiss as a relativist proposition is our own existence, as we move into a new age more culturally diverse than the present. The question "who am I" may be not only the beginning but also the ultimate destination of a curriculum when political and social perspectives have disintegrated.

Understandably, the images derived from information technology often appear to us more real than the propositions of classical philosophy; consequently, we are tempted to see computers as substitutes for teachers, as role models for critical thinking, and even as evaluators of abstract truth. It is refreshing to find Lyman turning the tables and asking liberal education to evaluate this technology. He outlines some interesting possibilities, including adding a new curricular component to help students sort out the claims about truth that are being made by digital forms of knowledge.

Yarmolinsky presents two radical and concrete measures by which an institution may curtail its spending without shirking its obligation to have a teaching focus. One would place a greater burden on the faculty to participate in the hard financial decisions; the other would realign some of the faculty around new units of instruction, thereby freeing them from the burden of existing alliances.

Boyer's redefining of liberal learning as an expanded form of scholarship has a strategic element. By insisting that discovery, integration, application, and teaching are equal parts of the academic gown, colleges and universities will create a climate in which this expanded form of scholarship will happen not just among faculty but among students as well.

The reaction of the symposium to the proceedings is contained in the statement that makes up the appendix. This statement was hammered out in small group discussions during the course of the event and adopted in the final plenary session. It is a distillation of the total experience, not just the content of the individual chapters in this book. It demonstrates that educational reform today is indeed an incremental process, one that is going on now in many institutions. Rethinking liberal education does not require tearing down the old but, rather, making adjustments in it. The statement reflects the practical, reasoned approach of administrators willing to examine sometimes radical propositions and reflecting how to do more with the resources they have or anticipate having. As such, it seems to us a pragmatic and yet optimistic declaration that may provide a guidepost in the journey to a new century.

2

A Historical Perspective

Bruce A. Kimball

While envisioning liberal education for the twenty-first century, we must not forget that our visions are shaped and conditioned by historical context, or tradition. Indeed, the very fact that we discuss something called "liberal education" demonstrates the influence of tradition. The general precept is well known, but the nature of this particular tradition is often misconstrued, due not only to neglect but also to genuine intentions to rescue or correct the tradition. To be sure, this particular tradition is long and complex, and it is doubtful that anyone can claim to understand fully the current situation of liberal education in light of its tradition, particularly in this era of postmodern interpretivism and deconstruction. This brief essay will therefore make two, more modest claims. First, I hope to demonstrate that, contrary to the conventional perception, the tradition of liberal education is not uniform and continuous but full of variety, discontinuity, and innovation. It has been and is a conflicted tradition. Second, I wish to argue conversely that innovative proposals made for liberal education at the end of the twentieth century often belong to the tradition, although this heritage is generally not recognized by either the proponents or their opponents.

These two points, I suggest, indicate the richness and complexity of the tradition and its value, as well as its influence, for those seeking to envision what the next century of liberal education may and should hold. This is not to say that the tradition is boundless, that liberal education is all things for all situations, or that it is without blemishes or addictions, even cancerous growths. But liberal education is what we have and what we are, after centuries of trying to get it right, and we can no more wipe the slate clean and start entirely afresh here than we can in any other human endeavor. We can certainly try to change and improve in the coming century, but change and improvement imply understanding of and comparison with the past. To provide perspective on the recent experience of liberal education in the hope of informing such normative judgments regarding the content, the structure, and the process of liberal education is the task of this essay.

The historical variety and discontinuity of the content of liberal education is demonstrated quintessentially in recurring debates between "ancients" and "moderns," or "battles of the books," in the memorable phrase of Jonathan Swift, who published *The Battle of the Books* in 1704. During the late nineteenth and early twentieth centuries, a debate of this type raged in the United States over whether Greek and Latin classics would continue to be required for the bachelor's degree in liberal arts.[1] But this debate, which has historically subtended several different disciplinary and intellectual perspectives, is more conventionally associated with the seventeenth- and eighteenth-century confrontations between emerging natural sciences and humanistic disciplines, on the one hand, and between classical and "modern" literature, on the other. While these confrontations may have more directly influenced liberal education in our own time, historians have come to attribute the origins of the ancients/moderns debate to fourteenth-century Italy, where budding humanism began to challenge the regnant scholasticism of the universities. Even this attribution, however, overlooks the debate that took place during the Middle Ages between *antiqui* and *moderni* who advocated conserving and speculative interpretations, respectively, of the *artes liberales*.[2]

Some will be skeptical of the variety and discontinuity appearing in these battles; they will assert that there is essential continuity in a bookish and canonical approach to liberal education. In response, it may be wondered whether such skeptics are anachronistically demeaning educators in the past, who surely thought they were disagreeing about something significant. Meanwhile, others will respond that, bookish or not, the assignment of reading in a curriculum makes a difference. It matters whether one reads Plato or Marx, Machiavelli or Virginia Woolf. Furthermore, these debates addressed not merely the composition of reading lists but also the question of whether the content of liberal education referred to a method of inquiry no less than, or even more than, a body of texts. This question was certainly involved in the lengthy debate concerning the role of natural sciences in the liberal arts, while it arose even more prominently during the late twelfth- and thirteenth-century reformulation of the liberal arts by the *moderni* in the newly founded universities.

At the heart of that reformulation was training in dialectical inquiry within the formal structure of the disputation, which employed as its primary tool the "new logic"—the deductive reasoning related in several of Aristotle's newly recovered treatises. Although these and other treatises of Aristotle were read to and glossed for medieval students, who copied them, it is a serious error to overlook the essential methodological purpose of this scholastic liberal education. No less serious is the error of inferring from the highly formal character of the deductive syllogism and the disputation that this method was merely "verbalistic and trivial—a kind of word chess—a verbal game." Such an inference is, in part, the legacy of older historiography that deprecated the Middle Ages and has not yet been superseded by the appreciative medieval historiography of recent decades.[3]

To recognize the integrity of scholastic method, one need only recall that modern courts of law employ a similar, highly formal, "verbalistic . . . kind of word chess." Whatever one's view of courts of law, the fact remains that they constitute the sanctioned means for resolving disputes in our society and that they share with scholastic disputations putatively neutral rules for conducting debate in order to resolve an issue on its merits apart from the interests of the parties involved. We do not seem to be able to improve on this approach. By the same token, if one has ever come away from a debate over some contentious ethical issue, such as abortion, or from a debate between candidates for elective office and felt dissatisfied because the two parties did not even identify their fundamental differences, let alone address them, then one can appreciate the scholastic disputation. The scholastic disputation required that the questions be precisely identified, that each party restate the other's view before proceeding, that both parties specify and enumerate the reasons for their views, and that each party specifically address each reason enumerated by the other and explain why it is not convincing, all the while employing rules of deductive reasoning in order to avoid fallacious arguments. After discussing these scholastic requirements with me in a conference, one undergraduate who was reluctantly preparing to make her class presentation on scholastic method suddenly exclaimed enthusiastically, "This is great! Everyone should debate this way all the time!" Whether or not that is true, this undergraduate had come to appreciate, along with scholastic method, the variety and discontinuity in the "traditional" content of liberal education.[4]

I now want to address the traditionalism of recent innovative proposals for this content, and it bears mention at the outset that much of the "postmodern" thinking denoted by such terms as "deconstruction," "hermeneutics," and "interpretivism" echoes the views of ancient sophists such as Gorgias and Protagoras, whose indirect influence on the liberal arts of grammar and rhetoric has been significant.[5] Somewhat more directly related to the content of current undergraduate education is the new claim that Greek learning, traditionally regarded as the fount of the liberal arts, stems from Africa, primarily via Egypt. The recent debate about the merits of this claim need not be repeated here. What has not been sufficiently appreciated is that this "Egyptian-spoils" claim has a significant place within the tradition of liberal education, specifically in the Christian appropriation of pagan learning in Antiquity.[6]

Faced with pagan criticism asserting that such sophisticated Christian doctrines as monotheism were derived from Greek philosophy, early Christians invoked the popular legend that Plato had traveled to Egypt; then they added the gloss that while in Egypt, Plato took from the Hebrew scriptures his doctrines that fit Christian teachings. Justin (c. 100–c. 165), Clement of Alexandria (d. c. 215), Origen (c. 185–c. 254), and Ambrose (c. 340–97) thus turned the pagan criticism back on itself by reversing the direction of the borrowing, and Augustine (354–430) transmitted the argument in his influential *On Christian Learning*:

> Did not the famous bishop [Ambrose], when he had considered the history of the pagans and found that Plato had traveled in Egypt during the time of Jeremias, show that Plato had probably been introduced to our literature by Jeremias so that he was able to teach or to write doctrines that are justly recommended? . . . Thus from a consideration

of times it becomes more credible that the Platonists took from our literature whatever they said that is good and truthful than that Our Lord Jesus Christ learned from them.[7]

Subsequent Christian writers on the *artes liberales,* such as Cassiodorus (487–583), relied on Augustine's authority and bolstered claims for the biblical origins of the seven liberal arts with citations that included Proverbs 9:1 ("Wisdom has built herself a house, she has erected seven pillars") and Exodus 25:37 ("You are to make lamps for it, seven of them, and set them so they throw their light"). Another claim, less daring than the idea that Plato had drawn directly from the Hebrews, was the argument, common in the ancient world, that the Greeks generally derived their learning from the Egyptians. By supplying the premise that the Egyptians had derived much of their learning from the Hebrews during their enslavement in Egypt, certain Christians inferred that Greek learning came from the Hebrews via the Egyptians. These arguments were credited to different degrees at different times. Augustine, for example, later retreated from the view I quoted above. Nevertheless, the claim for Egyptian origins of Greek learning was a commonplace for centuries in Christian discussion of the liberal arts.[8] The recent innovative claim for "Afroasiatic" origins of Greek learning thus employs a traditional strategy and rationale, albeit a more sophisticated scholarly apparatus.

Another new proposal for the content of liberal education that can be located within the tradition is the incorporation of knowledge from other cultures. It scarcely needs to be said that this issue has become highly politicized and has engendered strong feelings and words on the part of advocates and opponents. All the more striking, then, is the reformulation of the Christian liberal arts in light of pagan and Islamic learning during the twelfth and thirteenth centuries. This reformulation has been carefully studied and analyzed by twentieth-century historiographers, but its radical character has generally been overlooked in discussions about infusing liberal education with material from other cultures, to the discredit of both advocates and opponents.

This reformulation was not a mere shift in Christian apologetics. It involved a sea change in conceiving the significance, the nature, and the sources of knowledge, of method, and of inquiry. Nor was it a kind of indirect or subconscious borrowing; the external influence was explicit and direct. Nor was the reformulation accomplished without conflict, even official interdiction.

Reading Aristotle's ethics, natural philosophy, and metaphysics was officially condemned due to their humanistic and pragmatic views, in addition to specific points of conflict with established Christian doctrine. Nor was the *status quo ante* of slight stature or brief tenure; the "seven liberal arts" that Aquinas (1225–74) declared to be no longer sufficient as curricular or epistemic schema had framed liberal education for some eight centuries. Finally, the role of the pagan and the infidel in reformulating the content of the liberal arts was not derogated or diminished but was recognized by the honorific titles of "the Philosopher" for Aristotle (383–322 B.C.) and "the Commentator" for Averroës (Ibn Rushd, 1126–98).[9] This recognition, it should be emphasized, was conferred during the period between the late twelfth and late thirteenth centuries, when eight of the nine European crusades were conducted against the Muslims. Islamic culture was certainly regarded as "infidel" at the same time that masters of the liberal arts receptively translated, employed, and honored Islamic texts and their authors. We modern masters have our own pagans and infidels, of course. Those who argue that teaching them would invigorate the liberal arts need only look to the tradition that those excluding them sometimes claim to defend.

Consideration of the twelfth- and thirteenth-century reformulation of the liberal arts leads directly to the topic of the structure of liberal education, because that reformulation emphasized the organization of knowledge to such a degree that the structure itself became the content and the distinction between structure and content dissolved. This point is well known, and handbooks and essays about liberal education often recount how "three philosophies"—natural, moral, and metaphysical—became enshrined as categories in liberal education and were combined with the seven liberal arts in the course of the thirteenth century. What is not appreciated is the innovative character of this epistemic and curricular organization. Scholastic philosophers did not borrow this formulation; rather, it appears that they integrated the Aristotelian division of philosophy (theoretical, practical, productive) with the Stoic (natural, moral, logical) and then combined that integrated system with the long-standing seven arts. In this fashion, they arrived at an original formulation, which was ingeniously rationalized as learning a deductive method of inquiry through the *trivium* and extending that method to number through the *quadrivium*, to sensory experience through natural philosophy, to human affairs through moral philosophy, and finally to the nature of being itself through metaphysics.[10] It is worth repeating that this structure and rationale have many antecedents but no direct precedent in Greek, Christian, or Islamic sources.

If the three philosophies represent an innovative structure in the tradition of liberal education, the antecedent schema of seven liberal arts betokens the variety and discontinuity in the structure of liberal education at a much earlier period. Throughout antiquity there existed little consensus over the number, the identity, or the order of the liberal arts.[11] Aristotle noted the disagreement over the content, structure, and purposes of education in his day, and Cicero (102–43 B.C.) stated nearly a dozen different versions of the liberal arts. A different dozen were subsequently offered by Philo of Alexandria (20 B.C.–A.D. 50), and two centuries later Clement of Alexandria (d. c. A.D. 215) listed the arts in a half dozen different ways. Only about the time of Augustine and Martianus Capella in the early fifth century did a consensus emerge around the *septem artes liberales*.[12]

Consequently, traditional structures of liberal education, such as the three philosophies and seven liberal arts, have not been the object of unbroken allegiance or duration, contrary to the intimations of many twentieth-century educators, particularly Progressive educators. The traditional structures have been discontinuous and innovative. Ironically enough, this point requires emphasis, not so much in regard to those older, traditional structures but in regard to modern, traditional structures to which twentieth-century professors cling. Perhaps the exemplar in this regard is the academic major.

The academic major is a relatively recent innovation, having arisen near the beginning of this century as an outgrowth of modern academic disciplines and departments. Establishment of the major was also a reaction to the fragmentation of liberal education that arose in the late nineteenth century through widespread adoption of the "elective principle," whereby undergraduates could choose their courses. The balancing of election with a major was signaled by the retirement of Charles W. Eliot, champion of the former, and the inauguration of Abbott Lawrence Lowell, advocate of the latter, as president of Harvard in 1909. Within a decade, the now-conventional system of distribution and concentration was widely adopted,[13] and today we seem to take for granted the allegiance to and duration of this century-old structure, while many wonder why earlier professors clung mindlessly, and for such a long time, to the seven liberal arts and three philosophies. Indeed, it is striking that amid the late-twentieth-century cacophony of debate about undergraduate education—even about the academic major itself—no report or study, to my knowledge, has seriously considered doing away with the academic major.[14] Meanwhile, considerable evidence suggests that the academic major is a fossil.

We know that the academic disciplines on which the major is based are "blurring," merging, being reconceived and reconfigured. This blurring is particularly evident in the humanities and social sciences, where the development is generally celebrated. But even in the sciences—notwithstanding their familiar and seemingly firm delineation into mathematics, biology, chemistry, and physics,—departments and majors can now be found in physical biology, biological physics, biochemistry, physical chemistry, chemical physics, mathematical biology, mathematical chemistry, and so forth. The disciplines are blurring here as well. Meanwhile, science departments are often heard to lobby for increasing the number of courses required for their major, on the one hand, due to the expansion of knowledge in their fields. Yet scientists affirm, on the other hand, that no one can command all the knowledge even in a subfield of mathematics, biology, chemistry, or physics. In light of this expansion of scientific knowledge, already beyond the ken of any one scientist, the call to increase the number of courses in the science major seems analogous to arguing that twelve courses is closer than ten to infinity. This paradox, like the blurring of the disciplines, raises questions about the rationale for the structure of the science major.[15]

There is reason to doubt not only the principled rationale for academic majors as foundations of coherent disciplines but also the instrumental reasons for continuing those majors. Professional schools in medicine, law, and business do not require specific majors and even discourage prospective applicants from selecting a major designed to prepare them for the profession. Don't try to learn medicine, law, business, and so forth as an undergraduate, say the leading professional schools; we will take care of that. Broaden yourself and prepare for life in general. The instrumental rationale for academic majors is fast weakening in regard to Ph.D. programs as well, particularly in the humanities and social sciences, where disciplines are blurring most rapidly and where the reservoir of applicants is becoming shallow in some fields. More important preparation for Ph.D. study than an undergraduate major in the corresponding field is one's development of the ability to reason, the command of language, a quantitative capacity, and a deep well of general knowledge.

Finally, students are simply not pursuing academic majors in the liberal arts. In the vast majority of colleges and universities throughout the country, arts and sciences departments teach service courses and nurture a handful of majors, whose existence serves to console the faculty that it is still a disciplinary department like the one from which the faculty earned their Ph.D.s. In response to this exodus of undergraduates out of liberal arts majors, some colleges have introduced general concentrations in "humanities," "Western civilization," or "social science" in the hopes of enticing more students to remain in the liberal arts under fewer strictures, a process that contributes to the blurring phenomenon just described.

Consequently, the principled rationale, the instrumental rationale, and the actual phenomenon of the academic major seem to be expiring. The fossilized structure of majors organized around disciplinary departments still exists, even though principle, utility, and student preferences suggest that it is nearing extinction. "So why keep the fossil on display?" one must ask the hundreds of colleges and universities where only a handful of students show up to view the exhibit. Liberal arts faculties, it appears, cling resolutely to this, their own traditional structure of liberal education, not appreciating that discontinuity and innovation have historically characterized such structures and that the academic major may be no more innovative, compelling, or enduring than the three philosophies or the seven liberal arts.

Conversely, recent innovative proposals concerning the structure of liberal education have a tradition. For example, women's studies, African American studies, and ethnic and area studies of various types have begun to petition for status as full-fledged academic disciplines. In certain respects, these petitions themselves belong to the tradition: Christine de Pizan (1365–1420), Bathsua Pell Makin (1608?–75?), and Virginia Woolf, among others, eloquently argued that the structure of liberal education, properly understood, includes the experience of the "other." Thus, Pizan portrayed Lady Reason identifying many a woman who "had such a noble mind and so loved and devoted herself to study that she mastered all seven liberal arts." Further, said Lady Reason, "Rest assured, dear friend, that many noteworthy and great sciences and arts have been discovered through the understanding and subtlety of women, both in cognitive speculation, demonstrated in writing,

and in the arts, manifested in manual works of labor. I will give
you plenty of examples." And in the seventeenth century, in the
first treatise in English that argued on behalf of higher education
for women, Makin wrote:

> Why should the seven Liberal Arts be expressed in Womens Shapes?
> Doubtless this is one reason; women were the Inventors of many of these
> Arts, and the promoters of them, and since have studyed them, and
> attained to an excellency in them: And being thus adorned and beautified
> with these Arts, as a testimony of our gratitude for their Invention, and as
> a token of honour for their Proficiency; we make Women the emblems of
> these things, having no fitter Hieroglyphick to express them by.[16]

Notwithstanding these examples, it may be capricious to suggest that tradition incorporates the responses and criticism aris-
ing from those excluded from the tradition. The current appeals
that women experience should inform liberal education and may
therefore constitute a more genuinely innovative proposal for either content or structure than any discussed earlier.

Be that as it may, the traditionalism of the variety and discontinuity of the structure of liberal education is revealed by consideration of the petitions mentioned here. The formal debate
prompted by such petitions tends to focus on the questions of
what is the nature and definition of an academic discipline and
whether the petitioning field fits that nature and definition. Meanwhile, it is generally recognized that the outcome of the formal
debate will entail significant political and financial implications
for the institution and for the individuals. But the influence of
these implications on the formal debate, particularly concerning
the nature and definition of an academic discipline, is often not
carefully considered or, at least, carefully stated. Thus, a few new
disciplines, such as computer science, arose almost by spontaneous generation and gained disciplinary status in liberal education due to the relevance and marketability of their subject matter,
which simply overwhelmed initial resistance and thorough debate
about whether they fit some notion of an academic discipline. In
addition, the argument, however muted, that the increasing com-
puterization of society justifies the establishment of computer
science departments is like the argument that the increasing
cultural diversity of our society justifies establishing departments
that address the new cultures. However, this likeness has not
generally been persuasive or even noticed, although the latter
argument has been made by some advocates of multiculturalism,

who invoke the demographics of the "New Majority" on behalf of teaching these new areas.[17]

More persuasive than these few recent precedents demonstrating political and financial implications in the debate over the new studies is that the petitions on their behalf recall the long-standing variety and innovation in the structure of liberal education. Most of the current departments and disciplines of the arts and sciences are adolescents, historically speaking, having arisen in the late nineteenth and early twentieth centuries. It was not until that point that psychology emerged from philosophy and that modern language departments appeared, prompted by the founding of the Modern Language Association in 1883. "The coming of the vernacular language into an assured position . . . is not yet everywhere admitted; even in the countries where it is not assailed directly, there are sharp controversies as to the status of such study," noted one observer in 1911. Meanwhile, the disciplines of economics, history, political science, and sociology were only gradually hatching out from their nineteenth-century nest in "political economy" and "moral philosophy." Among the some 600 colleges and universities in the United States during the 1910s, only one-quarter claimed to teach something called "political science," merely one-tenth "sociology," and less than one-tenth "anthropology." The emergence of all these new fields was shaped as much by circumstance and opportunism as by epistemic imperatives.[18]

Given this background, the approach of deriving a definition of "academic discipline" from the current panoply of arts and sciences and then evaluating new fields by that measure may involve a serious anachronism about the organization of the liberal arts. What appears to some disciplinarians to be the evolution of academic disciplines through a kind of epistemic selection may also be interpreted as a kind of winners' history. The structure of liberal education has been various and discontinuous; it might even be said that the emergence of new fields calls the structure into question, rather than vice versa. In any case, a necessary step in considering the status of new fields is reexamining the nature and stability of the structure of liberal education, rather than assuming that the structure is natural and stable. In the late twentieth century, as suggested here in regard to the academic major, all signs indicate that our present structure is undergoing dramatic transformation, yet this indication rarely seems to inform the consideration of petitions from new fields for disciplinary status.

In the process of liberal education, no less than in its content and structure, the variety and innovation of the tradition is evident, and the lecture, often regarded as uncomplicated and conventional, demonstrates this point convincingly. Criticism of the lecture has been voiced loudly throughout the twentieth century, and by 1972 a review of the research attempting to evaluate the effectiveness of the lecture listed ninety-one studies, apart from hundreds of polemical and expository essays on the topic. Amid this literature, perhaps the most persistent strain of criticism is directed against the underlying pedagogical model of "transmission" from teacher to student implied by the lecture—a model that Paulo Friere called "the banking concept of education" and that he linked to oppressive and hierarchical personal relations in the larger society.[19] Within the academy, criticism of "transmission" has been heard most vociferously from advocates of case method teaching, whose popularity has grown inversely to that of lecturing, both in professional fields and in liberal education. "Certainly, [case method] is vastly superior to the mind-numbing lecture system it replaced," these advocates hold.[20]

This inverse relationship between the lecture and case method was observed soon after the invention and adoption of case method teaching in law by Josef Redlich, who conducted the most penetrating study of the early development of case method for the Carnegie Foundation for the Advancement of Teaching. A German-trained law professor from Austria, Redlich expressed regret about the trend; he argued for the introduction of lecture courses into the legal curriculum and suggested that the degree of reliance on lectures indicated the "scientific" character of the jurisprudence in American law schools.[21] However, Redlich's opinion did not influence the future course of case method instruction in the United States.

What *was* influential was the gradual adoption of case method from law by Harvard Business School, which increasingly deprecated and eschewed lecturing during the twentieth century. In the course of this displacement of lecturing by case method, a number of advocates in the Harvard Business School informed case method teaching with concepts and metaphors drawn from John Dewey and Progressive education: that knowledge is dynamic, multiform, and relative; that learning requires the "active participation" of the student; that the instructor must appeal to the student's interest; that conceptual learning comes primarily through experience and implementation; that learning is a cooperative and democratic enterprise; and that, in light of the foregoing points, the presentation of problems to students is the chief means of teaching.

> What these points seemed to imply about lecturing was that the mere act of listening to wise statements and sound advice does little for anyone. In the process of learning, the learner's dynamic cooperation is required. . . . It would be easy to accept the unanalyzed assumption that by passing on, [through] lectures and readings . . . the accumulated experience and wisdom of those who have made business their study, the desired results could be achieved. . . . This assumption, however, rests on another, decidedly questionable one: namely, the assumption that it is possible by a simple process of telling to pass on knowledge in a useful form. This is the great delusion of the ages. If the learning process is to be effective, something dynamic must take place in the learner. . . . We cannot effectively use the insight and knowledge of others; it must be our knowledge and insight that we use. . . . The case plan of instruction may be described as democratic in distinction to the telling method, which is in effect dictatorial or patriarchal.[22]

In addition to these invidious points of comparison between lecturing and case method, it was frequently said that cases may legitimately be interpreted in different ways. This doctrine that cases give rise to "multiple interpretations" and that "following the business tradition there is no one 'right' answer in discussions of decision-making cases" was then carried over into the most recent adoptions of case method by other fields in professional and liberal education.[23]

Before attempting to demonstrate the variety and innovation within the traditional process of lecturing, which such recent critics ignore, it is worthwhile to note the incoherence of their invidious criticism. The first point of incoherence is the assumption that lecturing involves "transmission" while case method, for instance, does not. Yet it is well known that case-method classes are often quite large, sometimes more than sixty students. If we take a modest thirty students for the class size and two hours for the class period, it is evident that, on average, each student may talk for only four minutes and must listen for 116 minutes. Students in a case method class must spend most of their time listening to someone else transmitting material to them, so the problem with lecturing cannot derive merely from its involving "transmission."

The second point of incoherence lies in the assumption that listening does not involve the student actively and dynamically.

Surely most students would affirm that rock music makes "something dynamic take place" in the listener; therefore, the act of listening per se cannot be considered passive. More to the point, virtually everyone can recall an occasion when they have listened to a speaker for an extended period of time and been involved, informed, and inspired. One thinks, for example, of Martin Luther King Jr. giving his "I have a dream" speech in Washington, D.C. Doubtless, one can also recall lectures that have been as compelling, if less emotionally moving. The act of listening itself does not preclude involvement by the learner.

The third point of incoherence lies in the inconsistency toward interpretivism. The interpretive approach is both endorsed and overlooked: cases are said to be interpreted in several ways, while lectures are assumed to be transmitted without interpretation. This inconsistency is compounded in statements asserting that lectures "convey information . . . to students, but [students] do not analyze, synthesize, or evaluate it."[24] Yet it is difficult to see how either conveying or interpreting can avoid involving analysis, synthesis, and evaluation. In fact, critics of the lecture method would do better to fault lecturing not on the basis that transmission occurs but that it does not and cannot occur—that lecturers intend to transmit their material but cannot. Such criticism, which I have never encountered, would be perhaps more significant, but admittedly it would have to apply equally to other processes in liberal education and would require a thorough rethinking of case method teaching as well. Be that as it may, most defenders of the lecture endorse the idea of transmission, arguing that teachers know something worth telling to students. Consequently, both critics and defenders of the lecture tend to assume that lecturing involves transmission of material from teacher to student, notwithstanding certain incoherent aspects of the criticism.

Turning now to the traditional process, let us observe that the academic lecture, in a formal sense, originated in the *lectio* of the medieval university, and transmission of material was of course involved, particularly due to the reliance on expensive, handwritten texts in the age before printing.[25] However, it is crucial to recognize that, from the very founding of the universities, interpretation was explicitly regarded as being concomitant with transmission. This point is well conveyed in the conventional method of lecturing described by a thirteenth-century master to his students at the University of Bologna:

it is my purpose to teach you faithfully, and in a kindly manner, in which instruction the following order has customarily been observed by the ancient and modern doctors and particularly by my master, which method I shall retain. First, I shall give you the summaries of each [topic] before I come to the text. Second, I shall put forth well and distinctly and in the best terms I can the purport of each [topic]. Third, I shall read the text in order to correct it. Fourth, I shall briefly restate the meaning. Fifth, I shall solve conflicts, adding general matters . . . and subtle and useful distinctions and questions with the solutions, so far as divine Providence shall assist me. And if any [topic] is deserving of a review by reason of its fame or difficulty, I shall reserve it for an afternoon review.[26]

Although this complex combination of transmission and interpretation was sustained by the *praelectio* among Jesuits and among humanists, such as Desiderius Erasmus,[27] the university practice of lecturing declined considerably over time, leading to such criticism as the often-cited remarks of Samuel Johnson, which were recorded by Boswell in the eighteenth century.[28]

Having arisen as an innovative practice in the thirteenth century and then declined, lecturing underwent further discontinuity in the American colleges whose pedagogy was dominated by recitation, with some declamation on themes. In fact, lecturing was introduced into American education as an innovative process complementary to those prevailing modes.[29] In legal education, for example, lectures on the common law, which had been introduced to Oxford in 1758, were held for the first time in America in 1782 at Tapping Reeve's proprietary law school in Connecticut, and as Josef Redlich happily noted, they constituted a notable advance over the apprenticeship model that had previously obtained in the colonies.[30] Early in the nineteenth century, colleges began offering "courses of lectures," which were appended to the regular curriculum and usually devoted to "modern" subjects. In this fashion, "modern" content and "modern" process were correlated in college catalogues, and these "courses of lectures" appeared with increasing regularity and prominence through the mid-nineteenth century, signifying that recitation remained the conventional process of liberal education but that resistance to unorthodox "modern" studies was gradually weakening.[31]

This eighteenth- and nineteenth-century innovation of the lecture required the professor to interpret and transmit a topic, rather than a text, and thus involved a new dimension of analysis and synthesis, if not originality. The "intensive and systematic" preparations that John Quincy Adams made between 1805 and

1808 for his year of lectures as Boylston Professor of Rhetoric and Oratory at Harvard College demonstrate the weight of responsibility that lecturers felt in this regard. The ancillary yet leavening role that the lectures and lecturer played in the mid-nineteenth-century colleges was both mirrored and reinforced by the contemporaneous vocation of public lecturer. This short-lived vocation served as a way station for intellectuals such as Ralph Waldo Emerson, who found the ministry no longer, and the college faculty not yet, a suitable position for their inclinations and talents.[32]

This innovation in educational process was further stimulated by the often-misconstrued example of the German university, where the lecture (*Vorlesung*) became "the systematic presentation of a growing field of knowledge by the research workers or advanced students in the field." Indeed, Friedrich Paulsen argued in his acclaimed *German Universities* (trans. 1906) that the lecture was not only compatible with but also necessary for "the independent acquisition and augmentation of knowledge" in a university devoted to "the principle of freedom of research and teaching."[33] American reformers embraced this idea early on. In 1825, George Ticknor, who had been impressed by the rigor and stimulation of lectures at the University of Göttingen, endorsed the lecture system at Harvard, while criticizing two central features of that system: that students were compelled to attend lectures and that they were not compelled to take notes. Likewise, at the University of Michigan during the 1850s, reforming president Henry Tappan established university lectures, which he associated with the German university and with intellectual rigor and stimulation. At the end of the nineteenth century Americans were still looking to German university lectures for models of process, even as the tradition of lecturing was once again changing dramatically.[34]

At that point, sustained criticism of the lecture as a process of liberal education began to appear for the first time. Paulsen took note of this new phenomenon in Germany, and in 1890, Henry Sidgwick published what appears to be the first widely circulated criticism in English. Sidgwick began his "Lecture against Lecturing" by observing that his view "was not shared by most of the persons whose experience give them adequate means of forming a judgment; but . . . I think it now desirable to publish it—giving due warning to the reader that it is a heresy." And one of the early respondents called Sidgwick's heresy "an original and suggestive essay against the system of professorial lectures."[35] When such criticism began to appear in the United States, its tentative tone was coupled with acknowledgment of popular dissatisfaction: "As a means of imparting information the academic lecture . . . occupies an important and conspicuous place in modern university teaching. There is a widespread feeling, however, shared alike by teacher and student, that lectures on the whole are irksome and unprofitable."[36]

Criticism of the lecture, fueled at least in part by the rise of pragmatism and by new doctrines in psychology, subsequently became such a dominant theme in discussion of process in liberal education that it appears today to be a traditional complaint against a uniform and enduring phenomenon. In fact, however, the variety, discontinuity, and innovation among the scholastic *lectio*, the collegiate "course of lectures," the nineteenth-century university *Vorlesung*, and the twentieth-century pedagogical staple are manifest.

Conversely, the traditionalism of certain innovative proposals for process in liberal education is apparent. One of the leading contenders, for example, is Gerald Graff's noteworthy proposal that educators should "teach the conflicts."[37] Drawing upon the broad movement in academic thinking represented by literary theory, hermeneutics, and poststructuralism, Graff insightfully observes that the conflicts now roiling within many academic departments over the nature of knowledge and the disciplines are generally not presented to the students. Rather, such conflicts are normally withheld by the faculty in order to maintain the appearance that the faculty have some consensus, and therefore understanding, about what ought to be known, taught, and learned. Graff proposes that such conflicts ought to be presented in the curriculum, even placed at the heart of liberal education, inasmuch as they constitute, he says, what the disciplines are now really about. Moreover, this presentation ought to include the actual process of debate and conflict among the faculty themselves, rather than reserving or hiding any disagreements and uncertainties from the students. Through this approach, Graff maintains, liberal education becomes authentic, because it becomes what the liberal arts teachers are actually thinking and studying.

This proposal to "teach the conflicts" certainly differs from much of the tradition of liberal education, which, in many periods like the current one, has not encouraged faculty to expose their disagreements about the formal curriculum. The entrance of

"modern" languages and sciences into the nineteenth-century
American colleges through student societies, adjunct scientific
schools, and vacation terms exemplifies the phenomenon of institutions preserving the formal curriculum from the conflicts that
were then dominating intellectual and educational discussion.
However, the tradition is not uniform in this respect. In the residential colleges and halls that were established around scholastic
universities during the fourteenth, fifteenth, and sixteenth centuries, tutors, who themselves often taught in the university, presented to resident students the humanist and religious learning
that contravened, if not contradicted, the teaching that the same
tutors gave in their university classes. When the significance of
university degrees eroded, this ancillary tutoring became part of
the formal liberal education, and ultimately tutors assumed the
place of professors in the teaching staff of colleges in the American
colonies.[38]

The formal incorporation of "teaching the conflicts" is exemplified even more clearly in the disputations of the thirteenth-
century universities. The contentiousness of the scholastic masters has often been lamented due to its contribution to the ossi-
fication of scholastic philosophy. Yet this very contentiousness,
perhaps not unlike that of certain modern advocates of the movements noted here, fostered the public display of disputes among
the masters and students in the formal setting of the university
disputations, which served pedagogically to give both masters and
students examples of and practice in the process of liberal education. Also, the scholastic liberal education emphasized structure
and process at least as much as content—and this emphasis is
shared by many advocates of the movements that have led to the
proposal to "teach the conflicts."

Another example of the traditionalism of innovative proposals
for process in liberal education lies in the recent emphasis on
building community. Over the past decade there have been loud
and persistent calls for "the creation and strengthening of communities *within* colleges" and the transformation of the college into
"a community of learning," a "community of imagination," and "a
moral community."[39] Not only do such current proposals belong to
the tradition but also in this last instance I would suggest that
there is a direct lineage to the character and conception of residential colleges and halls mentioned earlier. Those colleges and halls
were founded by humanist scholars, Protestant burghers, and
Catholic orders precisely in order to provide a harboring commu-

nity and to foster a communal sense of commitment to a moral and religious vision of liberal education.[40] In fact, these institutions represent the origin of the community ideal that is now so commonly invoked. Here, too, the change called for today belongs to the tradition.

Several historical implications for rethinking the content, structure, and process of liberal education have been suggested here. First, I have tried to demonstrate that the tradition of liberal education is not uniform and continuous but full of variety, discontinuity, and innovation. It has been and is a conflicted tradition. Second, and conversely, I have attempted to show that innovative proposals made for liberal education at the end of the twentieth century often have been part of the tradition. Another way of stating these two points is that the tradition and the innovation— really, the ways of the insider and the outsider—are often not as easily identified as those envisioning liberal education for the twenty-first century might be led to assume. More precisely: what appears to be the tradition, or the insider, viewed in the current context, may be considered the innovation, or the outsider, when a much longer view is adopted, and vice versa. A further point is that the specific examples discussed, which are hopefully informative in their own right, indicate that the content, structure, and process of liberal education are less clearly distinguished over time than one might surmise. The curricular content, the organization of studies, and the mode of teaching and learning—to use three correlative categories, out of all the possibilities—often overlap or merge, particularly when liberal education attempts to inculcate methods of thinking or inquiring. Mindful, then, of the elusiveness of these distinctions and the privileging they imply, whether for the tradition or the innovation, let us undertake to consider the current situation and future prospects of liberal education.

Notes

1. See, for example, "A New Battle of the Books, or Throwing out the Middle Ages," *Nation* 99 (1914): 315–16.

2. Swift is often credited with the metaphor "battle of the books," which is echoed today in W. Bliss Carnochan, *The Battleground of the Curriculum: Liberal Education and the American Experience* (Stanford, 1993). But the metaphor has an older and no less prominent antecedent from the early thirteenth century: Henri d'Andeli's *The Battle of the Seven Arts: A French Poem by Henri d'Andeli [La bataille des VII ars]*, trans. Louis J. Paetow (Berkeley, 1914). Variants of the phrase "ancients and moderns" were widely

employed in succeeding centuries, and the literature on the topic is enormous. See the classic works Hubert Gillot, *La querelle des anciens et des modernes en France* (Paris, 1914); Anne Elizabeth Burlingame, *The Battle of the Books in Its Historical Setting* (New York, 1920); Richard F. Jones, *Ancients and Moderns: A Study of the Rise of the Scientific Movements in Seventeenth-Century England* (St. Louis, 1961). On the origins of the debate, compare Cesare Vasoli, "La première querelle des 'anciens' et des 'modernes' aux origines de la Renaissance," in *Classical Influences on European Culture, A.D. 1500–1700*, ed. Robert R. Bolgar (Cambridge, U.K., 1976), pp. 67–69; Albert Zimmermann, ed., *Antiqui und Moderni: Traditionsbewußtsein und Fortschrittsbewußtsein im späten Mittelalter* (Berlin, 1974).

3. The quotation is from Harry S. Broudy and John R. Palmer, *Exemplars of Teaching Method* (Chicago, 1965), p. 68, relying on F. W. Winterton, "The Lesson of Neo-scholasticism," *Mind* 51 (1888): 397–400, which also served as the authority for Ernest C. Moore, *The Story of Instruction*, 2 vols. (New York, 1936, 1938), 2: 359–63, and John S. Brubacher, *A History of the Problems of Education*, 2d ed. (New York, 1966), p. 180.

4. I would like to note the relevance of this point to Sheldon Hackney's welcome call for a national conversation about significant public issues. What I find so refreshing about this call, if I understand it correctly, is that it addresses not so much particular issues as the underlying issue of how one conducts a discussion or debate in an intelligent and civil manner. Hackney's courageous call for a national conversation is thus, from my perspective, an explicit challenge to the kind of discussion of public issues conducted by demagogues on radio talk shows and to the politicians who pander to them.

5. I have discussed some of these echoes in "The Historical and Cultural Dimensions of the Recent Reports on Undergraduate Education," *American Journal of Education* 96 (1988): 293–322, and "Rediscovering the New Liberal Education: Curricular Implications of the Recent Knowledge Revolution" (plenary lecture to the annual meeting of the Association of American Colleges, Washington, D.C., January 1991).

6. The most prominent authority giving rise to this view is Martin Bernal, *Black Athena: The Afroasiatic Roots of Classical Civilization* (London, 1987). Ironically, Bernal is thoroughly appreciative of the historicity of this Afroasiatic view; in fact, this historicity is his whole point.

7. Augustine, *De Doctrina Christiana*, trans. D. W. Robinson Jr. (Indianapolis, 1958), bk. 2, ch. 28, p. 43.

8. Cassiodorus, *Institutiones*, ed. R. A. Mynors (Oxford, 1929), bk. 1, ch. 28; bk. 2, ch. 3; Augustine, *De Civitate dei*, bk. 8, ch. 12. Biblical quotations are from *The Jerusalem Bible*. See Gerard L. Ellspermann, "The Attitude of the Early Christian Latin Writers toward Pagan Literature and Learning" (Ph.D. diss., Catholic University of America, 1949); Simone Viarre, "A propos de l'origine égyptienne des arts libéraux: Alexandre Neckam et Cassiodore," pp. 583–91, and Silvestro Fiore, "La Théorie de Bernard Silvestris *Aegyptus parturit artes* et les préceptes Persans du *Damdad Nask*," pp. 575–81, in *Artes*

Libéraux et Philosophie au Moyen Age, Actes du quatrième congrès international de philosophie médiévale (Paris, 1969).

9. See, for example, the 1215 condemnation of Aristotle's natural philosophy at the University of Paris, recorded in H. Denifle and E. Chatelain, eds., *Chartularium universitatis Parisiensis*, 4 vols. (Paris, 1889–1897), 1:70. Thomas Aquinas, *Expositio super librum Boethii* DE TRINATE, quae 5, art. 1, resp. 3, in *St. Thomas Aquinas, The Division and the Method of the Sciences*, ed. Armand Maurer (Toronto, 1953). A starting point for learning about the reliance on Islamic learning is Mehdi Nakosteen, *History of Islamic Origins of Western Education* A.D. *800–1350, with an Introduction to Medieval Muslim Education* (Boulder, 1964).

10. Thomas Aquinas presents a succinct statement of this formulation in *Commentary on the Nicomachean Ethics*, trans. C. I. Litzinger (Chicago, 1964), bk. 6, lect. 7, no. 1211. An excellent discussion of the emergence of this formulation is James A. Weisheipl, "Classification of the Sciences in Medieval Thought," *Mediaeval Studies* 27 (1965): 54–90.

11. Aristotle, *Politics* 1337a34–42; Cicero, *De Oratore* I, 9–11, 56–63, 158–59, 187; III, 57–58; *Orator* 113, 115–20; *Brutus* 151–54; *De finibus* I, 72; III, 4; *Partitiones Oratoriae* 80.

12. See the helpful tables in Henri I. Marrou, "Les arts libéraux dans l'antiquité classique," pp. 5–27, in *Artes libéraux et philosophie au moyen age: Actes du quatrième Congrès International de Philosophie Médiévale* (Paris, 1969).

13. Laurence Veysey states, "In the late nineteenth century, subject majors had not at first been universal in the new universities, despite their emerging departmental structure. . . . By 1910 just about all American colleges and universities had embraced the subject major" ("Stability and Experiment in the American Undergraduate Curriculum," in *Content and Context*, ed. Carl Kaysen [New York, 1973], pp. 1–63).

14. See, in particular, the reports on the academic major sponsored by the Association of American Colleges: *Liberal Learning and the Arts and Sciences Major*, vol. 1: *The Challenge of Connecting Learning* (Washington, D.C., 1990); vol. 2: *Reports from the Field* (Washington, D.C., 1990). Rudolph H. Weingartner discusses the undergraduate major in his insightful book *Undergraduate Education: Goals and Means* (Phoenix, 1992), ch. 5.

15. Compare the views of Joseph J. Schwab, *Science, Curriculum, and Liberal Education: Selected Essays*, ed. Ian Westbury and Neil J. Wilkof (Chicago, 1978); *Science for Non-Specialists: The College Years, Report of the National Research Council's Committee on a Study of the Federal Role in College Science Education of Non-Specialists* (Washington, D.C., 1982).

16. Christine de Pizan, *The Book of the City of Ladies*, translated by Earl Jeffrey Richards (New York, 1982), bk. I, chs. 29, 33; Bathsua Pell Makin, "An Essay to Revive the Ancient Education of Gentlewomen," *First Feminists, British Women Writers, 1578–1799*, ed. Moira Ferguson (Bloomington, Ind., 1985), p. 134; Virginia Woolf, *A Room of One's Own* (New York, 1957), ch. 1.

17. See, for example, M. F. Green, ed., *Minorities on Campus: A Handbook for Enhancing Diversity* (Washington, D.C., 1989); C. S. Pearson, D. L. Shavlik, and J. G. Touchton, eds., *Educating the Majority: Women Challenge Tradition in Higher Education* (New York, 1989). Cf. Peter N. Stearns, *Meaning over Memory: Recasting the Teaching of Culture and History* (Chapel Hill, N.C., 1991).

18. Quotation is from T. Corcoran, S.J., *Studies in the History of Classical Teaching, Irish and Continental* (London, 1911), p. 212. A good place to begin examining the extensive literature addressing this emergence of academic disciplines and departments is Alexandra Oleson and John Voss, eds., *The Organization of Knowledge in Modern America, 1860–1920* (Baltimore, 1979). The argument and facts here are drawn from my own account in *The "True Professional Ideal" in America: A History* (Oxford, 1992), ch. 4.

19. Frank Costin, "Lecturing versus Other Methods of Teaching: A Review of Research," *British Journal of Educational Technology* 2 (1972): 4–31; Paulo Friere, *Pedagogy of the Oppressed* (1970), rev. ed. (New York, 1993), ch. 3.

20. William Epstein, "The Classical Tradition of Dialectics and American Legal Education," *Journal of Legal Education* 31 (1981): 422. See, for example, Henry O. Fuchs, "Outside Reality in the Classroom: Cases," *Journal of English Education* 60 (1970): 745–47; Richard F. Jones, "The Case Study Method," *Journal of Chemical Education* 52 (1975): 460–61; David C. King, "Using Case Studies to Teach about Global Issues," *Social Education* 38 (1974): 657–58; Joseph P. McAdoo, "An Investigation of the Case Method as a Means of Teaching Concepts of Speech-Communication" (Ph.D. diss., University of Missouri, 1974); Louis C. Mancuso, "A Comparison of Lecture, Case Study, and Lecture-Computer Simulation Teaching Methodologies in Broadcast Economics," *Southern Journal of Educational Research* 10 (1976): 1–12; Jack B. Rogers and Forrest E. Baird, *Introduction to Philosophy: A Case Method Approach* (Cambridge, Mass., 1981); Marcus G. Singer, "The Teaching of Introductory Ethics by Case Method," *Monist* 58 (1974): 616–29; Karl H. Vesper and James L. Adams, "Evaluating Learning from the Case Method," *Engineering Education* 60 (1969): 104–6; M. Walder, "The Use of Case Studies," *Education in Chemistry* 11 (1974): 58–60; Ira L. Winn, "Case Study as an Integrative Tool for Environmental Education," *Social Studies Review* 13 (1974): 21–23.

21. Josef Redlich, *The Common Law and the Case Method in American University Law Schools* (New York, 1914), pp. 41–47.

22. Quotation is from Charles I. Gragg, "Because Wisdom Can't Be Told" (1940), in *The Case Method at the Harvard Business School*, ed. Malcolm P. McNair (New York, 1954), pp. 6, 9, 10, 11. See statements by Melvin T. Copeland (1920), Arthur S. Dewing (1931), and Malcolm P. McNair (1954) also included in this collection. See also C. Roland Christensen, *Teaching and the Case Method* (Boston, 1987), pp. 17–34.

23. Quotations are from Gary Sykes, "Foreword," p. vii, and Katherine K. Merseth, "Cases for Decision Making in Teacher Education," p. 52, in *Case Methods in Teacher Education*, ed. Judith H. Shulman (New York, 1992).

24. Cheryl Givens Fischer and Grace E. Grant, "Intellectual Levels in College Classrooms," in *Studies of College Teaching*, ed. Carolyn L. Ellner and Carol P. Barnes (Lexington, Mass., 1983), p. 58.

25. The associated ambiguity between lecture as in "reading" and lecture in its pedagogical sense continued for centuries and is clearly expressed in John Stewart (1749–1822), *Prospectus of a series of lectures, or A new practical system of human reason, calculated to discharge the mind from a great mass of error, and to facilitate its labour in the approximation of moral truth, divested of all metaphysical perplexities and nullities; accommodated to the most ordinary capacities, in a simple method, which dispenses equally with the study of the college, or the* lecture *of musty libraries* (Philadelphia, [1796]). Emphasis added.

26. Quoted from "Odofredus Announces His Law Lectures at Bologna," in Lynn Thorndike, *University Life and Records in the Middle Ages* (New York, 1944), p. 67. Although Odofredus here describes lectures in law, the practice in other faculties and universities seems to have been quite similar. Thus, Hugh of St. Victor (1096–1141) noted that *lectio* addresses "three things: *litteram, sensum, sententiam*. The *littera* is the agreeable order of expression, which we also call construction. *Sensus* is a kind of easy and open significance, which the *littera* displays at the first look. *Sententia* is a deeper meaning, which is found only by exposition and interpretation. Among these things the order to inquire is first *littera*, then *sensus*, then *sententia*" (*Didascalicon*, bk. 3, ch. 9). My translation from Latin text is quoted in Martin Grabmann, *Die Geschichte der scholastischen Methode, nach gedruckten und ungedruckten Quellen*, 2 vols. (Freiburg im Breisgau, 1909–11; reprint, Graz, 1957), 2: 242–43.

27. Corcoran, *Studies in the History of Classical Teaching, Irish and Continental*, ch. 15; Desiderius Erasmus, "*De ratione studii*, that is *Upon the Right Method of Instruction*, 1511," no. 10, 526F–528C, trans. William H. Woodward, in *Desiderius Erasmus Concerning the Aim and Method of Education* (Cambridge, U.K., 1904), pp. 173–74.

28. James Boswell, *Boswell's Life of Johnson* (1791), edited by George B. Hill and L. F. Powell, 6 vols, (Oxford, 1934–1950), "Talking of Education," aetat. 57.

29. In the 1780s, when the professor of divinity at Yale College first introduced for students "two exercises called 'lectures' . . . one was discussion by the professor on some topic of positive or controversial divinity; the other a catechetical exercise on the first" (Mary L. Gambrell, *Ministerial Training in Eighteenth-Century New England* [New York, 1937], p. 75).

30. William Blackstone, *A Discourse on the Study of the Law* (Oxford, 1759), pref.; Samuel H. Fisher, *Litchfield Law School 1774–1833, Biographical Catalogue of Students* (New Haven, 1946), p. 1; Redlich, *The Common Law and the Case Method in American University Law Schools*, pp. 7–8.

31. For example, the *Catalogue . . . of Dartmouth College for the Academical Year* (1852–53) lists as a supplement to the regular curriculum "courses of lectures" in the modern subjects: anatomy, physiology, history, rhetoric and belles lettres, chemistry, geology, mineralogy, astronomy, and natural philosophy, as well as theology and moral philosophy (p. 28).

32. Quotation is from J. Jeffrey Auer and Jerald L. Banning, Introduction, to *Lectures on Rhetoric and Oratory by John Quincy Adams* (1810; reprint, New York, 1962), no page; Donald M. Scott, "The Profession That Vanished: Public Lecturing in Mid-Nineteenth-Century America," in *Professions and Professional Ideologies in America*, ed. Gerald L. Geison (Chapel Hill, N.C., 1983), pp. 12–28; James R. Lowell, "Emerson the Lecturer: Ralph Waldo Emerson," in *Great Teachers, Portrayed by Those Who Studied under Them*, ed. Houston Peterson (New Brunswick, N.J., 1941).

33. Harry S. Broudy, "Historic Exemplars of Teaching Method," in *Handbook of Research on Teaching: A Project of the American Educational Research Association*, ed. N. L. Gage (Chicago, 1963), p. 21; Friedrich Paulsen, *The German Universities and University Study*, trans. Frank Thilly and William W. Elwang (London, 1906), pp. 63, 212. Ironically, Paulsen mistook the scholastic lecture as "the mere transmission of a definite body of accepted truths" (p. 63).

34. George Ticknor, *Remarks on Changes Lately Proposed or Adopted in Harvard College* (Boston, 1825); Henry P. Tappan, *University Education* (New York, 1851), passim; Thomas N. Bonner, "The German Model of Training Physicians in the United States, 1870–1914: How Closely Was It Followed?" *Bulletin of the History of Medicine* 64 (1990): 18–34.

35. Paulsen, *German Universities and University Study*, p. 189; Henry Sidgwick, "A Lecture against Lecturing" (1890), reprinted in *Miscellaneous Essays and Addresses* (London, 1904), p. 340; William Knight, "A Defence of University Lectures," *Contemporary Review* 58 (1890): 291. Thirty-seven years later, Sidgwick's essay was still the primary target for Arthur Quiller-Couch, *A Lecture on Lectures* (London, 1927), passim.

36. Frederick H. Pratt, "The Dangers and Uses of the Lecture," *Educational Review* 24 (1902): 484.

37. Gerald Graff, *Beyond the Culture Wars: How Teaching the Conflicts Can Revitalize American Education* (New York, 1992).

38. A path into scholarship on the college movement in these regards may be found in Alan B. Cobban, *The Medieval English Universities: Oxford and Cambridge to c. 1500* (Berkeley, 1988); Anthony Grafton and Lisa Jardine, *From Humanism to the Humanities: Education and the Liberal Arts in Fifteenth- and Sixteenth-Century Europe* (Cambridge, Mass., 1986); John Morgan, *Godly Learning: Puritan Attitudes towards Reason, Learning and Education, 1560–1640* (Cambridge, U.K., 1986).

39. *Involvement in Learning: Realizing the Potential of American Higher Education, Final Report of the Study Group of the National Institute of Education on the Conditions of Excellence in American Higher Education*

(Washington, D.C., 1984), p. 33; *Integrity in the College Curriculum . . . The Findings and Recommendations of the Project on Redefining the Meaning and Purpose of Baccalaureate Degrees*, Association of American Colleges (Washington, D.C., 1985), p. 26; Sharon Parks, *The Critical Years: The Young Adult Search for a Faith to Live By* (New York, 1986); David H. Smith, "The College as a Moral Community" (plenary lecture for the Lilly Endowment Workshop on the Liberal Arts, Colorado Springs, June 1993).

40. This lineage is evident in Francis Oakley's good book *Community of Learning: The American College and the Liberal Arts Ideal* (New York, 1992).

3

The Importance of
Mission

Susan Resneck Pierce

In fall 1993 the University of Puget Sound Board of Trustees accepted an offer from Seattle University to assume sponsorship of the Puget Sound School of Law. Although we had not been seeking an alternative home for the law school, we board members responded to Seattle University's initiative as we did because we believed that transferring the law school would clarify to all our constituents the University of Puget Sound's mission as a national liberal arts college. We were also convinced that the law school— which had been established in 1971 and was located in a renovated department store in downtown Tacoma, a ten-minute drive from Puget Sound's main campus—would be better served by becoming part of an institution firmly committed to professional and graduate education.

The action illustrates how two very different universities can work together to ensure that each offers those programs that best fit its mission. For Puget Sound, the decision further exemplifies our determination to focus our resources, financial and human, on what we do best—a determination that grew out of the awareness that we cannot (and should not) try to do and be everything.

The aftermath of the decision, however, dramatizes something very different: that even though the rhetoric of higher education in the 1990s is characterized by calls for institutional focus and for funding only the endeavors that are central to that focus, the pressure from multiple constituencies makes it very difficult for colleges and universities to move beyond talk to action. Furthermore, although most universities are not likely to face the directly comparable choice of transferring a program, this situation demonstrates instructive principles to all institutions: it is essential that their governing boards be absolutely clear about institutional mission and ensure that resources are allocated accordingly; it is equally important that institutional mission grows out of institutional strengths; and it is crucial that boards select and support presidents whose vision is consistent with their own.

Puget Sound has deliberately been true to these principles for some time. For example, in the mid-1970s, cognizant of changing demographics and determined to establish itself as a national institution known for excellence in teaching, the university moved away from its goal of becoming a large comprehensive university with a substantial number of professional programs and redefined itself essentially as a liberal arts college. In keeping with this mission, the board closed satellite campuses in Seattle, in Olympia, and on military bases; eliminated an array of graduate programs; and capped the "main campus" or undergraduate enrollment at 2,700 students.

Although this redefined mission ran counter to the "bigger is better" belief held by many private colleges in the 1960s and 1970s, the strategy worked. Puget Sound was awarded a Phi Beta Kappa chapter in 1986. SAT scores have jumped 135 points since 1980. In 1993 we were added to the Watson Foundation list of top liberal arts institutions, and that same year we received more than 4,000 applications for 688 freshmen spaces. Some 70 percent of our incoming students come from outside the state of Washington. Retention is at an all-time high. Fund-raising is going well. Our endowment has grown in the last twenty years from $6 million to more than $90 million.

In addition to seeing the law school transfer as beneficial to the university as a whole, the board also believed it made sense for the law school, in both the short term and the long term. For example, we were impressed by Seattle University's plan to build a new building for the school on its main campus, something that campus boundaries had made impossible at Puget Sound. We noted the possibilities of joint degree programs between the law school and Seattle University's graduate programs in business administration and public policy. We recognized that because the school will remain in its current location for nearly six years and because Seattle University agreed to assume all faculty and staff contracts, including faculty tenure, no member of the current faculty, staff, or student body would face an abrupt change.

The decision to transfer the law school had the added benefit of avoiding some difficult future choices, including the possibilities of decreasing the school's size (at more than 800 students, it is currently the largest law school in the state) or maintaining the current size but creating a separate mission as a large law school of opportunity driven substantially by enrollment considerations for the foreseeable future. Neither option was appealing—particularly the first, because it almost certainly would have meant eliminating faculty, staff, and programs. Then, too, the possibility that Seattle University or another institution might open a new and competing law school in Seattle was daunting, given that a healthy percentage of Puget Sound law students and most of the evening students live closer to Seattle than to Tacoma.

Puget Sound is not alone among college campuses that have come to believe they must allocate resources in keeping with their mission and that identify institutional fit as a criterion for evaluating both new and existing programs. Indeed, in today's economic climate, even America's most financially secure institutions have begun to consolidate or eliminate programs as a means of using resources more effectively. For example, Wesleyan University is closing its master's program in education because the program was not fully integrated into the campus and because closing it will save $200,000 per year. Dartmouth is considering the same move. MIT has made known its plan to eliminate 400 faculty and staff positions over the next several years and to decrease its graduate programs by 10 to 12 percent, and the University of Pennsylvania is phasing out several departments.

Despite all the benefits of the law school transfer, the board did not come to its decision easily. We knew that some Tacomans would keenly feel the loss of the school, which lay in the center of a downtown struggling to revitalize itself. We also spent a good deal of time deliberating about the process. All of us preferred broader consultation but in the end concluded that a public process would have jeopardized the transfer. We also were concerned that a protracted public debate would seriously damage the law school if the arrangement fell through.

The response of several of the university's external constituencies to the law school decision indicates that we were right to be nervous about community reaction. Although most observers acknowledged the validity of the transfer in terms of institutional mission and the law school's future, several critics denounced the university for putting its well-being above that of downtown Tacoma. Arguing that the trustees' obligation to the city should take precedence over their responsibility for the university, the local newspaper, in a series of hostile articles, op-ed pieces, cartoons, and editorials, mounted a campaign to fuel community opposition.

Tacomans associated with efforts to revive the downtown, including community leaders and elected officials at the local, state, and national levels, also exerted pressure. One disgruntled attorney circulated a letter announcing his efforts to persuade his clients to eliminate the university as their beneficiaries. A group of five citizens formed an ad hoc group called Save Our University Law School (SOULS), which marched in front of the law school. Others mistakenly charged that the city had funded the law school building. (The truth here is that we put $11 million of our own resources into the building, including the repayment with interest of the loans we had secured with the city's help.)

The event not unexpectedly gave rise to other kinds of criticism of the university. For example, some were unhappy with the university's selectiveness in admissions, which they interpreted as elitist. Others complained that the discussions with Seattle University had been confidential. One critic condemned the board for behaving like members of a corporation rather than a family. A disgruntled alumnus worried about the football team.

After a month of such criticism, the board met with our local congressman, the city manager, and a prominent banker. We listened to their concerns and then voted unanimously to reaffirm the decision, believing, as we had originally, that by transferring the law school we were being true to our responsibility as trustees.

In retrospect, I have realized that much of the negative reaction stemmed from the widely held notion that because educational institutions are involved with a host of constituencies, they are obliged to serve them all. Those who subscribe to this notion simply did not accept the board's premise that our primary constituency is our students and that our primary responsibility is the well-being of the university.

Such feelings are on some level understandable, for in addition to their basic elements—students, faculty, and staff—academic institutions benefit from and/or must accommodate the often-dissimilar interests of alumni, parents, donors, accrediting agencies, foundations, corporations, the press, local communities, and federal, state, and local governments. As the law school decision indicates, sometimes these external constituencies endorse a college or university's educational mission. At other times, they are convinced that we should instead function as social service or community service agencies or even as surrogate parents.

Such notions are, I believe, also related to the growing expectation that educational institutions should make up for inadequacies in other parts of our society. Elementary and secondary schools have in recent decades been asked to do far more than teach. Rather, teachers and staff are now called on to satisfy a plethora of social, psychological, and physical needs no longer met by families, religious, and community organizations, and to some extent the government.

It is not surprising that higher education is now being confronted with the same sorts of nonacademic demands. These demands are not, I want to stress, frivolous, nor can they be ignored or taken lightly. But unless we find a way to address them responsibly, in ways consistent with both our mission and our resources, they will in time threaten the essential health of many of our colleges and universities, just as they have damaged many of our elementary and secondary schools.

In addition, most colleges and universities are faced with a series of other nonacademic pressures that deflect institutions from their commitment to teaching and learning and that drain resources. These include a new consumer mentality on the part of students and their families, expanding governmental regulations, the new American inclination to litigate all grievances, weaknesses in our elementary and secondary schools, and changes in the country's political and social attitudes.

These new demands and the resulting claims on institutional resources are coming at a time when colleges and universities are especially fragile because of the rising costs of academic programs, particularly those associated with rapidly developing computing technology, scientific equipment, and library materials. In addition, many institutions that have for a number of years deferred maintenance in order to fund other priorities are now faced with decaying physical plants and serious equipment needs; Yale, with its billion-dollar deferred maintenance bill, is the most prominent example. The result: on many campuses, the teaching faculty — and the libraries, technologies, and facilities that support them — are either competing for limited funds with nonacademic programs, often unsuccessfully, or are simply playing catch-up. Both circumstances are detrimental to the academic enterprise.

There is a special irony to this deflection from academic priorities. Simply put, even though American colleges and universities are among the few institutions that profess to be — and generally are — dedicated to reflection, analysis, and the making of reasoned and informed judgments, all too many campuses seem to be losing their sense of academic purpose, apparently without reluctance and often without even particularly noticing it. All too many of these institutions seem almost routinely to add programs and staff in nonacademic areas in an incremental fashion without considering the cumulative effect of this diversion of resources from academic pursuits.

Some of these new demands on higher education simply grow out of the reality that colleges and universities are no longer predicated on Mark Hopkins's famous notion that the best teaching takes place with a professor seated on one end of a log and the student seated on the other. Rather, most educational institutions are exceedingly complex. Typically, they now include hotels in the form of residence halls, restaurants in the form of food services, health clinics, counseling centers, placement centers, and health clubs. They require sophisticated marketing, public relations, and fund-raising operations. They depend on successful fiscal management, strong investment policies, and solid legal counsel. They employ personnel administrators, loan officers, and grants administrators; community service coordinators and career counselors; security staff; and landscaping, custodial, and maintenance crews. Most run libraries, bookstores, and computer stores. They produce in-house newspapers and magazines. They have computer programmers and technicians on staff. Some operate museums of natural history. Others have their own art museums. Some even have their own real estate offices, telephone companies, book and journal publishing houses, hotels, travel agencies, movie theaters, and venture capital arms.

This multiplicity of functions is in part the product of important and sometimes obvious educational notions (for example, that healthy students learn better than students who are ill and that a residential campus is likely to promote learning). Yet other functions are a response to the reality that colleges and universities are like small villages or sometimes even medium-sized cities, which are assumed by their inhabitants to provide such desired features as well-lit pathways, appropriate parking, and a safe environment. When making a choice about college, many prospective students and their families look first for a talented faculty, a favorable student-faculty ratio, a first-rate library, an attractive and well-maintained campus, and state-of-the-art science and computer facilities. Many also expect modern facilities and a great many special programs and services. For example, they frequently seek residence halls that can accommodate computers, microwaves, compact disc players, and VCRs. They want up-to-date recreational facilities with all the latest workout equipment. They expect food that is nutritious, tasty, and varied enough to satisfy diverse dietary preferences. They look for overseas study programs, writing and math skills centers, special advising programs, summer internships, community service opportunities, and sophisticated career planning and placement centers.

Some students and their parents also now expect a good many personal services. It is unclear whether the current generation of students brings with them greater psychological needs than earlier generations did or whether they are merely evidencing another form of a growing American entitlement mentality; what *is* clear is that colleges across the country have been adding staff and programs to address these needs. For example, most campuses now routinely offer counseling support and educational programs for students from dysfunctional families, those with eating disorders or drug or alcohol problems, and those who are struggling with their sexual identity or who have been victims of various forms of harassment and abuse. They also offer gynecological exams, birth control, and AIDS-prevention workshops.

I am not arguing against the worthiness of such efforts to address the psychological and social needs of our students. Quite the contrary: like every other administrator and faculty member I know, I worry about how best to help troubled students. Moreover, all of us recognize that students suffering emotional or physical distress are less likely to learn than are those who are psychologically and physically healthy. But the costs of providing such help are as evident as the benefits. And so the question becomes one of degree—of just how much an institution of higher education can and should do to promote the emotional well-being of our students. To put it another way: At what point does the responsibility of parents, social service agencies, and the students themselves for addressing these larger social problems end, and at what point does ours begin? If, as is likely to be the case, we decide that we all share that responsibility, how do we find the appropriate balance?

These are not abstract problems. I expect that every dean of students can tell stories of parents who expect colleges to meet whatever needs their sons and daughters bring with them to campus. In the last five years, I've kept track of some of the anecdotes I've heard from colleagues across the country: the parents who insisted that the counseling staff guarantee their suicidal daughter's well-being so that the rest of the family could take their annual vacation; the mother who was angry that her emotionally unstable son had been convinced to take a medical leave, because she believed the leave would jeopardize his chances of being accepted into a top graduate school; the mother who was dismayed to learn that the admissions staff was not meeting the plane of her eighteen-year-old son when he arrived at the local airport; the father who was outraged that his son's university refused to sponsor a flying club because of concerns about increased insurance costs and increased potential liability; and the family that asked the president's secretary to locate a kennel for their daughter's dog.

Other costs associated with being competitive in a difficult marketplace are also growing. Many colleges have increased their financial aid budgets, often quite dramatically, in ways that have drained resources from academic and other programs. Even though conventional wisdom suggests that institutions should dedicate no more than 20 percent of tuition revenues to financial aid, an increasing number of institutions with enrollment problems are doubling that percentage. Many of these institutions rationalize this increased commitment of financial aid as a good business decision in those cases when a student meets the institution's academic standards and the cost of educating that student is less than what the student can afford to pay. To my mind, this is a dangerous strategy, because it typically commits resources for four years (unless the institution engages in "bait-and-switch" tactics) and deflects resources from other areas of need. Many colleges have also invested substantial resources into the admissions effort itself, developing expensive videos, computer disks, and glossy publications. Because most private colleges and universities are tuition-dependent, they are reluctant to take chances with their major source of revenue.

Declining enrollments have in fact hit some campuses hard. Since such decreases are almost inevitably accompanied by reductions in operating budgets, and often by the elimination of faculty and staff positions as well, some institutions are relaxing their admissions standards to bring in a sufficient number of students. Others, faced with structural deficits but healthy admissions possibilities, are increasing the size of their student bodies in search of increased revenue to deal with budgetary deficits.

None of these steps—overspending financial aid budgets, diluting standards, or precipitously increasing enrollment to balance the budget—are happy ones, since all have a potentially negative effect on the quality of academic programs. Although public institutions are facing different sorts of budgetary pressures, bred of low tuition and fees and declining revenue from state and federal sources, they may provide the best evidence of the correlation between the level of an institution's resources and the quality and kind of academic programs it can offer. For example, it often takes students in the California public university system five to six years to graduate, simply because they cannot get into the courses they need. In some of the country's major research universities, undergraduates are taught primarily by teaching assistants or in classes so large (some with a thousand or more students) that the classrooms are outfitted with TV monitors. Some of these institutions have even abandoned general education requirements, because they are no longer able to guarantee students access to the courses.

The lack of solid academic preparation among many college-age students is putting further pressure on college and university budgets, particularly at a time when institutions are competing for students. Because many American secondary schools no longer require a rigorous college preparatory track for many students, first-year college students often arrive with academic credit for extracurricular activities or academically soft courses in lieu of a rigorous program grounded in the study of English, mathematics, science, foreign language, and history. These students end up spending at least part of their college years learning what they should have studied in high school, and college courses are subsequently watered down to accommodate their lapses.

The only way for institutions to avoid this sort of downward spiral in the academic preparation of their student body is to adhere to or even raise their admissions standards. But in today's climate, many institutions do not believe they have the luxury of selectivity, or a position of great enough security that they can enforce rigorous admissions requirements. Such enrollment pressures may also be driving some institutions to relax their grading standards, although the national scandal of grade inflation may stem less from this sort of economic consideration and more from the growing sense on the part of students that anything less than a B is an unacceptable grade and the unwillingness of faculty to uphold standards in the face of student expectations. (The underpreparedness of college students argues against the movement to limit college degrees to three years as a way of combating the high costs of postsecondary education. Such a model might be feasible if students were leaving our high schools with a solid educational foundation rather than, as is often the case, in need of remedial work.)

Other changes in America's social and political climate have also had a substantial effect on college campuses, which no longer are sanctuaries from the larger society. Instead, colleges and universities are being buffeted by the same discontentments and pressures that are threatening America's social contract. These changes in the nation's social and political landscape have also begun to erode, slowly but persistently, the commitment of many institutions to teaching and learning and, even more particularly, to the open and spirited examination of ideas that has always been at the heart of our educational system.

For example, and perhaps most tellingly, many campuses are beginning to undergo a kind of balkanization that is leading not to greater understanding and tolerance but rather to a new kind of separatism, as faculty and staff alike give way to pressures from various groups. Indeed, students are all too often separating themselves by race, ethnicity, gender, and sexual orientation. They seek segregated housing, campus organizations and, in some extreme instances, even courses. For example, in the spring of 1993, a group of Hispanic students and faculty at UCLA conducted a successful hunger strike, driving the university to create a separate Hispanic studies department in lieu of its existing interdepartmental Hispanic Studies program, despite the fact that most Hispanic and other faculty members opposed the move.

Campuses are also fraught with growing instances of intolerance and with a fervent unwillingness on the part of victims of such intolerance to let it go unchallenged. In 1993, for example, two much-publicized incidents took place: African American students at the University of Pennsylvania destroyed thousands of copies of the student newspaper in protest over what they viewed as racist reporting, and Jewish students at Brandeis did the same because their student paper had run ads from an anti-Semitic group that argued that the Holocaust was a myth.

The 20 October 1993 edition of the *Chronicle of Higher Education,* selected at random, suggests just how widespread the tendency toward balkanization is. The cover pointed to the University of Mississippi's battle over the flying of the Confederate flag, while the two-page "In Brief" section devoted itself mainly to reporting the following instances of campus intolerance: a dishwasher at Iowa State University, who had provoked student protests because he sported tattoos of a swastika and the letters KKK on his arms, was assigned a new job; death threats prompted two African American students at the University of Rhode Island to move out of their campus dormitory rooms; Hispanic students at Brown protested what they considered the university's lack of commitment to Hispanics; the University of St. Thomas in St. Paul decided to continue to display a poster of Margaret Sanger, the founder of Planned Parenthood, despite a complaint from an antiabortion alumnus; minority students at Rochester Institute of Technology praised a special orientation program designed to help them adjust to college; a Muslim student at Iowa State threatened a "jihad" or holy war against a white professor of African American studies because of a disagreement over Afrocentrism; and a so-called prankster poured laundry detergent into a new sculpture at Yale that honored women.

What many of us find especially distressing are the apparently growing numbers of racist and anti-Semitic incidents, of what people are now referring to as hate speech. Sometimes these events appear to be the work of members of the campus community, but often they are products of external groups. For example, in summer 1992, the White Aryan Nation blanketed libraries, student unions, and residence halls at a number of campuses in the Pacific Northwest with fliers celebrating the lynching of blacks and the horrors of the Holocaust.

In response to such incidents, some campuses have tried to legislate speech as well as conduct, even though such speech codes are likely to make individuals skittish about interacting with anyone different from themselves and are as likely to encourage a new spirit of censorship and self-censorship. The real danger, of course, is that the very notion that colleges and universities are places where all ideas, however controversial, can be responsibly explored and debated in an atmosphere of informed, deliberate, civil, and often fervent discourse is now endangered. The notion that a college campus should be the setting for such an examination of ideas is further jeopardized by other social currents. The country's penchant for litigation, for instance, has thrust many matters that once would have been considered internal into attorney's offices and courtrooms.

This moving of problems from an informal arena to a formal one often makes their resolution more difficult and the costs associated with adjudicating them very high. As significantly, in some instances, this tendency toward litigation is likely to compromise academic standards. The American Disabilities Act is one such case in point. Clearly worthy in its intention, the act nevertheless is sufficiently ambiguous that it has given birth to a whole new area of litigation, including threatened suits from students with learning disabilities who, after some kind of academic failure, are now arguing that the faculty is obliged to somehow accommodate their learning difficulties enough to enable them to graduate.

The fear of litigation has also had other effects on how educational institutions and the individuals within them function. For example, many faculty and staff members now refuse to provide references for fear of being sued if the assessment is unfavorable. Some faculty are reluctant to write letters for tenure and promotion reviews, even though such reviews are at the heart of every institution's search for excellence, because recent court rulings no longer guarantee confidentiality to participants in such reviews.

The social climate has also led some faculty to avoid being alone with students in any setting, including their offices, for fear of being charged with sexual harassment. Indeed, because of this fear, a professor I know at an East Coast university will neither take graduate students on site visits nor give them rides home from campus, something he used to do routinely. Such decisions suggest just how far away we have moved from Mark Hopkins's vision of the faculty member and the student sharing a log and intellectual exchange.

Even when litigation seems frivolous, it needs to be taken seriously because of the staggering costs of fighting suits. In 1993, the *Wall Street Journal* reported two such incidents. In the first, an undergraduate sued Princeton because he was injured after he climbed onto and then fell off the roof of the small commuter train at the university-owned train station. In the second, Brown University was sued by a student who, while taking a shower in a dormitory room with her boyfriend, slipped, fell against a soap tray, and injured herself. Her complaint: that the soap tray was somehow faulty. Both cases suggest something about the failure of individuals in our society to take responsibility for their own actions; nevertheless, both Brown and Princeton were forced by these suits to go beyond pronouncements. Each found itself in the midst of a formal legal proceeding.

New governmental regulations and reporting requirements are also requiring colleges and universities to commit additional resources and staff time to administrative rather than academic functions. New federal regulations in the areas of athletics, campus security, alcohol use, and international students and faculty have all necessitated either new or reallocated staff positions. Financial aid regulations—complicated, cumbersome, ever-changing, and not always logical—also require large staffs, and staff members in turn require ongoing training just to keep up with the changes. With these experiences in the background, many college administrators have objected to the proposed new layer of governmental involvement with the accreditation process.

The challenges facing those of us on college campuses are varied and abundant, and they are likely to become even more insistent in time. For that reason, we faculty, administrators, and trustees must insist that our institutions have established a sense of purpose, a mission that is feasible and that guides both policy and operational decisions.

Once our institutional mission has been defined, we must be actively vigilant in ensuring that this mission is always our touchstone. It does not benefit us or the long-term interests of our institution to let a series of ad hoc decisions shift institutional direction without recognizing that such a shift has taken place. Nor does it serve us well to allow resources to be diverted from that mission. Indeed, many colleges and universities have become debilitated by their tendency to fund every good new idea without considering whether the costs associated with that idea were central rather than peripheral to the institutional mission.

On a more practical level, as we ask for and respond to new demands for resources, we need to view those requests in light of existing programs and positions. In other words, we need always to consider whether what is being proposed could be funded by eliminating something that no longer is a priority. In the growth periods of the 1970s and 1980s, many institutions tended to engage in incremental budgeting. But by adding new costs to their base budget through a series of discrete decisions, without either deleting other expenses or securing new sources of funding, many of even our best colleges and universities developed substantial structural deficits.

We also need to recognize that innovation for its own sake is not necessarily desirable. Or, to state it more simply, new is not necessarily better; *better* is better. In that light, we must reaffirm and adhere to academic standards, regardless of the forces—whether litigation or the competitive marketplace—that encourage compromising those standards.

Most of all, the contemporary climate requires a certain kind of leadership and a certain kind of courage to make the kinds of decisions that we believe will serve our institution's best interests, even when those decisions are unpopular with one or more of our constituencies. Such leadership is especially difficult on college campuses, where change is typically slow in coming and where custom requires that elaborate processes be followed before action can be taken. For these reasons, those who lead on college campuses need to try to educate their various constituencies about the complexity of the issues facing higher education generally and their own institution in particular.

There are no gimmicks when it comes to excellence. And on college campuses there is no substitute for a commitment to the kind of excellence that inspires students to gain necessary skills and new knowledge—that brings them to new levels of intellectual inquisitiveness, academic discipline, and accomplishment. In the end, then, we faculty members, administrators, and trustees need to make sure our decision making embodies the very values that our institutions profess to teach: the importance of reflectiveness, deliberate and reasoned judgment, and informed choice. This is what we can and should do best, and our students and the larger society deserve no less.

4

Some Thoughts on Curriculum and Change

Leon Botstein

It should go without saying that in the twentieth-century history of American higher education, each significant curricular reform movement has had a distinct political agenda. This is particularly true for initiatives designed to create decisive changes in the shape of the undergraduate curriculum. In those circumstances in which a political movement and an institutional initiative have coincided, a distinct political purpose can be discerned in what the institution required of its students and how the program was articulated.

The historical moment was certainly at issue in the case of the reforms of the 1930s. Men such as Robert Hutchins, Stringfellow Barr, and Scott Buchanan saw in the idea of a core curriculum a way to realize their ideal construct of democracy. The Great Books concept and the variants of the core at Chicago had at their root a notion of natural rights and the social contract. Inherent in that framing of the body politic were concepts of freedom and civic responsibility. The objective was clear: one needed to educate young Americans—the elite of the nation—to steer the country away from the extremes of fascism and communism. Radical reform was imperative, since during the Great Depression both of these alternatives appeared politically viable.

In the post–World War II era, the Cold War framed most of the discussion about the curriculum. This claim may seem odd, but on closer inspection, beginning with Harvard's general education reform from the early 1950s, the concept of the university, until the late 1980s, was substantially defined by a consciousness of how much the United States constituted an alternative to political unfreedom. The elective-course system in its new Harvard form, combined with distribution requirements and an enormous premium on undergraduate specialization, was a kind of metaphorical mirror of the idealized free marketplace of ideas. We were convinced that we were training young people to cherish the advantages of free choice and liberty in a world in which the grim alternative of totalitarianism was not a mirage but a present danger.

The political significance of specific curricula has changed with time as the circumstances that led to their formulation have disappeared. The Great Books curriculum was once allied with a politics sympathetic to democratic socialism. Scott Buchanan, for example, was an admirer of the kibbutz. Stringfellow Barr would be appalled by the fact that the Great Books idea has become the exclusive province of modern neoconservatism. Likewise, the elective system of the departmentalized curriculum exemplified by that at Harvard in the late 1960s—the model for most other institutions—ironically became viewed by left-wing radicals of the era as oppressive and excessively restrictive. This critique would have astonished the opponents of the elective system and even the Progressives of the 1930s.

This brief historical reflection is significant from our point of view simply because one can hardly imagine a time in history when the political occasion for curricular change was more pressing than it is now. In order to discuss the present occasion and its consequences, one needs to dispense with the self-serving claim that there is something akin to an apolitical, or nonpoliticized, curriculum. The organization of knowledge and certainly the modes of its transmission are inherently part of a fabric of social ideas and action. One does not need to make pretentious references to older traditions of the sociology of knowledge or to more fancy and recent methodologies to argue that what we are doing now is not value-neutral. The current system is not, after all, a benchmark of objective standards simply because it is what we are used to. One need only find out what the values are and come to some resolution about whether one shares them. Asking a student to major in a department defined a certain way and to pass through some set of requirements is explicitly didactic. How is that major defined in the context of other potential ways of organizing knowledge? At the end of the argument, the defenders of any institutional arrangement can be permitted the luxury of arguing on the basis of tradition and authority. They may even wish to say that what they are doing is right and true. But I suspect that the mere reference to excellence, standards, and self-evident truths in discussions of curriculum fools no one—especially not those who make such claims.

That is not to say, of course, that such words don't mean anything. They certainly do. Any curriculum must defend scrutiny with respect to standards of rigor, method, discipline, difficulty, and truthfulness appropriate to the finest traditions of the university. Curriculum, ultimately, is a strategy among possible strategies. It is a tactical decision within the larger context of teaching and scholarship. Whatever decision is made, the content and conduct of the curriculum through which the decision is realized must conform to the university's standards regarding inquiry, scholarship, and argument, no matter how heavily laden those terms are with "Eurocentric" conceits regarding objectivity, evidence, and truth. That's who we are, and if one wants to call our modes of inquiry subjective or "political," so be it. As Wittgenstein noted long ago, it may not be important for what I believe is true to somehow be "absolutely" true. We might be happy to settle for a very high probability. Unreasonably skeptical questions or suspicions do not necessarily require a response.

Given that what we are doing now is not in any sense a value-neutral model, we then can ask what strategically would be the best curricular arrangement for the end of this century and the beginning of the next. In order to answer that question, one has to be clear about one's objectives. How do we want young people in college to think, and about what? Why do we want them to think about these things? What would we wish them to learn? What questions do we wish to encourage them to ask? Do we have any particular commitment to how they reflect and communicate about issues? If we think that nothing needs to be changed but that students should study what they seem to want to study in the existing arrangements, we ought to be clear about why we think that. And one hopes the answer is not merely a function of habit or convenience or possibly narrow self-interest. Are there particular habits of mind, subjects, or skills that we consider particularly appropriate?

Behind these kinds of questions lies the larger issue that faculties today are particularly loath to ask—the kind of question that previous generations, circa 1914 or 1933, seem to have had less trouble asking and answering. This issue has to do with the role of the university in society and the kind of society the individuals in the universities wished to support through the traditions of reason and learning. To put it more bluntly, until recently our predecessors accepted the assumption shared by David Hume and Thomas Jefferson—the eighteenth-century belief that through education and the spread of reason, progress could be achieved. Even Hegel and his followers' nineteenth-century twist to the logic of history contained a commitment to the idea of human progress, of some temporal logic that would result in a future that was better than the past. Of course, this notion did not prevent outbreaks of cultural pessimism such as those supplied during the fin de siècle by Max Nordau and others like him, who feared something called nihilism. They feared the loss of optimism. Furthermore, the shadow of the Holocaust has been appropriately long. We no longer can believe easily that education will improve ethical behavior, that human progress will suppress barbarism and reason will triumph over madness, and that an educated citizenry is an insurance against political violence.

The tragedy of our current situation is that we desperately need to ask this larger question and to forge some agreement about an answer. The Cold War has ended, and an easy description of America's role in the world is no longer possible. Furthermore, defining freedom and democracy, and therefore civil society in the United States, merely by contrast won't do. As we watch the peoples of Eastern Europe struggle with little success to develop alternatives to communism through the use of so-called freedom, we recognize how complicated the process of politics and social organization is. Moreover, the economic and social realities within the United States are challenging in and of themselves. The aging of the population, the constant and senseless violence, the persistence of the race question, shifts in the distribution of income, and the changing nature of employment constitute one category of challenge. And the unavoidable question of the environment and its constraints provides a wrinkle that was unfamiliar to our predecessors.

If one adds to this description the more sensitive issue of ethics and values, one finds oneself in truly murky waters. No doubt issues of gender and sexuality are being played out in ways that have little obvious historical precedent. Within this entire panoply of unavoidably cliché-ridden descriptions of current issues, there is the unmistakable and legitimate concern for the reigning standards of education. Within our laudable advocacy for democratic access, we cannot avoid the fear that with increased certification comes inadequate achievement. From an educator's point of view, one of the most troubling issues is that of motivation. Is there for the American adolescent the social supports for the love of learning, for curiosity, for the discipline that must accompany inquiry and the access to the pleasure of the life of the mind? Social mobility and the desire for a better job have always been excellent motivators. However, in the context of widespread historical and cultural pessimism, it can hardly be said that most young people have gotten from their elders the sense of a shared belief that the future will be better than the present, even in terms of income and employment. In fact, in our history as a nation, we have never had a comparable moment in which, at any level of schooling, the encouragement of learning and curiosity has received less support, spiritually and practically, from the adult world.

And this brings us right back to the strategic decision of curriculum. How can we best motivate our undergraduates to use their minds, to extend their range of curiosity, and to utilize the traditions of the university? To what end, personal and social, might their efforts be directed? What vision of the individual as citizen and of the body politic lies underneath any curricular advocacy? To simply say that such concerns are individual matters that have nothing to do with how our colleges are organized or what they teach is a patent act of self-deception. Once again, the status quo itself may offer a positive argument. The only question is what kind of argument it is.

One needs to turn to a closer description of the issues whose resolution by faculty in strategic terms should, I believe, define curricular decisions. In my opinion, we should think about curriculum by asking what kind of general and specialized education (or majoring process) would help any undergraduate student deal with central issues whose substance outstrips the limits of journalism—issues that are undeniably unavoidable and central to the existence of each of us. Here are ten such questions.

1. How does the individual define himself or herself in terms of identity? Who am I? What am I? What does it mean to say that I'm of this or that group or male or female? What is the dynamic between the externally determined identity and the possibility of individuality? How can we understand differentiation in the definition of identity other than in one's particular name? What are the consequences of various definitions of being?

2. How does my conception of my own identity help me conceive of who someone else is? The definition of the other, in terms of nation, race, religion, or any other category, is a crucial problem. Bosnia is an extreme example of the need to encourage critical self-reflection on the many fictions and constructs of this existential problem. An undeniable political objective of the university should be the encouragement of resolutions that lead not to violence but to respect, civility, affection, and tolerance.

3. By what rules should individuals conduct their lives? The age-old issue of the conflict between so-called natural rights and societal obligations and rights is still with us. How should we resolve disagreements? What is our relationship to civil law? What is the distinction between law and an individual's personal system of moral values? What *is* our obligation to others? What do we do when we disagree with law? What is our relationship to the use of violence? What is the role of the state in regulating conduct? Can we construct a shared definition of civility? How do we then deal with poverty and illness—the misfortunes of others?

4. If in our personal lives we embrace a religious faith defined as commitment to transcendent truth, how does that faith square with any notion of civil society? Is belief an absolute, revealed truth reconcilable with tolerance of the other's, or is tolerating someone else's disagreement with one's own allegiances a sign of intolerable weakness in one's own religious commitments? In other words, does tolerance require a sacrifice of faith? The early-twentieth-century dream of a world of increasing secularization and the decline of the religious has not materialized, making this issue of the dictates of revealed truth a pressing one.

5. Are there procedures and rules, not only in law but in the conduct of inquiry, with which we can agree in order to avoid an unacceptable obliteration of the boundaries be-

tween truth and fiction? Is there some valid way for us to create a hierarchy that can be accepted broadly enough that we can avoid the idea that everyone's opinion about any subject is equally valid? There is a rumor that some theory of "standpoint epistemology" has been argued. Is there some alternative to a nonhierarchical and unlimited acceptance of subjectivity?

6. One of the ironic consequences of the remembrance and popularization of the Holocaust is that in the late twentieth century, the victim has become the metaphor for all ordinary life. Those who died in or survived Auschwitz were and are true victims. The legitimate, lifelong rage of the Holocaust survivors—the conviction that the world owes them something—is not, however, a generalizable strategy for our lives. Yet a pernicious legacy of the Nazis is the extent to which any individual now finds it possible to construe his or her own quite ordinary life in the image of the concentration camp victim, a powerless and helpless person. In this view the world is stacked against one to such an extent that the assumption of responsibility for one's own actions in life or the acceptance of the imperfect, gray, and messy character of life comes to appear unreasonable. We all have become victims of various forms of harm and abuse for which we ask redress. The generalized use of the victim status within wide sectors of society is not beyond critical inquiry. Moreover, the self-definition as victim immediately solves the causal and existential question: the individual need only find his or her victimizer. That process, just like the justification of one's status as a victim, is problematic. The unproblematic case of the Nazis has become the model for most of the situations of the highly problematic facts of everyday life that have developed in the second half of this century. As most Western religions make plain, life on earth was not designed to be an experience of painlessness, comfort, and happiness. The facts of life are to blame most of the time.

7. In today's United States, we encounter an extraordinary amount of bad faith with respect to our own capacities for thought. Why is it that—at a time when more adults than ever before have gone to college; when there is more schooling, statistically speaking, than at any other time in history—the quality of public discourse is so low? We complain

about the sound bite, about television, about the poor quality of newspapers, and about the manipulation of the political process by media tricks and image-making. There are even calls to censor TV because of its presumed influence. But I suspect the truth is rather different. No matter how many hours children and adults spend before the TV, virtually all of them know perfectly well that TV isn't real. We know that the discussion is poor, yet we hide behind our own laziness and blame some magical technology that mesmerizes. We permit ourselves to think in reduced terms about all the major issues and to sustain ourselves in a kind of stupor of thoughtlessness, thereby eliminating the much-hoped-for public realm whose existence was presumably made possible by the spread of literacy since the late eighteenth and nineteenth centuries and by electoral democracy. We imagine that ignorance and lack of interest are no longer our fault but are involuntary.

8. How is it possible, in an age of enormous technological dependence, in which significant innovations in biology, transportation, and information science are taking place, that the percentage of people who have any idea or notion about science and technology is steadily declining? Furthermore, owing to technology, what will be the future of memory and written language in the next century?

9. Given the changed external world, what does an American need to know about the world that is different from what previous generations needed to know? What objectives and imperatives are associated with the claims that, for economic and political reasons, an American growing up at the end of this century needs to learn to have a new relationship to the history and cultures of Africa, Asia, Latin America, Europe, East and West, and the rest? In this context we can also raise the local and global ecological and environmental questions. We need to define and teach a wider and more far-ranging sense of history.

10. Last but not least, do we not have to reconsider the reciprocal and dialectical relationship between intimacy and privacy, on the one hand, and the public and shared space, on the other? What do we make of the fact that the intimate has become public and that sexuality, once construed as a private matter, has become central in public discourse? This issue returns us to the discussion of the definition of

the individual and the boundaries between one's self and one's neighbor. This matter requires the critical evaluation of questions about the distinction between family relations and strangers and about the arrangements by which we develop intimate groupings as opposed to political groupings.

These ten points are only a beginning. But they represent generalized questions that can be derived from scanning almost any daily newspaper or watching a few hours of CNN. They can be gleaned from any encounter with daily life or any observation of what goes on in an American high school or in the homes of many Americans.

In terms of curriculum, the result may be a fixed curriculum with specific items ranging from texts to works of art and matters of science. Rumination on these issues can also lead to other kinds of curricular arrangements. But it seems evident that there should be some shared criteria. One might wish to argue that students should confront these kinds of issues in common, that the university must organize student encounters that do not derive exclusively from their subjective response to the question "What would you like to major in?" or "What are you interested in studying?" One might be tempted to argue that a certain uniform standard of literacy would be desirable for all. One might conclude that the study of philosophy and political argument might play a role not only as a subject but in defining what is read and how. Bernard Williams's new book on Homer is an example of how tradition might serve the present. One might find a central role for the teaching of the arts and sciences to nonartists and nonscientists. Statistics and mathematics might unexpectedly appear as crucial, and the selections we make in the name of history might take a particular shape.

But the criteria for the curriculum cannot be only what faculty determine as desirable in terms of input. We live in an age of terrifying historical pessimism. Idealism of any sort and candid optimism are at a premium. Therefore, the curriculum has to generate motivation and has to be measured by its efficacy in inspiring students over the short and long run. Too much of our time in curriculum battles has been wasted in two ways. First, we have concentrated exclusively on the small percentage of the student's time traditionally allocated to general education and have spent too little time rethinking the majority of the student's time, which has been allocated to the major. By the same token, we have spent too much time worrying about the first year of college and too little about the last year. Second, we have thought too much about turf and content. This is what has been wrong with the multicultural debate. I see no clear evidence that when we teach *X*, students learn *X* or anything obviously related to *X*. One needs to think about plausible hypotheses regarding what will really affect the habits of mind and the behavior of individuals in their personal and civic lives, five, ten, fifteen, and twenty years after college. The attitudes and behavior of the graduates of most of our institutions cast considerable doubt on any exaggerated claims about the efficacy of past curricula. Most of all, is there any evidence that we respect speech and language as action sufficient to influence our lives?

The primary difficulty, of course, is getting faculty to talk openly and candidly about such issues. It is even more difficult to get them to agree that something needs to be done. It is perhaps even harder for them to accept the compromise that any curriculum must in its nature reflect the strategic hypothesis. Administrators, for the most part, lack the courage or the power to assist in this process. But the overwhelming fact is that in the last decade of the 1900s, because of the mystical properties of ends of centuries (let alone of millennia), we face both a fantastic opportunity and a desperate moment. It should serve as an inspiration to design the curricular experience of undergraduates with a distinct point of view.

One might ask how the world would be different if we were to succeed. We might be permitted to dream that there would be less tolerance of violence and hatred and therefore less of it. Not only might the Oklahoma tragedy and the L.A. riots have been avoided and the tragedy of Bosnia averted but also we would have had less fascination with the Bobbitts, the Menendez brothers, Tonya Harding, and O.J. Simpson. Perhaps we would not swoon over Stephen Spielberg and console ourselves that watching a Hollywood film will do some kind of good. The daily newspaper would focus less on personalities. The level of discourse about all these things, if they existed at all, would be different, whether in the *New York Review of Books* or *People*. We would create a world in which the manner and character of people in public life would be different. We might subject those who seek public office less to reflexive and hypocritical criticism, therefore giving ourselves the ability to hold them to a much higher standard than we do ourselves. And finally, we would take greater responsibility for our own lives, without blaming others, so that we might be able to accept the imperfection and the pain of suffering that inevitably will be our lives—not with equanimity, anger, or resignation but perhaps with the irrational response of getting up each morning and trying again and being satisfied with the fractional progress that comes from sustained idealism and ambition. Most of all, we might create a world in which language meant something again—in which people appropriated it for their own uses and made it their own and, through the creation of a public life, found both communication routes and the boundaries amid the open space of intimacy. This development might make our legal freedoms more than useless or irrelevant ideas or mere legitimations for doing harm to others. For those of us in the university, the love of creation and inquiry could flourish and render critical reflection an ethically significant act. It is only at this level of discourse that the particulars and details of curricular arrangements can be suggested, argued, and agreed on.

5

The Search for American
Liberal Education

Frank F. Wong

Liberal Education and the American Context

When Charles William Eliot launched his radical reforms at Harvard
in the late 1870s, he was convinced that the fixed curriculum,
based on English liberal education models, was ill-suited to the
democratic spirit, the cultural diversity, and the rapidly changing
circumstances in America. By introducing the free elective system, he hoped to develop in students the habits of self-reliance
that he regarded as essential to the American democratic system.
Seventy years later, in a post–World War II climate of concern
about the "unifying purpose and idea" for American education,
Harvard issued a new version of liberal education in its famous
Redbook. To address the new American circumstances, these reforms reduced rather than increased choices for students. These
benchmarks of American higher education notwithstanding, the
final chapter of a widely respected study by Bruce Kimball, published in 1986, opens with the observation that there is no "distinctively American view of liberal education."[1]

This observation contains an irony that raises interesting and significant questions. After such high-profile efforts as those made at Harvard, why is there no clear model of American liberal education? And if there is no such model, do we need to develop one, especially in the context of the dramatic changes affecting American society today—changes that in many ways are more radical than those faced by Charles William Eliot? Why, in this latest round of debates about the core curriculum in our colleges and universities, has the issue been posed in terms of the primacy and purity of Western civilization rather than in terms of the adequacy of our educational models to address the realities of America in the late twentieth century?

These questions are even more striking when one considers the almost complete reversal of roles and the dramatic changes in orientation that have occurred in the relationship between the United States and its cultural ancestors in the Anglo-European world. While in the late nineteenth century Great Britain was extending its rule to much of the rest of the world, and other European nations were its chief competitors for imperial influence, in the late twentieth century the United States stands alone as the remaining superpower of the world. In that earlier period, cultural influences flowed primarily from the Anglo-European world to the United States, but now cultural influences flow primarily from the United States to other parts of the world. When Eliot was president of Harvard, the United States was almost entirely oriented toward the Atlantic community in terms of commerce and culture, but in our own time, Bill Clinton, the president of the United States, has declared that the economic future of the United States lies in Pacific Rim trade, and the influence of non-Western cultures on the United States is increasingly evident. Immigrants coming to the United States in the nineteenth century were overwhelmingly from the Anglo-European world. Immigrants coming to the United States in the late twentieth century are overwhelmingly from Asia and Latin America.

Limits of the Traditional Model

In examining the history of curricular reform in American higher education, we see clearly the reasons for the absence of an American model of liberal education. While the Harvard reforms were concerned with adapting traditional models of liberal education to American circumstances, the reforms did not challenge essential assumptions built into those models. Some of these assumptions seriously inhibited the possibility of even considering an American model of liberal education. The Oxford model of liberal education that flourished in America was best articulated by Matthew Arnold. He believed in a concept of high culture, mediated through great books, which contained the best that had been thought and written. In practice, this translated into the assumption that the best ideas contained in the texts of Western civilization were universal—they applied to any time and any place. If liberal education equaled universal truth, then there was no need to distinguish an American model of liberal education from an English model of liberal education. Arnold's model of liberal education, like the Great Books program advocated by Robert Hutchins at the University of Chicago, was valid for all cultures. You could apply the model to different circumstances, but the model itself was timeless and not related to place. Even as Eliot grew determined to respond to changes in American society, he promoted publication of the Harvard Classics, which assumed a great books notion of liberal education.

Arnold's emphasis on liberal education as high culture also discouraged consideration of a distinctive American model. In nineteenth-century England, liberal education as high culture was suited to a class-conscious society in which gentlemen of the aristocracy were groomed for leadership responsibilities. But this high culture was self-contained, self-perpetuating, and comfortably insulated from the rapid changes occurring in other parts of the society. In fact, Arnold's liberal education envisioned not only a self-contained but also a harmonious culture, and this concern for harmony and order easily translated into a fear of rapid change, which represented disorder. Although Eliot was concerned with responding to the many changes occurring in American society, the model of liberal education he used had its own built-in limitations that kept it from achieving that purpose. These limitations were to appear repeatedly in many, if not most, subsequent efforts to reform liberal education in America. The self-contained high culture became that of the American college professor rather than the English aristocrat, and efforts to create new forms of liberal education inevitably sparked internal arguments among professors rather than efforts to develop a new model appropriate to the changing realities of the larger society. Given that from the outset college teachers were largely oriented toward Anglo-European culture, the internal debate was not likely to emphasize distinctive American features or requirements.

Impact on Curricular Development

This unwitting and almost unconscious dependence on an Anglo-European model of liberal education has had pervasive impacts on how American higher education has approached those areas of the curriculum that we variously call liberal education, general education, or core education. One impact has been succinctly described by philosopher John Searle. According to Searle, our notion of liberal education has emphasized extreme universalism, on the one hand, and extreme individualism, on the other. Our objective has been to provide individual students with the intellectual skills to liberate themselves from their provincial origins so that they could identify with universal humanity. In this kind of liberal education, there is no place for particular cultural identities. To be concerned about what it means to be an American is to undercut the cosmopolitan aspirations implied by universal truths.

Another impact of this model is the almost blind assumption that liberal education must be monocultural because it is universal. This is unsurprising, since many efforts to establish liberal education began with Western civilization courses that virtually presumed that Western civilization was coterminous with universal truth. The notion that Western civilization might be one of many high civilizations that have struggled imperfectly to express their aspirations for universal truth was alien to this approach. The emergence of anthropology as an academic discipline, however, began to erode the traditional concept of Western civilization as the one universal civilization.[2] This emergence has paralleled our growing awareness of the existence and integrity of cultures other than our own. That awareness, in turn, has reached a peak in our own time, because global interdependence and communications have forced on us the reality of multiple cultures in constant contact and interaction with each other. In addition, we have a newly acute sense of the pluralism that has always been a feature of American culture. Such developments have dramatized the discrepancies between these realities and our traditional approaches to liberal education.

Still another impact of the traditional model of liberal education is the failure to confront the contradictions between the aristocratic basis of Anglo-European approaches and the democratic, scientific, and technological realities of American life. When Robert Hutchins and Mortimer Adler launched the Great

Books curriculum at the University of Chicago, John Dewey criticized it because of this contradiction. In Dewey's vision, American education should reflect American society: it should be explicitly democratic and should give emphasis to the aspect of liberal education that Bruce Kimball identified as the Socratic, scientific method of open-ended truth-seeking, as opposed to the great books approach, which venerated established traditional values. Dewey's approach did not just acknowledge and accommodate the cultural pluralism of American society; it also reflected the multiplying pluralism of the disciplines within the academy. This came from the explosion of new knowledge that was generated by the scientific method. Dewey's insistence on connecting theory with practice and education with experience reflected the American tradition of philosophical pragmatism rather than the European tradition of Platonic idealism.[3] Because of the Anglo-European orientation of the most visible advocates of traditional liberal education, Dewey's American approach has received little attention in the repeated efforts to restore or reform liberal education in the American academy.

Dewey's recognition of the growing dominance of the scientific method and the resulting growth in specialization within all the academic disciplines anticipated one more impact of the traditional model of liberal education. While it was possible for advocates of the traditional model to turn away from the rapid changes that led to increased pluralism in the larger society, it was not possible to ignore the increased academic pluralism within the academy. In fact, most debates about liberal education, general education, or core curricula in the past half century have essentially turned around the question of how to reconcile the traditional aspiration for a common, shared academic culture with the separating tendencies of specialized academic disciplines. Those disciplines were increasingly shaped by the different research interests of the faculty. The core curriculum adopted by Harvard in 1979, which helped set off the latest wave of reforms in general education across the academy, was acknowledged by insiders to be a compromise that tried to balance the faculty's research interests with their desire to impart to students a sense of a shared academic culture.[4]

In terms of maintaining this kind of balance, the history of these kinds of reforms in the past several decades is not very promising. Because of the dominance of the research ethos in higher education today, most faculty members do not have a sense of a shared academic culture (much less a loyalty to such a culture), and their research priorities inevitably erode the effectiveness of core curriculum reforms. Significantly, the struggle between the ideal of a traditional liberal education and the pluralism of academic specialization has obscured the larger issue of whether liberal education needs to respond to the increasing cultural pluralism of the larger society.

Compartmentalization of Liberal Education

In another sense, however, academic specialization and the research ethos reinforced the tendency of the traditional liberal education model to separate itself from the larger society and from activities that were considered nonacademic. This tendency is expressed in the comment, often heard among liberal education advocates, that the academy should honor and recognize only "learning for its own sake." Normally, this belief translates into an attitude in which any applied learning, especially learning associated with vocational or professional education, is scorned and considered less than worthy. Needless to say, this attitude can become effective insulation from the changing winds in the larger society and easily exempts those in the academy from taking seriously the need to respond to such changes.

Ironically, while many in the academy regard liberal education as the opposite of academic specialization, in recent decades liberal education has tended to become a separate academic specialization in itself. This is revealed in different ways. Some scholars of higher education have voiced dismay that the number of pure liberal arts colleges is declining; they perceive this decline to be caused by the increase in professional programs in liberal arts institutions. This outlook implies that liberal education has a function totally separate from that of professional education. In many if not most universities, liberal education is either a segregated college or a segregated portion of the curriculum. This, again, separates liberal education from other aspects of education and implies a form of specialization.

Other trends in higher education have also encouraged the compartmentalization of liberal education. In the last decades, the increased specialization in the academic sector has been paralleled by an increased specialization in the administrative sector. As faculty members have turned more and more toward their specialized research, they have become less and less concerned with those aspects of students' lives that are not focused on the purely academic. At the same time, student services and athletic programs at universities have expanded dramatically. Each has developed its own multiplying specialties such as career counseling, remedial study, recruiting, and so on. Personnel in these specialties sometimes become more involved than the academic faculty in those aspects of students' character development and values formation that once were assumed to be part of traditional liberal education. This ironic outcome is another aspect of the failure of the traditional model of liberal education to respond to the rapidly changing circumstances within the American environment.

Search for a Distinctively American Liberal Education

Our analysis shows that the traditional model of liberal education—heavily oriented toward Anglo-European assumptions about the universality of high culture mediated through great books—has discouraged any serious efforts to develop a distinctively American approach to liberal education, despite repeated reforms aimed at helping the academy adjust to rapid changes in American society. This analysis contains a significant implication. As the inclusiveness of the American experience reaches beyond the Anglo-European experience in the late twentieth century, the need for an American view of liberal education has dramatically escalated. It is not too much to say that we are long overdue for a serious exploration of this issue. Where and how would such an exploration begin?

Debates that have emerged recently in the academy's so-called "culture wars" have often implied that a traditional liberal education, based on a "Eurocentric" view of Western civilization, and the contemporary needs of a pluralistic America are mutually exclusive. However, framing the issue in this manner is both simplistic and misleading. Significant aspects of the traditional model of liberal education can and should be retained in any American view of liberal education. After all, our views about education and culture essentially evolved from Anglo-European roots, and some, if not all, of those views continue to be appropriate for the conditions we face today. At the same time, the limitations of the traditional views of liberal education, many of which were noted in the foregoing analysis, need to be recognized and replaced by ideas that more effectively address the changing realities of America and the educational requirements those realities dictate.

Unity in Pluralism

We need not abandon the aspiration of traditional liberal education to find universal truths because we have discarded at least the conscious *presumption* that Western civilization alone possesses the universal truth. Although this distinction may seem subtle, its consequences are dramatic. A goal of finding universal truths acknowledges the need for some standard that transcends particular cultures so that we are not trapped in a meaningless cultural relativity, but it also recognizes that there must be open and equal transactions between cultures in order to determine what those broader standards might be. Bruce Kimball's useful typology, in which he identifies the two main strands of the liberal education tradition, can be applied here. One of these strands is made up of the known cultural truths used to develop character and leadership; the other comprises the Socratic-scientific search for truths that are continually unfolding with new experience. In effect, an American model of liberal education would take the Socratic method and apply it to cultural truths, thus establishing universal truths as aspirational rather than presumptive.

Although some recent critics of traditional liberal education have dismissed any notion of universal truth as inherently contradictory to the requirements of cultural pluralism, the combination of the search for universal truths with the reality of many different cultures is deeply and distinctly American. As many observers of the American scene have noted, the Declaration of Independence appealed for the equality of all human beings, a universal claim that permitted American immigrants from many different European cultures to unite in opposition to the British crown. Gunnar Myrdal identified democratic ideas as a universal American creed that provided the *unum* in *e pluribus unum* — the unity in the pluralism that was the United States.

If we accept democratic ideas as one of the conceptual cornerstones for an American view of liberal education, revising the traditional model of liberal education has other significant ramifications as well. The Matthew Arnold view of a pure, high culture mediated by the great books of Western civilization for gentlemen of the aristocracy should be replaced by a view of culture that is less pure, less static, less removed from the larger democratic society. This view of culture would be more open-ended and more multicultural, and its development would be more dynamic. Great books from many different cultures and civilizations would provide the basis for a continuing dialogue about which aspects of these human cultures apply broadly to the general human condition and which are tied only to a particular culture. This view of culture would not repudiate the accumulated wisdom of the past but would require its application to present and future issues, with the open possibility that it might be revised or revitalized. This approach to culture would be more anthropological than metaphysical, more comparative than culture-bound in its method.

The Integrating Vision of Liberal Education

In our search for an American view of liberal education, we do not need to abandon the traditional ideal that emphasized integrated learning aimed at the whole student. This integration included character development along with intellectual development, practical knowledge combined with academic knowledge, and education for who they are as well as for what they will do. Insofar as liberal education is a distinctive aspect of higher education, this integrating vision is the essence of its distinctiveness. In addition, we should remember that the roots of American higher education were planted by the early New England liberal arts colleges, which were dedicated to this vision of an integrated, whole-person education nourished in a residential community. Subsequently, of course, American higher education developed other kinds of institutions, such as land grant universities and community colleges, both of which emphasized service to society rather than detachment from it.

Ernest Boyer, president of the Carnegie Foundation for the Advancement of Teaching, has suggested a "New American College" model that implies a distinctively American approach to liberal education. This approach applies the integrating vision of the early American liberal arts college to other distinctive aspects of American higher education so that they can be expressed in a single institution. The traditional model of liberal education had an aversion to involvement in the larger society and its needs. The New American College's approach would extend the scope of liberal education to engage the needs of the larger society in a spirit akin to the distinctively American land grant university. Colleges that have assisted local school districts in improving the quality of public education exemplify this broader scope of liberal education. Universities that provide local governments with studies and proposed solutions to environmental problems also illustrate the application of American pragmatism to liberal education.

In a similar way, the integrative priority would be applied to the relationship between what we call general education and the more specialized education of academic and professional disciplines. Rather than rigidly segregating the general education courses from the courses required for a major, whether in the arts and sciences or in applied professional areas, educators would make a conscious effort to provide a theoretical and practical connection between these sectors of the curriculum. This scheme would involve structured efforts to have the teachers of these different kinds of courses engage in conversations about how students can apply the knowledge and skills taught in general education courses to the more specialized courses in the field major. Such efforts would help reestablish liberal education as the intellectual foundation of all academic disciplines and reaffirm the importance of some shared vision of learning within the faculty.

In this New American College model, the traditional American liberal arts college vision that connects character development with academic learning would be restored. This connection has been significantly eroded in the past several decades by the withdrawal of faculty involvement with student behavior and the simultaneous emergence of professional student-life bureaucracies. While it is unlikely that faculty concern with student life can be restored to nineteenth-century levels, a different kind of connection can be established by asking faculty and student-life staff members to collaborate in building academic components into residential life programs. This living-learning focus would promote the integrative vision of the liberal arts in a new and more challenging context.

A New American College model is less a particular set of institutions than general ideas that can be applied to a variety of different kinds of colleges and universities. The model draws strength from the American experience, which, in higher education, is embodied in wide institutional diversity. In liberal arts colleges, the model would challenge the traditional ivory tower syndrome and open up new ways of viewing vocational and professional fields. In large research universities, the model would be more effectively applied in schools or divisions than across the entire university. In comprehensive universities, especially the small, private institutions with strong liberal arts traditions, the new concept provides an opportunity to integrate its existing components in synergistic ways that make the whole much more than the sum of its parts.

This integrated American approach to liberal education would need to engage the challenge of academic specialization in a fresh and different way. As I have noted, previous efforts to restore the liberal education vision in higher education have repeatedly been eroded by the dominance of the research ethos and the fragmentation brought about by academic specialization. But it is important to emphasize that specialization itself is not the problem. No one can deny the strengths and advantages that specialization brings in developing new knowledge and high levels of competence. The problem comes when specialization is so dominant and so narrow that it becomes disconnected from other fields of learning, from the broader issues of human values and the human condition, from the needs of the larger society, from the personal development needs of students, and from students' honest concern about how their education will help them make a living. The problem facing any liberal education reform is "disconnected specialization." The initial challenge is to envision a practical way to reconnect the academic specializations so that liberal education's integrating vision is given priority.

Primary-Care Education

An analogy from the health-care field may provide a useful comparison for addressing this issue in higher education. As many have observed, the dominance of the health-care system by medical specialists has created a situation in which the needs of the whole patient are lost or subordinated to the treatment of a particular part of the patient's body. There is great advantage in being treated by a heart specialist, an eye specialist, or a bone specialist if those specialists have not lost sight of the fact that good health is the result of a whole human system working well in an integrated way. But the pressures of specialization too often result in a disconnection from these larger concerns. As a result, the medical field today, according to many expert observers, desperately needs more and better trained primary-care physicians whose priority concern is to appropriately connect specialized care to the needs of the whole person.

In a similar way, an American approach to liberal education that invokes the integrating vision of the early liberal arts colleges needs to develop a new model of faculty activity. This model could be appropriately called the "primary-care professor." These primary-care professors would have an essential concern for the whole student. They would teach in ways that would have some influence on what students believe and how students behave. They would teach their subject matter in ways that relate to other academic disciplines, and they would not presume that their own discipline had exclusive claims to truth. They would be concerned not only with how knowledge is produced but also with how it is taught, integrated, and applied. They would be concerned about how the general skills and knowledge of liberal education connect with the professional or vocational skills that students will need in order to earn a living. They would be interested in determining how the wisdom and knowledge of the academy can be applied to the urgent problems of the larger society and the wider world.

This primary-care model of faculty activity would complement the academic specialist model that presently dominates the culture of our colleges and universities. Just as the primary-care physician relies on medical specialists to provide the appropriate expertise based on the needs of the patient, in a similar way the primary-care professor would outline the optimal ways for a particular student to use academic specialists to achieve the learning goals considered best for that student. In the ideal New American College model, all professors would have some of the attributes of the primary-care professor, and there would be a balanced distribution of traditional academic specialists to best serve the needs of the whole student.

Some people in the academy would argue that the integrating vision of liberal education is obsolete or at best a nostalgic longing for a lost golden age. If one were to interpret integration as a unity of knowledge of the kind sought by medieval philosophers, such an argument would be valid. But the integration needed today is more modest. It is perhaps better described as a sense of continuity or connection across the borders of academic and administrative specializations. While this vision might appear to go against the grain of an era in which knowledge and information continue to expand at exponential rates, there are significant indications that larger imperatives may be driving us toward increased connections between fields of knowledge. Much of the cutting-edge research now taking place in the sciences, the social sciences, and the humanities is explicitly interdisciplinary—whether biochemistry, international studies, or cultural studies—and most of the urgent problems that cry out for the application of new wisdom and knowledge require an interdisciplinary approach, whether environmental studies, health care, or the new world order.

To facilitate this kind of American approach to liberal education, colleges and universities need to develop structures and incentives to encourage and reward continuous conversations at the intersections of the varied specialities in our institutions. These intersections must include not only those between academic disciplines but also those between arts and sciences disciplines and professional disciplines, between faculty and administration, between different cultural groups on our campuses, and between the academic community and the larger society. In our current structures and incentive systems, these kinds of conversations are inhibited or even discouraged. But unless such conversations come to be conducted on a continuous basis, the quest for an American model of liberal education will make little progress.

Conclusion

Although efforts to reform liberal education in America have frequently been concerned with adapting to the country's changing circumstances, they have not been equally concerned with developing a more appropriate model to engage these changing circumstances. Our analysis suggests that as we approach the twenty-first century, the traditional liberal education model, which has its origins in Anglo-European culture, needs to be replaced by an American liberal education model that has its origins in American culture and experience. While this model need not discard all aspects of the traditional model, it should be more democratic, more multicultural, and more responsive to the needs of American society. At the same time, it should take the universal aspirations and the integrating vision of the traditional model and reinterpret them in the context of the cultural and academic pluralisms that constitute major influences in the country and the academy today. As a part of this search for an American liberal education, we might profitably explore a new model that accepts and affirms the cultural and academic diversity presently found in our colleges and universities. At the same time, this model would apply the priority of integration by promoting conversation and creative development at the intersections of the now-divided sectors of academic departments, general and specialized education, academic life and student life, and college and community. At the end of this search, we may find a truly new American college that reflects an American model of liberal education. This innovation could in turn give us a renewed sense of academic community and at the same time enrich our service to American society.

Notes

1. Bruce Kimball, *Orators and Philosophers: A History of the Idea of Liberal Education* (New York: Columbia University Press, 1986), p. 205.

2. W. B. Carnochan, *The Battleground of the Curriculum: Liberal Education and the American Experience* (Stanford: Stanford University Press, 1993), p. 104.

3. John Dewey, *Democracy and Education: An Introduction to the Philosophy of Education* (New York: Macmillan, 1916), pp. 94–117.

4. Phyllis Keller, *Getting At the Core: Curricular Reform at Harvard* (Cambridge: Harvard University Press, 1982), p. 164.

6

Restructuring for the Twenty-First Century

Stanley N. Katz

Today, as the demographics and culture of America change, the demands made on any number of social, cultural, and educational institutions that had their origins in the traditions of Europe and earlier American history seem almost impossible to reconcile. The current demand that these institutions serve all members of American society—people of a multitude of backgrounds, cultures, and interests—and at a higher technological level than ever before, gathers increasing weight, weight that threatens these institutions.

At the same time, those with a vested interest in universities, museums, social services, and arts organizations desperately try to shore up their beloved institutions from within, with the result that no one is pleased. Reform attempts seem to lead to the creation of yet more bureaucracy, further stifling institutional ability to respond to the new needs. Goals apparently so simple and clear as "We must better educate our youth to compete in the new world economy" become complicated and muddled.

To complicate all the more this process of "change"—to use the current buzzword—we are coming to realize that in tinkering with our traditional institutions, we no longer have confidence in the traditional ways of passing along our values, nor is there a strong consensus on what those values are. William E. Brock, chairman of the Wingspread Group, which was convened to study higher education, states that we must pass along to the next generation the "critical importance of honesty, decency, integrity, compassion, and personal responsibility in a democratic society."[1] Who could disagree? The problem is that people of goodwill no longer necessarily define terms such as "integrity" and "personal responsibility" the same way.

So while everyone of every political persuasion is able to agree that something must be done, it has become almost impossible to agree on what to do. Goals become either so idealistic that they are laughable or so watered down, in order not to offend any interest group, that they are useless. In today's political climate, it is clear that to call for "major reform" plays well in the press but can actually forestall any needed change. Therefore, though many people present complex, detailed visions of how to "reform" liberal education, I believe it might be best to instead suggest incremental changes based on specific educational goals that can start now, not five or ten years from now.

While the answers to the problem of how to educate our children for a complex, often uncertain, and rapidly changing world ultimately lie in making major structural changes in the university, actually making such changes will not be an easy task. Emotional and political ties to the "old ways" constantly frustrate change—even if those "old ways" are really memories of what things were like when we were twenty years old, as opposed to real knowledge of the historical traditions of the university. Clearly, small reforms in procedure and modest changes in curricular requirements—changes that will make a significant difference in the lives of the current generation of students and can also facilitate larger structural change twenty years down the road—represent the most attractive solution to the current "problem" of liberal higher education.

But when we study the university in the hope of finding solutions to address the changing needs of our society, the apparent problems posed by liberal higher education must be seen as reflections of underlying institutional complexity—of the fact that there is simply no such single entity as "the university." There are many different types of institutions of higher learning—research universities, liberal arts colleges, community colleges, and so on—and they serve widely divergent functions for our society. The diversity among institutions of higher learning cannot be overstated, and this diversity greatly complicates any general prescriptions for educational reform. No one needs to be reminded, at this point, that there are no easy answers. But in diversity is opportunity, and the possibility that higher education can meet the challenges posed by a changing society has never been greater. We have the opportunity to revisit the needs of education in a large democracy.

The fundamental problem is not a dearth of innovative approaches but the question of how to shape the reforms so that they are persuasively linked to creative responses to societal changes. We have a good idea of what we ideally desire from teachers and students, and we have seen examples in which enthusiastic teachers and students have performed exceptionally well in a variety of institutional settings. But what institutional arrangements, in general, will promote the talents and enthusiasm of as many teachers and students as possible? Beyond this, is the best organization of intellectual life also the best structure for the cultivation of democratic citizens?

One approach toward educational reform that is both mindful of the multiplicity of institutions of higher learning and cognizant of the urgency of social problems involves focusing primarily on the reorganization of undergraduate education. It has come to be the common wisdom (vide the Wingspread Report) that the teaching of undergraduates is severely neglected—and some observers make charges more serious than those of neglect. While I think such charges are at best exaggerated and at worst malicious, I believe deeply that undergraduate education can be significantly improved if we can agree on its goals.

In this essay, I shall focus on undergraduate education in the research university, since universities are the sector I know best and since undergraduate instruction is the most common activity across the range of our tertiary educational institutions. It is my conviction that undergraduate education often serves as the last and best chance postsecondary students have to broaden their intellectual horizons and to prepare for the great demands that society will place on them. In addition, undergraduate education provides the best circumstances in which democratic values can be inculcated or reinforced. This is the subtext of undergraduate education: that whatever the curriculum, the very institutional processes through which learning takes place must also serve to inculcate a respect for democratic values.

This focus on undergraduate education, however, raises an important question: how can we reform tertiary education without also addressing some of the problems posed by secondary schooling? I should like to argue for a closer relationship between secondary and tertiary educational institutions and for the provision of greater continuity in the schooling of college-bound students. This will require, at the very least, both improvement in the content of the high school curriculum and enhanced attention to pedagogy in postsecondary education.

For the past twenty years or more, enlighted college leaders have led attempts to enhance secondary school teaching through university–high school alliances in fields such as foreign language teaching and American history. The natural scientists have been very active in this regard as well, as have many of the professional learned societies. But we need to do much more to intensify and broaden the link between school and university, especially to institutionalize the regional and local relationships between secondary and tertiary education.

My own organization, the American Council of Learned Societies, has for the past three years been sponsoring university-based programs for the development of K–12 humanities and social studies curricula, in the belief that primary and secondary school students and their teachers deserve access to the most current knowledge of university humanists. There is no more reason for these students and teachers to operate with the American history of the last generation than there is for them to learn the biology taught to their parents. We have had a tremendous response from the ACLS teacher-fellows and from their university colleagues. It goes without saying that there are also large opportunities and responsibilities for the universities in their capacity as teacher-trainers.

For me, the essence and potential of the school-university relationship is reciprocity. The schools have something to contribute to postsecondary institutions beyond the students whom they inevitably funnel to them. Primarily, I think, this contribution lies in their pedagogical expertise. For all of the traditional professorial scorn of education schools and of pedagogy as a discipline, great progress has been made in cognitive psychology and the development of pedagogy over the past several decades.

The challenge to higher education is to reexamine its own pedagogical assumptions in light of the new psychology and recent developments in school teaching. The critics of higher education complain that we do not devote ourselves sufficiently to teaching, but the debate about college teaching seems entirely quantitative—that is, are we teaching *enough*? The more serious question is whether we are teaching *effectively*, but we cannot even begin to analyze that question until we have a theory of learning. In other words, what effects do different teaching methods produce?

The higher education debate has focused on curriculum, but even when we are agreed on what to teach, we must know how to do it well. Schools and schoolteachers can help us, and we ought to put them to work in the universities in a variety of ways. Imagine, for instance, a high school social studies master teacher working with the university professor responsible for a freshman history survey course. Might she not provide invaluable assistance in the training of teaching assistants, the critique of the professor's teaching methods, and even (God forbid) the professor's "lesson plans"? This example seems to me only the most obvious one; I believe that there will be a great many similar modes of interaction between schools and universities.

More important, I want to suggest the possibility of reconceptualizing the last two years of high school and the first two years of undergraduate education as a single unit. This unit should not be a seamless one, however, as we must be heedful of the special role compulsory secondary education plays in society, as well as the need for specialized research. I quite understand that not all secondary students go on past the twelfth grade, but nevertheless I think we might usefully conceive of grades eleven to fourteen (an interval that in itself is a useful concept) as the crucial years for liberal education. Why not think of these as the Liberal Arts Years?

We worry about the "preparation" of secondary school students for college work, but beyond elementary questions of literacy and numeracy we are not very clear about what we expect, except that "our students do not know as much as they used to." I wonder. By what standard? I don't think I knew very much when I graduated from New Trier High School in 1951, although a year earlier *Life* magazine had declared New Trier to be the best high school in the United States. Every nation in Europe thinks of the preuniversity period when students are roughly fifteen to nineteen years of age as crucial years for inculcating the liberal arts, and they certify such accomplishment by the *baccalaureate* or *abitur*. Maybe the French and Germans are onto something. Could not ongoing collaboration between secondary schools and the managers of freshman/sophomore collegiate education produce some interesting and sensible sequences of courses and other learning experiences? Rather than recruiting university faculty to collaborate with schoolteachers in inventing model high school courses, as the College Board is now doing in its important Pacesetter program, why not place these courses in the context of the general education we expect college-bound youngsters to achieve before doing specialized "upperclass" work in the university? Some of the structures for beginning this work are already in place. I will not pretend that I feel confident of the precise content of the liberal education to be prescribed for grades eleven to fourteen, though I will confess that I am an only modestly reconstructed admirer of the Harvard Redbook of 1945. I believe that there must be a significant core of common knowledge based on history, large ideas, and significant texts, though my notions of the parameters of commonality have certainly expanded since my own "general education" experience at Harvard in the early 1950s. This is hotly contested ground in higher education these days, and I will only say I believe that a great many viable understandings of liberal or general education are currently in place in our colleges and universities.

Ironically, at the end of the twentieth century, the liberal arts seem to have become ever more practical, though neither the critics of undergraduate education nor the public at large seems to be aware of this fact. Americans are living longer and changing careers more often in a world whose demands they cannot predict. The sociologists and labor economists tell us that today's college graduate should expect to hold five or more different types of jobs during his working life. Our society needs citizens who can rapidly adapt to the changing needs of the growth and technological development of the economy, who also have an unprecedented degree of specialized knowledge; yet those young people will be best served by an education sufficiently liberal and unspecialized that they are primarily trained to be broadly knowledgeable and to think clearly and creatively. Postindustrial economies place little value on the retention of specialized knowledge but instead emphasize basic numeracy and literacy (including computer literacy). This situation strikes me as a tremendous opportunity for the humanist to claim more space and time in the undergraduate curriculum, at the very least in the last years of high school and the first years of college.

We also have the opportunity and obligation to take up the social realist challenge laid down by Jane Addams nearly a century ago:

As the college changed from teaching theology to teaching secular knowledge the test of its success should have shifted from the power to save men's souls to the power to adjust them in healthful relations to nature and their fellow men. But the college failed to do this, and made the test of its success the mere collecting and dissemination of knowledge, elevating the means into an end and falling in love with its own achievement.[2]

Similarly, in the early years of the nineteenth century Edward Copleston defended liberal higher education as a means of saving us from our worst selves by establishing a social bond.[3] Though this was a radical notion at the time, it seems quite a sensible suggestion as the twentieth century ends. I have already confessed that I will not try to prescribe the content of liberal education, except to assert that the humanities must form a significant portion of its core. But I think some tested humanities approaches seem particularly useful in creating the common intellectual terrain that must underlie liberal higher education.

Consider the possibility, for instance, of a requirement that all university freshman (or, better still, eleventh graders) enroll in a course where a common text—such as the U.S. Constitution and the documents that place it in chronological context (I have in mind Bernard Bailyn's magnificent Library of America volumes, *The Debate on the Constitution*)—formed the basis for an extended exploration of, say, the role of law in a democratic society. With such a core set of texts, it should be possible to link this threshold humanities course to other learning activities during the Liberal Arts Years of the liberal education experience, bringing to bear different disciplinary perspectives and chronological and cultural contexts. I could imagine (and have taught) a subsequent course that analyzes the dilemmas of constitutionalism and the rule of law in contemporary societies making the transition from socialism to capitalist democracy.

The next step, I would hope, would be to establish connections to other sorts of liberal learning experiences across the range of the sociology of knowledge. These connections are easiest to imagine in the humanities and social sciences, since, at least from a historical perspective, they are so closely related to one another. But it seems possible, especially through the history of science, to link at least some of the initial, nonspecialist exposure to the physical and life sciences to whatever body of text or ideas is chosen as the core experience. My feeling, frankly, is that the content of a particular set of core ideas is less important than the process of taking a comprehensive and interrelated approach to a common learning experience.

The likely outcome of this reform is a focus on thinking skills and the communication of ideas, which are the basic tools the general population needs in order to face our rapidly changing world. We have found in the schools that one of the most effective ways to communicate ideas is to reify them by placing them in historical context or to represent them as historical figures. Ideas can be grasped by undergraduates as a narrative and thus can be seen as an expression of citizens reconciling themselves to the playing out of human history.

Another aim of this proposal, then, is to stimulate conversation and encourage clear thinking and communication in a social environment, to deepen interest, and to facilitate commitment to ideas as emotion enters into these conversations. Students of widely divergent backgrounds, interests, and abilities will be compelled to create a meaningful conversation about these ideas. This will draw students into interdisciplinary experiences so that over time their attitudes toward learning and customary boundaries in learning will change. It may also be that teachers-in-training who have taken such courses can assist in teaching them at the college level, since the courses will be linked to related teaching activities in grades eleven and twelve.

Admittedly, this is not (with the exception of the suggestion that grades eleven through fourteen be somehow linked) a very startling proposal. In form it really harkens back to quite traditional notions of general education. But at least two innovations would be required to adapt general education to the current situation of higher education: the content to be covered would have to be broadened to take into account the multicultural realities of our society, and a broader range of pedagogical techniques would have to be used than were used when I was an undergraduate—especially methods of creating genuine exchange between teacher and student.

Implementing these reforms will require some significant organizational reform in undergraduate education. The current departmental structure has outlived the rapid increase of information and knowledge, as well as other fundamental changes in what we know and how we look at the world. This has happened because the departmental structure of today's research universities is largely an artifact of branches of knowledge that seemed distinct at the turn of the century but have remained distinct only for reasons of academic and administrative convenience.

This is not the occasion for an extended discourse on the state of the mind at the end of the twentieth century, but I do need to assert that late-nineteenth- and early-twentieth-century categories of disciplinary knowledge are no longer adequate. We have invented new disciplines and altered old ones. We work across disciplines and in nondisciplinary modes. Increasingly, we organize our research according to the subjects we study rather than the techniques we use to study them—urban studies, area studies, women's studies, and the like. Since the professoriat studies what it considers most important, we need to reformulate curriculum so that it corresponds at least in part to developments in research.

Yet most university departments correspond to the classical modern disciplines, while the newer approaches are relegated to committee or program status, without permanent budget lines. If the academic department is not the enemy of knowledge, it is almost certainly the foe of pedagogical reform. We have to find a way to place the facilitation of learning closer to the center of university decision making.

In the short term, this will require new modes of assigning faculty members new undergraduate teaching responsibilities and designing new learning experiences. For the purpose of undergraduate teaching at least, the faculty might better be organized thematically into discipline clusters. In practice, this move would restructure undergraduate education by consolidating faculty from different departments along thematic lines. In the short term, this only means new groupings of faculty for undergraduate teaching. For example, a theme such as "models of human behavior" could bring computer science (artificial intelligence), cognitive psychology, social psychology, and neoclassical economics together with aspects of sociology, history, and political science.

For the long term, these changes would set the stage for a consolidation of departments around these themes or even for some more radical reorientation of intellectual sociology. In the meantime, however, universities might begin to reconfigure themselves in other ways along lines already suggested by area studies, cultural studies, and multidisciplinary studies. Such a move would in fact take the direction that most faculty and students are already going. While the need for individual disciplinary training will persist in the foreseeable future, most of us now require training in more than one discipline. Increasingly, we do research across disciplinary lines, and we have to find ways to make the organization of the university look more like our own minds. We must also find a way to encourage and facilitate non- and multi-disciplinary teaching. Here again, what I propose has been tried before, at institutions as different as Hampshire College and the University of California at Santa Cruz.

The reorganization of undergraduate education around themes or areas of emphasis requires a rethinking of how we present the curriculum to students. Currently we organize upperclass undergraduates in terms of majors. But "majors," in their current incarnations, frequently do not advance the larger objectives of liberal higher education. They are narrowly conceived, ordinarily discipline-based, and often preprofessional in character. Ideally, we need to think more flexibly and imaginatively about the organization of upperclass student intellectual effort. This can best be achieved within broadly defined categories or "areas of emphasis." It should be within our organizational capacity to design a system that does not tie students' thematic concentration so heavily to the faculty's formal organizational structures. There is no good reason why faculty research (or even graduate teaching) should have to be symmetrical with undergraduate pedagogy.

A transition to a more thematic organization of student effort also argues for a reduced reliance on individual "courses" as the basic building blocks of the curriculum. Courses are a "mechanical" way to think about formal schooling at any level. Education needs a broader array of experiences including pro- and interactive projects that encourage students to find the deep connections between ideas, knowledge, and experience. Deep down we all know this, and we also recognize that it is apparently cheaper and more convenient administratively to organize instruction in uniform units. But if our colleagues in K–12 education are finding practical alternatives, we should be challenged to do at least as well.

Once students complete the Liberal Arts Years, they will be ready to apply themselves to deeper exploration of a specific area of knowledge—that is, to focus on a specific emphasis in their studies (in grades fifteen and sixteen). This area of emphasis should in some way mirror the larger consolidated groupings of the university. It will influence a student's choice of a college or university in the first place. Under this plan, a student will be able to engage both broadly and deeply in a specific area of emphasis. For instance, a student interested in economics may study a wide array of interrelated topics, such as politics, mathematics, history, and psychology, with a faculty no longer divided by department but now united by undergraduate teaching responsibilities.

At the beginning of this process of focusing on an area of emphasis, a student should be able to negotiate with a faculty member the outlines of her course of study and to develop the terms for a portfolio of educational objectives that will be used to evaluate the outcome of her studies. Here, cost and administrative imperatives will doubtless limit the range of possibilities, but even at the worst we should be able to present students with a reasonable range of thematic and pedagogical alternatives.

Which brings us to the problem of student evaluation. Once again, the recent experiences of elementary and secondary education seem to point the direction in which we should be going. We have learned that the most traditional sorts of testing mechanisms fail to adequately represent students' learning accomplishments, because they lack context. Tests are too often akin to "snapshots" of the mind, but in the true acquisition of useful knowledge the mind is engaged in process, and like snapshots, which freeze a split second of a complex action, tests often mislead and conceal more than they reveal.

An alternative is the concept of portfolio evaluation, which has become so important in school reform and which is now so much talked about in the context of faculty evaluation in higher education. If a test is akin to a snapshot, a portfolio is akin to a documentary film. The portfolio has two aspects: what it will consist of and how its contents will be determined. The portfolio could contain test scores, but these scores would be contextualized by the inclusion of essays, artwork, and so on. Further, following the suggestion of Ted Sizer, the evaluation might encompass "exhibitions" or performances, such as a debate, a dance recital, or a poetry reading.

It is not that snapshots will be eliminated but, to continue the metaphor, that they will be used in a richer context, a context in which a moving camera closes in, juxtaposes, and uses narration to convey richer meanings. This sort of portfolio can contain a wider array of information than the traditional academic record. It could also link academic work to community service, travel, and a variety of relevant noncurricular and nontraditional activities.

The contents of the portfolio should be negotiated between students and faculty. This will create some problems, such as how to establish comparability among the students being assessed, but the negotiation process itself must be seen as an important component of the process of education. Negotiation will compel teachers and students to think and communicate clearly about what they are doing and why they are doing it. The process will help scholars focus on undergraduate teaching and help students take the content of their education seriously. Academic standards are not uniformly applied now, and they will not be in the foreseeable future, either, but I believe that through this method we might actually enhance the appreciation of standards.

Teachers, too, can be well served by portfolio evaluation. Teaching encourages deep attachment to knowledge and new understandings. It is closely related to scholarship in ways that we are only just beginning to explore adequately. As such, teaching—especially undergraduate teaching—should be considered seriously in tenure decisions. Teachers should compile their own portfolios through negotiations with faculty peers, administrators, and students. These might include plans for curriculum development, reports on mentoring, videotapes of classroom performance, evaluations by students, and other materials that represent the performance of mutually agreed-on duties. Crucially, however, teachers must be evaluated in terms of what their students learn—in other words, there must be some systematic relationship between student and faculty portfolios. Student learning must distinguish good college teaching from teaching that is not as good. Scholarship and service, needless to say, would also be included in the portfolio—though I join with the many voices calling for more effective recognition and reward of the teaching component.

The reforms that I have outlined need to be implemented in light of a deeper understanding of the nature of learning itself. As I suggested earlier in this essay, we must take seriously what researchers are learning about learning. We are beginning to recognize what is done best individually and what is done best in groups. Educators are aware of different learning styles and different talents—indeed, the many lessons of cognitive psychology. The research university mocks its own intellectual ambitions when it fails to take heed of its own discoveries.

As we continue to study the changing sociology of knowledge, as well as the attempts to understand the learning process itself, we will no doubt be compelled to face some uncomfortable truths. As a result, our understanding of learning will deepen our understanding of the sociology of knowledge. We should prepare the institution to change as our understanding of understanding grows. Learning itself should become a focus of curricular and pedagogical planning. Moreover, the thematic organization of tertiary education should be revised and adapted both to our developing sense of how students learn and to our understanding of what we as scholars are learning. If there is one overarching aim to the reforms I have set forth, it is that they should provide higher education with institutional mechanisms that will promote such institutional flexibility.

Who will determine which reforms will be implemented? We all will. The democratic basis of the development of new programs depends on *continual* negotiation among interested parties. All the relevant stakeholders—trustees, faculty members, students, families, community representatives—have legitimate roles to play, depending on the problem to be solved. Together we must negotiate what liberal education is and what it should be. Within some reasonable limits of administrative convenience, we must try to adapt our institutions of higher education to the conditions of a changing society. To do so, we must be engaged in an ongoing process of mutual redefinition of standards and processes within our academic institutions.

Let me end by reiterating my major points:

- We should reorient the relationship between secondary and tertiary education to provide greater continuity in education.
- We should reorganize our efforts around the concept of the Liberal Arts Years.
- We should restructure the content and organization of tertiary education around major "areas of emphasis." We should organize the faculty thematically for the purpose of undergraduate teaching.
- We should make the learning process itself a focus of curricular and pedagogical planning and take greater account of what we are learning through our research in the ongoing intellectual reorganization of the university. We should evaluate students and teachers by more comprehensive and flexible means.
- We should continually negotiate what liberal education is and should be through a process that includes all the relevant stakeholders.

Notes

I should like to express my gratitude to my friend Jeffrey Edelstein for his intellectual and research assistance in the preparation of this essay.

1. William E. Brock, *An American Imperative: Higher Expectations for Higher Education* (Racine, Wisc., 1993), p. 1.

2. Jane Addams, "A Function of the Social Settlement" (1899), quoted in *Jane Addams on Education*, ed. Ellen Condliffe Lagemann (New York, 1985), p. 37.

3. W. Bliss Carnochan, *The Battleground of the Curriculum: Liberal Education and the American Experience* (Stanford, 1993), p. 29.

7

The Years before College

Howard Gardner

Participants in the past decade's discussions about precollegiate education speak informally of "waves" of educational reform. The first wave which took place in the early and middle 1980s, centered on attempts to ensure that students would secure the prerequisites for higher learning; this phase was often termed a quest for "basic skills" or the "basic literacies," though sometimes commentators spoke more bluntly about "getting the little buggers to work harder." The second wave, which occupied the late 1980s, called for the professionalization of teachers and of building administrators. There should be a higher caliber of teachers, teachers should have more control over the events in their classrooms, and management should occur, as much as possible, directly on site.

Commentators like Albert Shanker and Patricia Graham have pointed out that neither of these waves was controversial. No one could question the importance of basic skills, though the means by which they were attained, and the time by which they should be in place, merited discussion. By the same token, while some may have feared the negative consequences of too much teacher or building autonomy, it was scarcely correct politically to oppose this trend in too direct a fashion.

One area of potential discussion has remained conspicuously absent from the first decade of discussions. This missing wave could be termed "the primary purpose of education." Various goals were implicit in many discussions, of course; they ranged from the preparation of a skilled workforce to the education of a wise citizenry. But there was understandable reluctance to make this discussion overt, because educators' goals are too likely to conflict with one another: the reformer who values well-roundedness or individual excellence might well clash with the reformer who values the graduate steeped in science or in the classics of Western civilization. Since reformers have needed all of the support and as much consensus as they could garner, it is not surprising that such discussions have taken place far more frequently in the corridors at meetings or in writings by individuals like Allan Bloom or E. D. Hirsch,[1] who did not come from the ranks of precollegiate educators.

In this essay, I put forth and defend a straightforward goal for education, from kindergarten through college: the enhancement of understanding. I argue that the pursuit of individual understanding should be central throughout the educational enterprise. I contrast this goal with other viable options and discuss some of the formidable institutional and individual obstacles to the achievement of such an education. Based on my own collaborative work and that of others involved in educational reform, I then outline some promising approaches to an education that keeps understanding central and that might yield a population better ready to benefit from the unique strengths of the American college and university system.

Current Options and a Vision

To complement a trio of waves, I suggest that concepts of suitable precollegiate education can conveniently be grouped into three broad categories, two existing and one a vision. The traditional approach to education stresses the need for students to master certain basic texts and certain core disciplines. A graduate of a traditional secondary school would have read literary classical texts and studied such core subjects as history, geography, and mathematics; he or she would be well positioned to pursue higher disciplinary studies.[2]

Particularly important in recent American history has been the complementary progressive approach, which is much less directive. Rather than prescribing texts and subjects, the progressive curriculum encourages students to develop interests and to pursue them in ways that are personally meaningful.[3] Progressive education stresses ties to the community and to the work world, and the pursuit of projects that inherently resist disciplinary slotting. A graduate of a progressive secondary school would have developed expertise in how to tackle a problem and how to use knowledge productively; he or she would be well positioned to make judicious decisions about what to study, how to study it, and what use to make of it in later professional and personal pursuits.

Each of these approaches has its obvious strengths and limitations. Properly pursued, the traditional approach ensures a population that shares a common background and can participate meaningfully in learning and in learned communities. The risk involved in the traditional approach is that it prejudges certain works, subject matters, and approaches as inherently superior, thereby consigning rival values (and students or groups with idiosyncratic interests and backgrounds) to lower status. Properly pursued, the progressive approach engages students and stimulates an education that is personally meaningful. However, one also runs the risk that some students will fail to develop basic competences and that a shared set of values and understandings may not emerge.

I believe that it should be possible to meld certain precious aspects of traditional and progressive education and, in the process, secure an education that is better for most students and more defensible as well on intellectual grounds. Stated simply, this third approach takes as its goal the cultivation of understanding: the capacity to apply facts, concepts, skills, and knowledge appropriately in new situations. This approach emerges from the posing of certain basic questions that have always interested human beings; cultivates the acquisition of skills, literacies, and disciplinary mastery as means of approaching these questions in a more sophisticated manner; and in the end yields individuals whose answers to these questions are reasoned and seasoned amalgams of the disciplined and the personal.

Let me unpack this vision. In calling for a focus on understanding, I am placing cognitive and intellectual approaches at the center of the educational enterprise. This decision may hardly seem radical, particularly to an audience steeped in higher education; yet one only has to hear the deafening discussion these days about "self-esteem" or "multicultural sensitivity" or "caring relationships" or "mastery of the tradition" to realize that this goal has definite rivals. I also want to distinguish understanding from mastery or memorization. The person who understands has not just mastered a body of material, nor has that person committed to memory a set of passages or books or tests or texts. Rather, faced with a new situation, problem, or project, the individual knows how to use skills or information appropriately in order to pursue that challenge in an effective manner. To the extent that one judges oneself ill-equipped to handle that fresh challenge, one knows that one needs to "tool up" and has some ideas about how to do just that.

But what should one understand, and how should one go about achieving that understanding? It may once have been possible to state all the important truths, all the crucial tasks, all the central texts or disciplines, but this is not possible any longer. Nor can we ever expect the day to return where all knowledge, let alone all understanding, can possibly be attained by a single individual. The traditional approach deals with this issue by arbitrarily conferring hegemony on certain bodies of knowledge, usually those that have been honored by dominant sectors of the society in the past. The progressive approach confronts this issue by assuming that no knowledge is inherently more important than any other—that what students need is to gain a feeling for how they learn and eventually to make their own choices about where to direct their energies and their talents.

A focus on understanding, I believe, provides a healthy middle ground. At the cost of mixing metaphors, one might say that it gives one dry land without boxing one in. The dry land comes from the pursuit of what I call basic or essential questions. Anthropologists and historians tell us that individuals the world over have always been intrigued by certain basic questions about human existence. These questions were originally approached through art, myth, and religion, then through philosophy and other humanistic scholars, and more recently through the formal disciplines, especially the sciences.[4] These questions will never be completely answered by scholars, nor will the answer hammered out in one culture ever be completely adequate for those of different backgrounds. Nonetheless, these questions provide a common core or anchor for all human beings.

Without attempting to be exhaustive, let me list and categorize these major or essential questions:

Personal identity: Who am I? Where do I come from? What will I be?

Group identity: What group do I belong to, in terms of family, community, nation, religion? What does it mean to belong to that group and not to others? How do new groups get constituted?

Group relations: How does my group resemble or differ from other groups? How do groups relate to one another? Why do they fight? How might they get along better?

The physical world: What is the world made of? How did it get to be that way? Where is it going? What is known about time, space, matter, energy?

The natural/biological world: What about the world of nature — of plants, animals, other living things? How did it originate? How do humans relate to these other entities? What is the relationship between the physical, the natural, and the manmade? What does it mean to have a mind?

The world of symbols: What about those entities that are created by human beings — poems, songs, histories, myths, dreams, language? What is their status; what can be gained from them; what remains mysterious? How do they relate to the supernatural?

The true, the beautiful, the good: What patterns exist in the world? Where do they come from? How do we decide what is true, what is beautiful, what is good? How do these realms relate — or fail to relate — to one another? Is there a Higher Being?

I argue here that the pursuit of these questions should undergird all education. The syllabi, curricula, and pedagogy of school ought to be directed, as much as possible, toward the elucidation of these questions. An individual's understanding of the world is thus enhanced, so that he or she is in a stronger position to approach these questions in a powerful manner — using the skills and knowledge gained in education in a way that makes sense to that person and can be pursued in that culture.

Thus stated, the goal of understanding seems simple and straightforward enough. I must acknowledge, though, that understanding is anything but easy to achieve. To the manifold obstacles that stand in the way of an education for understanding, I now turn my attention.

Institutional Obstacles

Even in those instances in which understanding, as defined here, has been accepted as a (or even as *the*) legitimate goal for education, formidable institutional obstacles stand in the way of its attainment. At a minimum, teachers, administrators, and parents have to agree on what understanding would be like, how its attainment can be fostered, and how one might determine whether such understanding has in fact been achieved or enhanced. None of these features proves simple to identify, monitor, or achieve, particularly when instances of an "education for understanding" have so far been rare or nonexistent.

An enormous complicating factor is coverage. Over the years, educators have felt increasing pressure to cover the principal topics within a textbook, either because such coverage is essential for a subsequent examination or, to put it in mountain climbers' terms, because the material is "there." However, the greatest enemy to understanding turns out to be coverage. As long as educators—or, for that matter, students or parents—are determined to "get through" all of the materials in a text or a course, one can virtually guarantee that most students will lack any genuine understanding of that material. Understanding proves inseparable from making tough choices.

Except in special circumstances, most youngsters the world over attend classes where they are grouped together with at least twenty other youngsters, or, not infrequently, with thirty, forty, or even more. Such grouping virtually ensures that teachers must resort to battle-axe tactics, even where a scalpel or a gemknife is indicated. It would be much easier to determine whether understanding has been achieved, or, if not, what alternative approaches might be adopted, if there were but one or a handful of students for each teacher. Tutoring, which provides ample opportunity for in-depth exchanges between student and teacher, is a preferred route for gauging and fostering understanding; however, because of economic considerations, such Socratic methods rarely prove feasible.

A final complicating factor has to do with the increasing heterogeneity of students both in the United States and in other parts of the world. If one can assume that students have the same background and cultural experiences, speak the same language(s), and share the same goals and values, then one at least has the option of pitching lessons so that they can reach at least a majority of the students in the classroom. Nowadays, however, one often confronts a classroom in which none of these expectations hold. Virtually any effort to target a group of students is likely to be purchased at the cost of missing large numbers of students with different strengths, problems, and goals.[5] The attainment of universal understanding—hardly a simple achievement even in relatively homogeneous circumstances—becomes steadily more difficult as the variations among youngsters proliferate.

Individual Obstacles

A wholly different set of problems arises from the nature of individual learning. In the past, teachers have had the luxury of subscribing to what might be called the Teachers' fallacy: "I taught a great class; therefore the students must have learned." But thanks to a generation of research by cognitively oriented educational psychologists, we now understand the fallaciousness of this inference. As psychologists have looked closely at the achievements of students—even the best students in the best schools—we have come to appreciate how difficult it is to attain genuine understanding in the classroom.[6]

The initial "smoking gun" came from classes in physics. It turns out that even students who get A's in physics at redoubtable undergraduate institutions like MIT and Johns Hopkins evince only a superficial grasp of materials. Questioned at exam time about mechanical principles, they do fine. However, once school is over and the same students are questioned about the behavior of phenomena around them, such as household machines or street-corner demonstrations or backyard games, they fail to exhibit understanding: they cannot apply Newton's laws to a coin toss or to a Ping-Pong game. Worse, they answer much in the manner of young children, reflecting what I have elsewhere dubbed "the mind of the five-year-old" or "the unschooled mind."[7]

It would be a relief to declare that these signs of nonunderstanding are restricted to the forbidding world of physics, but they are not. Biology students fail to understand the principles of evolution; mathematics students apply algorithms without having any idea what they mean; history students do not appreciate the link between the kinds of analyses that they carry out with reference to past events and the operation of the world of contemporary experience; and arts students display aesthetic preferences and reasonings that prove to be indistinguishable from the proclivities and understandings of individuals who have never taken an art class.

In short, scores of studies across a dozen disciplines indicate that as long as students are examined only on what has been in the textbook, as long as students take a test for which they have been explicitly prepared, many of them appear to understand. But as soon as they are called on to apply school-gained knowledge in unfamiliar situations that require the same knowledge, these students reveal the superficiality and evanescence of the knowledge they have putatively obtained.

There is yet another obstacle to education for understanding. Until recently, most educators everywhere have been adherents of the One Best Method in the Uniform School. Recognizing the ambitiousness of schools' goals, and the limited amount of time and other resources at their disposal, teachers have generally taught and assessed all students in pretty much the same way. At the least, this approach has history and economics on its side.

But just as psychologists have documented the difficulties exhibited by students when they are expected to apply knowledge in new situations, psychologists now concur that students have quite distinct learning styles, strengths, and approaches, and that students can show their understanding in many different ways. A decision to present information in one way—say, a lecture—or to assess in one way—say, a short-answer test—is not simply dubious on the face of it. It means, additionally, that one is "playing" to students who happen to learn in that way, and, correlatively, that one is placing additional burdens on students whose strengths happen to lie in a quite different vein. An optimal education would approach and assess students in ways compatible with their personal strengths; yet such an education presupposes both a knowledge base and a pool of resources that currently do not exist.[8]

Promising Leads

It may seem that I have succeeded too well in laying out the obstacles to an education geared toward understanding. The institutional obstacles are formidable, and so are the obstacles stemming from the contours of human learning. Have we set out an exquisite and awe-inspiring goal, only to demonstrate that it is utopian rather than practical?

To my mind, the obstacles, while genuine and formidable, are not in any way crippling. To a large part, they derive from practices that have arisen for different reasons in the pursuit of different goals. Once one has rethought the purposes and the pace of school, it should prove possible to make significant progress toward the form of education that has been honored in these pages.

Consider, for example, the treatment of all children in the same way and the reliance on certain short-answer assessment instruments. These practices arise because of a misplaced belief that understanding is not important or an equally unwarranted belief that it will come about simply as a result of sheer exposure or sheer memorization. We now realize that understanding is not a necessary concomitant of exposure, and we also appreciate that students do not all acquire knowledge or come to display it in the same way. Thus, we are challenged to proceed in quite different ways—sacrificing coverage for uncoverage, striving to reach each student in a way that is comfortable for that student—in order to sculpt an education that stimulates understanding.

When one is trying to rethink practices that have run awry, it is useful to attempt to identify institutions that have had some success in similar enterprises. In our own work, we have drawn inspiration from two educational institutions—one very old, the other quite new.

The ancient institution is the apprenticeship. For thousands of years, particularly in preliterate cultures, individuals have learned what is important not through formal schooling but by close and constant interaction with experts who exemplify the kinds of knowledge and understanding to which the apprentice aspires. Interestingly, even in the most complex industrialized societies, we continue to use apprenticeship methods in certain pursuits that we prize—from doctoral dissertation studies to law clerking to medical internship. Formal testing is hardly needed in such surroundings, because both students and masters gain ample evidence every day about how understanding is proceeding and how it might be enhanced.

While apprenticeship may seem a superannuated practice for modern schools, it actually proves productive to think of the classroom in these terms. Teachers can benefit from thinking of themselves as masters of literacy, scientific thinking, or problem-finding, constantly exhibiting what it is like to use one's skills appropriately; students can benefit from thinking of themselves as novices bent on becoming journeymen and aiming toward the eventual production of a masterpiece. Among the many dividends of this approach is a student's deeper involvement in the assessment of his or her own progress toward important learning goals.

The contemporary institution of special relevance to understanding is the children's museum (and its educational brethren). In a children's museum, students are exposed to intriguing displays and provocative questions that immediately attract their interest and their characteristic style of learning. Individuals are free to work on new information in a way, pace, and strategy that makes sense to them. Students can bring questions and answers from the museum back to school, and they can also transport mysteries or concepts from school to the museum. As Frank Oppenheimer, founding director of San Francisco's attractive Exploratorium, once quipped, "No one flunks museum."

The children's or discovery museum harbors important lessons for an education aimed at understanding. It accepts as valid the student's own curiosity and approach. At the same time, it makes available attractive displays that distill much of the best thinking that has emerged from disciplinary (and interdisciplinary) scholars over the years.

Having singled out these two institutions, I feel the need to underscore one point. I do not call on apprenticeships because of a belief that students should be required to sweep floors for seven years, nor do I call on children's museums because of a conviction that every youngster should be required to play with bubbles or visit grandma's kitchen or observe electronically animated dinosaurs. Rather, I wish to argue that many of the practices in today's schools are ill motivated; they endure less because they have intrinsic (or lasting) value than because they have been around for a long time. "We have been doing things this way for so long that we know they are right," a Chinese educator once responded to a critical comment I had ventured. I like better what Joanna Martin, an American middle school teacher, tells her students' parents: "School does not have to be the way that you remember it." Important lessons for education can be gathered from other countries and from apparently remote institutions if we will only take the trouble to attend to them.

The Need for a Systemic Approach

Over the past ten years—and, for that matter, over the past 100 years—there have been many excellent educational programs in American schools. Wonderful projects, inspiring teachers, and productive youngsters have dotted the landscape. There are schools that are terrific today, and there are even schools that have been that way for decades, often against formidable odds. Why, then, has almost every informed observer been struck by the sameness, the mediocrity, the lack of spark in the vast majority of American schools?

The answer, I believe, is this. It is hardly easy to fashion a good classroom, a good teacher, even a good school in isolation, and it proves extraordinarily difficult, over the long run, to sustain quality and innovations. To ask people to do much more than they usually can do, and to ask them to continually surpass themselves for long periods of time, is just not the reasonable way to ratchet up quality. Most precollegiate schools in Germany and Japan and Israel are better than most American schools not because the educators or the students are inherently superior; these schools are superior, on the average, because systems have been put into place that allow and encourage people of ordinary talents to do competent work over the long haul.

Americans have had a faith—a quasi-religious faith—that school control should be local and that national efforts in pedagogy, standards, or assessment are doomed to be nefarious. I think that these fears are largely misplaced and that, thanks to the individuals who make textbooks and tests, we in fact have mediocre national standards already in place. But even those reformers who remain committed to individual American genius and who do not trust nationally oriented reform efforts one bit have gradually come to the conclusion that we need a systemic approach to educational reform.[9]

In my view, and in the view of many others in the "reform business," reform needs to be systematized in two ways. On the one hand, there needs to be a single coherent conversation among school folks, so that those who are concerned with the education of young children are talking about the same issues as those who are concerned with the education of college-bound seniors. In the absence of such a conversation, one either has de facto domination by the individuals who have the greatest responsibility for, and power over, the college admissions procedures, or one has a situation where there is little effective communication between the primary school teachers, who seek individuality and self-esteem, and the high school teachers, who want only to produce disciplinarians in their subject. One of the most disheartening aspects of education in America today is that teachers can rarely report what is actually being done in the classrooms of teachers who deal with youngsters who are two years older, or two years younger, than those under their own charge.

In addition to systematization within the building or along a "pathway" from kindergarten through high school, there needs to be systematization within a school district (or comparable jurisdiction). While it is not by any means easy to sustain a high-quality school, one often encounters at least one estimable school within a district. The existence of the much-honored James Madison School allows the harried superintendent to point with pride to at least one building; and JMS serves as a magnet for those teachers, administrators, and parents who are willing to put in a lot of uncompensated extra hours each week. However, if the American educational system is to be enhanced as a whole, we must go beyond this very scenario: the happy accident of a great principal or a tireless set of teachers or parents. And such bootstrap improvement on a wide scale means that resources, workshops, mission statements, and coherent pathways need to be worked out and monitored on a districtwide level. Certainly, it would be desirable for students who move from one side of the tracks to the other to expect that the education obtained on both sides will be equally good and perhaps even consistent with one another.

A number of educators, including our own research-and-development group at Harvard Project Zero, have recently sought to transcend ivory tower generalities and to create actual models of systemwide school change. Our own collaboration—with the Coalition of Essential Schools at Brown University, the School Development Project at Yale University, and the Educational Development Center of Newton, Massachusetts—is called ATLAS, or Authentic Teaching Learning and Assessment for All Students. This collaboration is self-consciously ambitious, striving to cover the gamut from pre-K to twelfth grade; to encompass curriculum, assessment, and instruction; to make optimal use of new technologies; to develop appropriate governance mechanisms within the school community; to ensure the continued learning of all participants; and to obtain necessary support and, if indicated, waivers from those who set policy in the district and the state.

Even to describe the basic assumptions and procedures of ATLAS is an ambitious project;[10] moreover, ATLAS has just begun and will in all likelihood evolve over the next several years. However, I will describe what is, for me, the central component of ATLAS, because it resonates deeply with my own vision of a good education.

At the center of the ATLAS vision is the individual learner, engaged daily, even hourly, in learning activities that are meaningful for him or her and that make sense from the perspective of the larger society. The vision is deeply progressive in that it begins with the child's personal interests, goals, strengths, and strategies; yet at the same time, there is a willingness to identify certain questions, topics, disciplines, and values as central within the ATLAS community. One may say that the vision is progressive yet rooted in tradition.

From the very first days of school, ATLAS students are introduced to the essential questions and themes that I mentioned above. Sometimes these questions are raised quite directly; it can be engaging to talk about who you are, or what the world is made of. But especially in the first years of school, the issues are often encountered in an implicit fashion, through myths or puzzles or knotty scientific conundra.

Throughout the school life, there is a continuing concern with these questions. In a sense, one should be able to approach any student, teacher, or parent on a given day, ask about the day's agenda, and receive an answer that can be couched in terms of essential questions and issues. However, that potential need not and perhaps should not be tested regularly; rather, the essential questions constitute a central theme or unspoken leitmotif of the school.

Literacies and disciplines are important, indeed essential, and central to any school geared toward understanding. If one wants to have a better understanding of the world, the self, and one's experience, one needs to have direct and detailed contact with the best that has been thought and done regarding these issues. But means and ends should not be confused. One must learn to read, write, and calculate not because these are good activities in themselves but because one will not be able to carry out historical analyses or physical experiments or interdisciplinary work about conflict or ecology unless one has acquired these basic literacies.

By the same token, one needs to be rooted in the major disciplines, even though it is not necessary that every student study every science, every art, every humanity. But, again, such mastery is not sought because of a desire to satisfy requirements of Carnegie units or advanced placement tests. Nor should the human disciplines be equated with bureaucratically defined "subject matters." Rather, one cannot begin to think about these questions in a sophisticated way unless one has been exposed to the methods, the thoughts, the contents, the skills, and the understandings that have evolved, often painstakingly, over centuries and even millenia.

Just how one should work out the conversation among basic questions, essential literacies, and the acquisition of disciplinary mastery is an excellent topic for school staff and interested members of the community to consider. Indeed, a school cannot succeed, at least in the United States, unless all of these individuals become stakeholders in such continuing discussions. From the work of schools in the Coalition of Essential Schools and other comparable institutions, we know that there are numerous ways in which to achieve pedagogical effectiveness and to educate students who do regularly exhibit enhanced understanding.

Veronica Boix-Mansilla and I have detailed one such approach to an education based on essential questions and oriented toward understanding.[11] According to this approach, students sample a set of questions that are considered important in their own community. Examples we have discussed include the nature of sickness and health, from the scientific perspective, and the nature of power and control, from the social studies perspective. As it turns out, nubby versions of these issues can be posed to youngsters of all ages in forms that intrigue and stimulate them.

According to the scheme we have developed, these questions are initially approached in a commonsense or intuitive way—the way of the five-year-old—and such an intuitive stance is appropriate. Over the next decade, students continue to revisit these questions, using, respectively and at least somewhat chronologically, enlightened common sense, protodisciplinary knowledge, and the "normal disciplinary knowledge" of secondary school. Only after students have passed through a sequence like this—only after they have worn the garb of some traditional disciplines—does it make sense to speak of metadisciplinary, multidisciplinary, and transdisciplinary knowledge.

Indeed, we question the now-widespread practice of invoking the term "interdisciplinary knowledge" for activities carried out in elementary school. While it is laudable to have theme-related curricula, where students approach problems in a variety of complementary ways, it is more precise to characterize these activities as commonsense in nature. A genuine interdisciplinary approach proves to be a difficult one to achieve, and it can only be legitimately undertaken, let alone carried off with success, at a time when individuals have achieved at least some rooting in the constitutive disciplines.

Elsewhere, I have dealt with various aspects of such an education, ranging from ways of addressing youngsters who display different profiles of intelligence to techniques for assessing students' and one's own understanding.[12] There is no need to deal further with these ancillary concerns here. The point to stress is that there are serious efforts afoot to educate for understanding in a systemwide fashion and that various reformers have written explicitly about the forms that such an education might assume.[13]

Getting the Signals Right

When I speak to audiences about these ideas, even those who find themselves in sympathy raise two difficult and related questions. The first is, "This sounds great, but how do we start?" In truth, to create an education for understanding is an enormously ambitious task, one that will take years if not decades to implement. There is no more certain road to failure than to try to implement everything initially, to watch one's school founder or fight or fail, and then to conclude, "It can't happen here." Indeed, one actual recurring nightmare I have is that I visit a Boston area high school ten years from now only to overhear the comment, "Ah, education for understanding: we used to do that!"

One who wants a chance for success in this ambitious undertaking might keep in mind a number of considerations. To begin, a school's educators need to have developed a consensus that some things are worth changing and that some energy for such an effort exists. It is best to begin with a widely felt need that can be addressed without too much fractiousness. At the same time, however, the school needs to set into motion some longer term plans, which will inevitably cut across interest groups and turfs.

Having a regular chance to meet, plan, and reflect on how one is doing is very important. And having skilled facilitators to aid in the process of learning how to talk with one another, and learning how to disagree civilly, is highly desirable. Lest higher educators be inclined to regard this need for mediation in a condescending way, I invite you to think about how difficult it is to have productive conversations about substantive business on most faculty committees, let alone among the faculty as a whole.

Ultimately, in terms of the vision described here, the purpose for such restructuring should be to focus on what I often call the "meat and potatoes" of school—a curriculum, pedagogy, and assessment based on understanding. This vision cannot be approached without the eventual initiation of a major set of changes across a school. In the effort to make this goal an exciting odyssey rather than a Sisyphean logjam, one can gain comfort from three considerations. (1) It is important to begin but at the same time not to expect to achieve everything overnight. (2) All teachers have some areas of understanding, and, working together, they have considerable resources for such a reoriented education. (3) Many other groups, such as those involved in the ATLAS collaboration, have now embarked on similar missions. They—indeed, we—are in a position to help and to provide useful models, cautionary as well as inspirational. In such challenges as the attempt to change the face of American education, it is certainly beneficial to have sympathetic fellow travelers.

The second, almost predictable question has to do with the signals between schools, particularly high schools and the tertiary institutions of college and universities. This question runs as follows: "I'd like my child to get such an education, but I can't sacrifice her. The colleges want high SATs and Carnegie units, and I can't risk an education based on uncoverage rather than coverage." Or as the organizer Ernesto Cortes Jr. once put it, "My [Hispanic] parents don't care about alternative assessment. They just want their kids to go to Yale."

In my opinion, despite their good intentions, most selective colleges and universities have been a reactionary force in this process. Though wanting—or, perhaps, appearing to want—students who understand, they have tended to support those institutions (like the College Board) and those vehicles (like SATs) that (at least until recently) have pushed for coverage and that reward superficial knowledge rather than deep understanding. Even when admissions committees actually reserve places for the deep but idiosyncratic students, the rhetoric tends to stress the need for the student who is a good test-taker, with a "modal" if not a "model" transcript.

In this regard, the power held by the leading "selective" colleges is enormous. If Harvard, Yale, and Princeton were suddenly to drop the SAT exam, this information would be spoken on every parents' lips, and rumbling in every student's stomach, within twenty-four hours. Hundreds of institutions in our country would instantly regroup. I do not favor change for change's sake, and I would certainly want to take a close look at any new methods proposed to assess student preparation for college. Yet it seems paradoxical that at the very time when most colleges are lamenting their students' lack of preparation, their leading spokespeople have been reluctant to think about ways in which incoming students might be differently prepared and differently assessed.

I invite those of you who are not satisfied with the American college student of today to think about how one might secure a future student body that is better able to take advantage of what the colleges can give today and what they might be able to give tomorrow.

Notes

1. Allan Bloom, *The Closing of the American Mind* (New York: Simon and Schuster, 1987); E. D. Hirsch, *Cultural Literacy* (Boston: Houghton Mifflin, 1987).

2. Mortimer Adler, *The Paideia Proposal: An Educational Manifesto* (New York: Macmillan, 1982).

3. John Dewey, *Democracy and Education* (New York: Macmillan, 1916).

4. Ernst Cassirer, *The Philosophy of Symbolic Forms* (New Haven: Yale University Press, 1953–57).

5. R. Snow and E. Yalow, "Education and Intelligence," *Handbook of Intelligence*, ed. R. J. Sternberg (New York: Cambridge University Press, 1982).

6. Howard Gardner, *The Unschooled Mind: How Children Think, and How Schools Should Teach* (New York: Basic Books, 1991).

7. Ibid.

8. Howard Gardner, *Frames of Mind: The Theory of Multiple Intelligences* (New York: Basic Books, 1983); Howard Gardner, *Multiple Intelligences: The Theory in Practice* (New York: Basic Books, 1993).

9. M. Smith and J. O'Day, "Systemic School Reform," in *The Politics of Curriculum and Testing*, ed. S. Fuhrman and B. Malen (Bristol, U.K.: Falmer, 1993).

10. *ATLAS Atlas* (Not formally published; copies available from Harvard Project Zero, Longfellow Hall, Cambridge, Mass. 02138.)

11. Howard Gardner and Veronica Boix-Mansilla, "Education for Understanding across the Disciplines" (paper presented at the conference on Teachers' Conceptions of Knowledge, Tel Aviv, June 1993).

12. Howard Gardner, "Assessment in Context: The Alternative to Standardized Testing," in *Changing Assessments: Alternative Views of Attitude, Achievement, and Instruction*, ed. B. R. Gifford and M. C. O'Connor (Boston: Kluwer, 1991), pp. 77–120; Gardner, *Multiple Intelligences: The Theory in Practice*.

13. D. Perkins, *Smart Schools* (New York: Free Press, 1992); Theodore Sizer, *Horace's School* (Boston: Houghton Mifflin, 1992).

8

Technology and Computer Literacy

Peter Lyman

What is "computer literacy," and what is its place in liberal education?

Liberal education is incomplete if it does not prepare educated people to address the presence of technology and, more important, the presence of technology's information products, in an informed and critical way. There are four reasons I say this.

First, the traditional liberal arts understanding of technology as machine, merely an "object" in relation to human "subjectivity," is an essentially aristocratic attitude that fails to acknowledge the way technology and information saturate the modern world in which educated people live and work.

Second, defining the computer as a mere machine is an uncritical ideology that enhances the technological mythology that computers are more objective than humans, thereby masking and legitimating the social power of technicians.

But, third, there is a deeper reason as well: technical objects are created within a technical culture that contains a powerful (if tacit) critique of liberal education, one that has the potential to replace liberal education in the modern world.

Finally, liberal education's dismissal of computers as mere machines distracts attention from the fact that technology's information products define modernity: mass communications mediate most of the information in our culture, and digital technology produces the images and information that saturate everyday life.

If liberal education is to come to terms with the significance of technology in the modern world, or to subject technology-mediated communication and information products to critique, liberal education must also become self-reflective about the technical objects that shape its own communications and information. What is the origin of the book form, as it has evolved from the codex, the journal, and the social organization of education around printed objects (the bookstore, the lecture, the library, the disciplinary society, scholarly publishers, the college)? What are the origins of the concept of creativity stemming from individual genius, and of the social construction of the "author" as property right holder? In some ways, higher education is the last social institution primarily organized around print technology and still resistant to information technology. Is this a testimony to the strength of the tradition of liberal education or a sign of its decline?

The Invention of Information

The very name "computer" is an anachronism, the persistence of which lends an authority of mathematical certainty to a technology that has long since evolved from computation alone to become a medium for communication and artistic expression as well. The name "computer" reflects the application of digital technology to calculation, the problem for which the computer was created; the idea of such an "engine" for calculation is as old as Copernican astronomy, and it attained its modern sense with Babbage. But Turing made the decisive conceptual discovery that separates computers from all other machines—the separation of the program or application from the mechanical technology of calculation. With the idea of the program, the calculating engine became a symbolic engine, for the same machinery can be used for different purposes.

In digital technology, the program is the culture of the machine; it enables the computer to operate through a symbolic language that is, in principle, infinitely flexible. If the silicon chip is the DNA, the applications program is the culture of the machine, legislating the structure and format of the information produced. This tacit technical authority is suggested by the term "user," which connotes an implication of dependency. During my ethnographic observations in Silicon Valley, I observed the way the term "user" described a pecking order of authority and dependence within the design of the computer: originally the designers of the chip referred to the writers of the operating system as "users"; then operating system writers called applications programmers "users"; and now applications programmers refer to consumers as "users." At each stage of design, choices are made that legislate the work of the user, defining the way in which information will be created, the interface that defines the human-machine relationship, and ultimately the organization of the cognitive work itself.

And this is the decisive fact about the culture of the computer: technical objects have a history, which, like any other text, is subject to interpretation. While the cultural matrix of the machine was taken from the culture of the engineers who created and used it, and was then instantiated in silicon, computers might have been designed differently. The military culture of the Office of Naval Research is still evident in the semantic construction of the user interface as "commands," a social relation more appropriate to the military than to the faculty office; in keys named "control," "escape," and "break," which suggest war games; and in vestigial remnants of military language in computer jargon, such as the "control-K" command, which is a mnemonic for "kill [text]," or in "documentation" that tells one what to do if the computer "crashes."

This military language persisted during the evolution of computer technology from mathematics to the cybernetic culture of "command and control." In the next stage, cybernetic control is applied to business data. In this period the image of the computer as "brain" evolved: mainframe computers were used to discipline the work of clerical keyboard workers at "dumb terminals." The "brain" image had more to do with the centralization of command and control in the workplace than with the quality of the computer's symbolic manipulation or "thought." Decisions were to be made by the computer program (or, more accurately, the computer programmer), not data processing workers. The technical design of computer systems as mainframes served by dumb terminals reflects the social organization of the military and business — hierarchical organizations with centralized, authoritative decision making. Today's "networked workstations" design originates with the decentralized authority of the scientific laboratory, now called a "client-server architecture"; it reflects the organization of work among white-collar professionals.

If computer "architecture" is derived from the social organization of authority at work, not the requirements of technology alone, the ideology of computer intelligence remains useful in concealing and justifying this authority. A lasting cultural heritage from this period is a change in the rhetoric of responsibility wherever computer information mediates human relationships: a manager can successfully avoid dealing with challenges to authority at work by blaming the computer, or a "computer error." While real computer errors—errors in calculation caused by mistakes in programming or data—do exist, management policies that have been deliberately programmed into the computer are often rationalized as "errors" when they are challenged. Because of the facticity of the machine, the cultural prestige of its intelligence, and a lack of understanding of the difference between a program and a machine, the quality of computer decisions and the origins of computer errors are rarely questioned.

The definition of the line between human responsibility and computer calculation might appropriately be the responsibility of liberal education, but the task of defining cannot be carried out without a far more substantial engagement with the nature of technology. To put the proposition in terms closer to the humanistic tradition, the computer chip and program are ultimately texts that may be criticized in the same manner as any other text and that might be rewritten to reflect the values and social relations of other social groups.

Computer technology has recently undergone another metamorphosis, from a technology of calculation and data processing to a medium for communication and the creation of new kinds of information. In the last decade, communication technology has fundamentally transformed the production, nature, and consumption of information so thoroughly that nearly every institution in society, with the possible exception of higher education, has been restructured.[1] One such restructuring has been the creation of new global institutions—multinational corporations responding to global markets created by worldwide mass communications.

This transformation has two distinctive characteristics that liberal education must address. First, everyday life has become saturated by mass media based on communication technologies. Second, the means by which information is created and consumed has been transformed by digital technologies. This may become known as the age of the invention of "information" and other new epistemological forms for the organization and legitimation of knowledge. According to the artist Frank Popper, this new culture of information will require that "people must respond with a different sensibility and a renewed perception, reflecting the changes in our knowledge and environment."[2] How should an educated person read these new texts, which present themselves ubiquitously in everyday life—both in the workplace where "information" gives technical authority to social relations and in the guise of consumer goods and entertainment that confound illusion and reality?

Print and Information

These changes in the role and presence of information in everyday life suggest that liberal education must rethink the privileged status of the book. This will require both a recognition of the printed book as a technology on which professional authority is built and a recognition of mass communication and digital information as primary cultural subjects that require critical attention. The modern world is saturated with information that is qualitatively different from print, yet liberal education does not prepare students to "read" such information as it presents itself in everyday life with the same critical sophistication that students read print in the college library or classroom.

Digital texts will not "replace" print any more than print replaced speech; they are fundamentally different means of communication. The problem is to differentiate the phenomenological quality of different media in order to understand their value for communication and, ultimately, for truth. Only then can we evaluate the social contexts within which different kinds of technologies should be situated. For example, how do different forms of communication affect the quality of a social relationship? Is it appropriate to send a love letter by fax? by electronic mail?

What is the phenomenological difference between print and screen, and what consequence does this difference have for the relationship between printed and digital information? It may be impossible for current generations to answer this question. "Writing" is governed by centuries of development of rhetorical rules for print, reinforced by our own childhood training to be literate; thus most of our judgments about the validity of printed information seem "natural," because they are habitual and tacit. And because the habit of reading makes the authority structure of print seem tacit, we often lose touch with the ways print serves as a "user interface" to information, or the social consequences of our rhetorical structures, in which some kinds of intelligences and learning styles are rewarded more than others. Is print the only kind of literacy appropriate for liberal education? At the least, one might ask for a pluralism of kinds of texts, a pluralism of the social relations they inhabit, and a tolerance for different learning styles in higher education.

Computers, on the other hand, initially seem to be an alien technology, although many of the rhetorical rules of the screen are still derived from print. Although "computer literacy" often means training to use computer applications, the computer is more likely to be illiterate than the user. What is most alien about computer technology is the residue of the military and business social relations that have been instantiated in the design. Perhaps this alien quality will disappear as intelligence is placed into every machine; today's cars, for example, have more computing power than the first mainframes.

The personal computer is an example of a countercultural machine. At this point in its development the personal computer is designed to be more like a musical instrument than a book or a machine. Using a computer is like giving a skilled performance in which the body and the instrument become one. It can be an experience like play, in which the sense of time disappears in an expressive moment. And, like any tool, the computer becomes solely an object to us only when it is broken or when we reach the limit of our skill. Sherry Turkle notes the emotional and cognitive engagement that computer use inspires and the way this relationship changes over the life course, as the computer becomes a medium for working through unresolved issues of psychological growth.[3] Here the interactivity of the computer makes it an "other"—more intelligent than a machine, because it is responsive, but not quite another self. What is fundamental here is that the personal computer makes it plain that knowledge is the result of a craft or a performance; obtaining knowledge is not a passive activity.

Yet the same thing has been said of the experience of reading a book: "The availability of a book to the hand, its presence on a shelf, its listing in a library catalog—all of these encourage us to think of it as a stationary object. Somehow when we put a book down, we forget that while we were reading, it was moving (pages turning, lines receding into the past) and forget too that we were moving with it."[4] Thus Stanley Fish describes not the book as object but the kinetic art of reading, when the book becomes a tacit extension of the hand and eye and we experience something like a dialogue with an author. Yet reading a book may also be an alienating experience, as any teacher who has ever assigned a beloved book to a class has discovered. Thus we might ask whether reading a book is a kinetic performance for readers of every social class and culture. If it is not, are the teachers of liberal education simply reproducing themselves? Surely the description of reading as a kinetic performance would seem more accurate if printed texts were read aloud to groups, rather than silently and in isolation; why then has reading become silent?

Similarly, it is difficult to separate the phenomenology of the personal computer itself from social context; for example, computing can be a powerful symbol of innovation in the midst of traditional institutions. One high school student told me that working in the computer lab was his favorite educational experience because it was the only one that wasn't supervised, because his teachers didn't understand what he was doing. At this point, then, the phenomenological differences may stem more from the cultural prestige of computers as a sign of the new and the future.

It is not accidental that computer technology has become a symbol of change and the future. The first-generation *personal* computers were often explicitly based on a critique of authority in business and education. Until the introduction of the IBM PC, virtually every personal computer company had been founded by a member of a social movement committed to democratic access to knowledge: the Altair (named after a fictional planet in Star Trek) was designed by an engineer who dropped out of the air force to build futuristic electronics; the Osborne computer was designed by Lee Felsenstein, a member of the Haight-Ashbury Diggers; IMSAI was based on EST; the Apple was designed by college dropouts Steve Jobs and Steve Wozniak.[5]

The most important case of a technology designed to cause educational change is the work of Seymour Papert, a mathematician at MIT who designed Logo, a computer language for teaching children geometry. Mathematics is a liberal art, yet in Papert's view the pedagogical practice of the liberal arts is in direct contradiction to their content and purpose. The political critique implicit in Logo is the belief that instruction in mathematics has the social function of filtering and tracking students (especially African American students, working-class students, and girls), but this filtering is a consequence of its pedagogy, not its content.

Thus Logo centers around a democratic pedagogy designed to empower students: problems are situated in everyday life, not in formal problem sets; problems are solved by group cooperation, not by individual competition; Logo requires performance and activity, while reading is passive; children learn Logo by solving problems and learning from mistakes, while mathematics as a liberal art is taught within a moral framework of right and wrong, in which a mistake is a sign of stupidity.[6]

This is the critique of the pedagogy of liberal education from the perspective of a technical culture that has created computer programs containing an alternative model of liberal education, a model for learning without teachers and schools. In Papert's case, the critique is derived from liberal education itself, for he requires us to examine the *practice* of liberal education as well as the theory. In practice, liberal education is more likely to be a passive mass education conducted by books and lectures than an active moral education conducted by dialogue in groups.

Is the prestige of the book in liberal education fully consistent with its goals and content, or is it a justification for passivity and the isolation of the individual student? The romance of the Great Books is founded in the importance of the author, which tacitly justifies the passivity of the reader. According to Foucault, the author concept reflects "a system of ownership for texts"; this system developed, he maintains, "once strict rules concerning author's rights, author-publisher relations, rights of reproduction and related matters were enacted at the end of the eighteenth and the beginning of the nineteenth century."[7] In scientific discourse, which emerged slightly earlier, the text finds meaning not in the context of its author's life work but in its truth value as established by "membership in a systematic ensemble, and not the reference to the individual who produced them." These two modes of reading and writing text, centered around "author" and "literature," exist in parallel today, roughly paralleling publication in humanities and sciences, books, and journals.

Yet, as Foucault concludes, there is no historical necessity that the author concept, "a role quite characteristic of our era of industrial and bourgeois society, of individualism and private property," remain unchanged. In the academic world, the author concept functions within a system of rewards, promotion and tenure, and social status. Thus the collective authorship contemplated by networked and digital texts is in fundamental tension with the economic and status structure of academic organizations.

Of course, the same criticism can be made of the forms of knowledge and social relations that gave birth to information technologies and, indeed, to the very notion of information. The word "information" is very old, originating in scholasticism. "In-form-ation," like "indoctrination," has at its etymological core the idea of giving form to the mind — to instruct, to train, to discipline. In modern usage, however, the word has assumed a connotation of neutrality: the prestige of the computer as calculator and brain has lent authenticity to the knowledge formats produced by computers. Like print, computers have distinctive rhetorical forms — data and databases, hypertext, computer-generated images and sound, simulations, spreadsheets, electronic mail — that have yet to be subjected to the same critical awareness as print. (In this process, we will come to be more aware of the tacit rhetorical structures of print — of, for example, the function and structure of the journal format as an "interface" to knowledge, or the function of narrative explanation.)

It is hard to define the place of technology in liberal education, in part because of the boundaries between the social contexts in which different information formats are used. We are often aware of the surveillance and social control implicit in information, for we confront it in our credit card bills every month; and we are aware of the saturation of everyday life with images, but we don't attend to it critically because it is framed as entertainment. Entertainment requires surrender to the rules of play, and play requires the spontaneous surrender of critical awareness in the interest of pleasure. Reading can also be in service to pleasure, but liberal education prepares the reader to distinguish different genres of print and to be aware of the rhetorical construction of claims about truth or the justification of authority or power. In a new liberal education, students will need to learn to deconstruct and analyze digital forms of knowledge and mass media in the same way.

Digital Criticism

A new liberal education must develop a digital criticism: an awareness of claims about truth or the justification of authority and power that is implicit in digital forms of knowledge, in a social world saturated with images consumed for entertainment, and in a work world constructed by information. Every medium may make a claim to represent the truth, each in its own terms, but liberal education has focused primarily on the truth claims of print. What is the relationship between our experience of images, social power, and the truth? How does digital representation change these relationships?

In a society in which images and information have the prestige of being real and true, can literacy be said to exist as a critical skill if it does not include the reading of images? Consider the relative authority of television and newspapers in the construction of public opinion and the election of political leaders, the authority of advertisements and information in the construction of economic life, and the authority of cinema or television and novels in cultural life. Are these forms of entertainment, or the social realms, of fundamental importance to liberal education? Computers mediate everyday life—the grocery checkout counter, the automatic teller, and the writing of texts, public opinion polls, credit cards,—and they do so largely on trust. Ultimately it is not the computer that liberal education must come to terms with; it is information, the knowledge made by the computer, the work of art constructed by computers, that tacitly makes the claim to be real and thereby true.

Walter Benjamin's description of the work of art in an age of mechanical reproduction raised an issue that liberal education has yet to consider: the camera and photographer dominate the scene within which pictures are produced, but the camera itself is never present in the picture.[8] This is the distinctive trait of communication in the modern world: the technology and social contexts that produce knowledge are concealed. A critical awareness of technology-based knowledge must always recover this hidden context.

For half a century, the definition of the photograph, the product of one of the first of the new information technologies, has wavered between a medium for artistic expression and a medium for the representation of reality. Richard Avedon recently said, "A portrait is not a likeness. The moment an emotion or fact is transformed into a photograph it is no longer a fact but an opinion. All photographs are accurate. None of them is the truth."[9] Yet today, photographer Robbert Flick says, "The truth has been locked out of photography; it is no longer a medium for representation. The computer is responsible for that." A photograph cannot be evidence, because a computer can exactly *simulate* any other mode of representation, real or imaginary, as the film *Jurassic Park* has made clear. Thus digital criticism must come to terms with simulation, with images that look and sound real but are not.

A foundation of digital criticism will be the distinction between the truth value of analog and digital, between representation and simulation, between an image that makes reference to the real and one that makes reference to a model of the real. "What is simulated is no longer the territory, an original substance or being, but a model of the real. . . . From now on it is the map that precedes, and thus generates, the territory."[10]

This substitution of an abstraction for a real referent is intrinsic to the digital, which translates all information into a universal binary code, recorded in standard electronic signals whether the content is music, text, or image. Unlike every previous medium for the representation of knowledge, digital information has no necessary analog to the real. This difference has fundamental impact on the use of knowledge. A printed text gains a certain authority from its facticity, while a digital text may, in principle, be modified by any reader. Copyright—the right to copy—is virtually unenforceable in digital networks. Digital information is, in its essence, always a unique performance by the reader, just as print, by its nature, makes possible the provenance of both authorship and a literature.

This is not a weakness, just a difference—one that requires a new sensibility and makes possible the invention of new kinds of representation of knowledge. Electronic journals are experimental tests of the value of the digital in regard to knowledge: the value of interactivity in constituting an academic dialogue (Psycoloquy); the value of malleability for managing information whose value is time-sensitive (Online Mendelian Inheritance in Man); the value of the graphic display of information (databases of three-dimensional models of the structure of molecules, based on X-ray diffraction data); the value of bulletin boards for distributing preprints in physics; the value of organizing the text around the reader's questions (hypertext); the value of databases for finding reference information (online library catalogs); the value of electronic mail for global communication.

These are no more than experiments, both because digital technology is still being invented and because the process of innovation is focused more on increasing the efficiency of print-based organizations than on creating new formats and new organizations for scholarly communication. But, fundamentally, innovation is limited because digital media are in tension with the social organization of higher education and its system of incentives and rewards. In contrast, digital technologies are reorganizing work in manufacturing and service industries and creating new kinds of entertainment industries. The refusal to consider digital creations as scholarship in promotion and tenure decisions has more to do with defending the social structure of education than with making judgments about creative contributions to knowledge.

There is also an internal contradiction within higher education. Often the new forms of knowledge created by the arts and sciences cannot be reproduced in print without a substantial loss of information. In the sciences, imaging technologies are used to visualize information in new ways, to create and manage new kinds of data, and to distribute texts by network because the value of information is time-sensitive. Print is increasingly used for the distribution of credit to the author, not for the distribution and access to knowledge. This tension may reflect the essentially conservative mission of liberal education, but it also signifies a withdrawal from engagement with the reality of economic, political, and social life.

What Is Computer Literacy?

The question "What is the place of technology in liberal education?" requires the redefinition of technology from "object" or "machine" (which are valid but not fundamental descriptions) to terms like "text" and "performance." This redefinition also implies a recognition of the technical foundation of print cultures and, thereby, an admission that books and information are different but not opposite. Even more fundamentally, it implies a broader investigation into the relationship between higher education, constituted by and centered on the production and consumption of print, and the work and social worlds in which information is embedded in sound, pictures, and spontaneous performances of social life, mediated by information as well as print. Provisionally, then, these might be the principles of the liberal art of computer literacy:

1. *Computer literacy has nothing to do with computer training.* If training is required to use computers, it is computers, not people, that are not yet literate; the need for training is a sign of poor design, which should not be rewarded in the marketplace.
2. *Computer literacy is related to the arts and to aesthetic education.* In many ways the tension between liberal education and technology parallels the estrangement between

the humanities and the arts. Technology is intrinsically related to the arts—in reality, it *is* one of the arts. Hence, aesthetic education is a foundation for digital criticism because it provides an education of the senses that one must have in order to develop a critical awareness of everyday life. Technology and its products require critical judgments that are essentially aesthetic.

An aesthetic education trains the body as a medium for constituting meaning, in complement to the way liberal education trains the mind. Just as clinical psychology trains the ear to hear the relationship between emotions and the meaning of words, liberal education should attend to meaning's physicality, not just its content. Just as ethnography trains the eye to see the relationship between language, space, and power, liberal education must educate the eye to "read" everyday life as a social construction.

However kinetic one's reading, books are no substitute for reflective practical experience, yet there is no substitute for books as a medium for reflective thinking. The issue is to define liberal education in a way that includes both.

3. *The history of science and technology, in its own terms, is a fundamental part of liberal education.* In the twentieth century, science and technology have been the foundation of the greatest expansion of knowledge and creativity since the Renaissance. Yet liberal education often stops in the nineteenth century and often seems to be unable to reconcile the past with either the theory or the practice of science. (Nor has liberal education come to terms with a global economy and an emerging global cosmopolis.)

    In the realms of digital information and mass communication, one must have an understanding of the technical realities in order to understand the structure and politics of information. It is not possible to criticize technology from a purely theoretical point of view. Computers have logical structures; more to the point, they also have histories and social contexts that define them. Unless they have experience with the crafts and concepts of science and technology, students will be at the mercy of computers.

4. *Knowledge is practice as well as theory.* Technical culture would require us to ask whether the pedagogical practice of liberal education in the modern university is fully consistent with its content and purpose. This is not simply a

technical question: Are the pedagogical practices of liberal education fully consistent with *its* content and mission?

As a corollary, is it possible for liberal education to follow the Socratic practice of finding its questions in the everyday world and returning there after whatever theoretical abstractions have been necessary?

5. *Mass communication and information technology are texts for the critical mind, different from print but not its opposite.* Although this is not programmatic, the first and most critical issue is to understand the use of technology as an ideology, a justification for authority in the workplace or everyday life, that precludes discussion of the merits.

Beneath this issue lies a most difficult epistemological problem: we have relied on print and its social organizations to authenticate knowledge, but we do not know how to evaluate the truth value of analog forms of the representation of reality (e.g., the photograph); nor have we begun to evaluate the truth value of digital information and images that simulate realities that have never existed in a manner fully satisfactory to the senses. Given that the everyday world is saturated with mass communications and, increasingly, with content based on digital technologies, liberal education must enable citizens to make reasonable judgments about the authority of information in the everyday world.

Notes

1. See, for example, Shoshana Zuboff, *In the Age of the Smart Machine* (New York: Basic Books, 1984). Zuboff writes about how work changes as technology saturates the workplace with information. It is odd that higher education, focused on the production of information and learning, is one of the spheres most resistant to this change.

2. Frank Popper, *Art of the Electronic Age* (New York: Harry Abrams, 1993), p. 58.

3. Sherry Turkle, *The Second Self* (New York: Simon & Schuster, 1984).

4. Stanley Fish, *Self-Consuming Artifacts* (Berkeley: University of California Press, 1972), p. 401.

5. Paul Freiberger and Michael Swaine, *Fire in the Valley* (Berkeley: Osborne/McGraw-Hill, 1984).

6. Seymour Papert, *Mindstorms* (New York: Basic Books, 1980).

7. Michel Foucault, "What Is an Author?" in *Foucault Reader*, ed. Paul Rabinow (New York: Pantheon, 1984), pp. 101–20.

8. Walter Benjamin, "The Work of Art in the Age of Mechanical Reproduction," in *Illuminations*, trans Harry Zohn (New York: Schocken, 1984), pp. 217–51.

9. Richard Avedon, *An Autobiography* (New York: Random House, 1993), quoted in *Newsweek*, 13 September 1994, p. 71.

10. Popper, *Art of the Electronic Age*, p. 175. Postmodernism has most fully come to theoretical terms with the presence of technology in the modern world, most notably in the works of Baudrillard, from whom this passage is obviously derived.

9

Constraints and Opportunities

Adam Yarmolinsky

Liberal education has always proved a challenge to deliver system-atically, if only because by its very nature it is difficult to specify. In the United States, institutions that seek to offer liberal educa-tion on the threshold of a new century operate under new or, at least, significantly more chafing constraints. This article exam-ines some of these constraints and suggests ways in which they can be relieved or accommodated.

The principle constraints discussed here are those of shrink-ing material resources, expanding and accelerating expectations, and increasing heterogeneity across the student body. In the face of these constraints, academic institutions from small liberal arts colleges to large research universities are no better able than other institutions to adapt themselves to changing circumstances—and perhaps a little bit less so.

Resource constraints stem from internal and external causes. The internal causes, I will argue, are the result of an economic anomaly. It is not possible for the direct delivery of liberal education to become significantly more efficient in the same way that other economic processes do, at least in part because liberal education is not something that can be "delivered": thus, there is a productivity lag behind other sectors in the economy. The institution cannot fully compensate for this lag by making improvements in the efficiency of other activities (e.g., computing or building maintenance).

The external causes, in the public sector, arise from the insistent demands for other uses of public funds, combined with continued popular resistance to tax levels comparable to those of other industrial democracies. In the private sector, the external cause is the declining capacity (or willingness) of families and individual payors to meet even a partial share of the cost of liberal education.

Other constraints result from expanding and accelerating expectations as students and their families demand that they be prepared for specific jobs or get a leg up on specific postgraduate professional training. In a sense this is the other side of the coin of employers' broader demand for higher education. As the proportion of jobs requiring undergraduate and graduate degrees has increased, the vocational aspect of higher education has increased accordingly.

Another set of expectations is expressed in public and legislative demands for greater accountability in higher education. In this realm as in other areas of both the public and the nonprofit sectors, there are growing demands for public demonstration of quantifiable results. Miscommunication and conflict between institutional leaders and public authorities, who are promoting accountability and defining expectations, weakens public acceptance of the idea of liberal education and even threatens its independence. At the same time that these constraints are pressing on institutional resources, the student body is becoming more diverse in age, ethnicity, and preparation, making for more difficulty in establishing and maintaining the educational community on which the pursuit of liberal education depends.

Further, that community is not well organized to deal with any of these problems, and it needs to find new ways to mobilize its talents and energies—from mentoring new teachers, to fostering more imaginative cooperation between faculty and staff, to involving faculty members in budgetary decisions.

Resource Constraints

The central economic fact about liberal education is that its core processes consume as much human labor as they did before the

Industrial Revolution—whatever the potential for economies at the margin. What this means is that over time, as productivity increases in the economy generally, the cost of liberal education must rise relative to the cost of other goods and services. There are other activities that share this characteristic: the arts, basic research, some aspects of primary medical care (which might explain part of the intractability of the health-care dilemma), and personal counseling and therapy. It is not coincidental that objective measurement of these activities is at best elusive.

Most of these activities are regarded as appropriate for some degree of public philanthropic support, as benefiting the public interest along with the interests of the individual who is directly affected. If, as has been said, taxes are the price of civilization, one can argue that liberal education, along with these other activities, is one of the more appropriate uses of tax proceeds. As the more mundane sector of the economy improves in efficiency, shouldn't some of the resultant savings be used for the public good?

Unfortunately, two current trends in public opinion work against the availability of public funds to make up for the relative increase in the cost of liberal education. First, there appears to be extraordinary reluctance to increase taxes at either the federal or the state level (despite our country's relatively low level of taxation compared to that of other industrial nations), and any increase at the federal level seems to be earmarked to reduce the deficit that accumulated in the federal borrowing binge of the 1980s. At the same time, there is a growing sentiment that higher education is a private rather than a public good, to be paid for by the student or the student's family, or by generous benefactors, rather than by the public purse. The traditional view, going back at least to Plato, that individual education is primarily a social benefit, a necessity of the good society, is being eroded. Nor does it bode well for liberal education that the one area where business seems willing and even anxious to pick up the tab is in the preparation of its employees for specific existing tasks, not through a general or liberal education.

The basic difficulty is exacerbated by problems of definition and of organization, since liberal education cannot be doled out to students in measured doses, like vitamin supplements. (In fact, it can't really be doled out at all.) The teacher's function is to facilitate, to conduct a joint exploration of ideas with students. In this way of thinking, teaching and research blend together; similarly, liberal learning is a continuum, not interrupted by departmental boundary lines. Thus the allocation of scarce resources between teaching and research among academic departments defies the application of settled principles.

Even before Ernest Boyer proposed broad new categories to extend the traditional limits of research, it covered a considerable range of activities, from extensive laboratory fieldwork to *gedenken* experiments and reflective reexamination of texts. One practical distinction is between funded and unfunded research. Yet funded research can in fact either add to or subtract from the institution's overall resources, as it may or may not buy faculty time, contribute to indirect overhead, or require matching capital or equipment contributions. The economics of joint products and joint inputs complicates, if it does not entirely frustrate, the computation of costs and benefits.

Academic departments are the basic units of accounting in all but a very few institutions. But departmental budgets are seldom subject to regular adjustment based on estimates of their contribution to the educational process. Departments tend to have their budgets the way Boston ladies have their hats. New ventures (including new joint ventures) are treated as budgetary add-ons, financed on a hope and a prayer, rather than as legitimate competitors for previously assigned dollars. Of course, there is good reason for fiscal conservatism, since the human resources, which by and large dominate the budget, are not easily interchanged. History is a stronger determinant than logic in the allocation of such resources as the number and seniority of positions, teaching loads, range of course offerings, even class size.

Within a university, the grouping of departments into schools or colleges adds obstacles to the pursuit of liberal education. Too often it is assumed that liberal education is the business of the school of arts and sciences—and therefore no business of the undergraduate programs in the schools of business, engineering, nursing, or social work, much less in the graduate schools of law and medicine. Or the arts and sciences may themselves be divided into schools of humanities, sciences, and social sciences, with liberal education implicitly limited to the humanities. This arrangement leads only too naturally to the suggestion that students should "get their liberal arts requirements out of the way" before proceeding to more serious vocational and prevocational study. And in the segmented universe of separate schools, the lion's share of new increments of scarce resources tends to go to the business and professional programs and to foster sponsored research, primarily in the sciences.

The scarcity of resources is borne in on all members of the academic community, and liberal arts faculty members cannot but be aware of the peculiar disadvantages under which they labor in the internal competition for resources. But what these faculty members generally do not feel is a sense of individual or collective responsibility for budget decisions, for the hard choices between academic and support services, among divisions and departments and even within departments.

In a sense, the faculty is the legislative body of the institution: no program of instruction can be offered, no student can graduate, no faculty member can be hired without its consent. In practice, every president serves at the pleasure of the faculty, since a vote of no confidence is almost certain to bring down the incumbent. Faculty consent may also extend to admission standards and to the size of the student body, and faculty participation is essential in decisions on administrative appointments, including the choice of a new president. Unlike other legislative bodies, however, the faculty seldom has any voice in budgetary decisions, which are the other side of the coin of every program decision.

Deeper faculty involvement in the budgetary process could be a prerequisite for action on the resource front. Putting to one side the role that faculty members can (and should) play in defending higher education appropriations in public forums, we can look at the contribution an economically sophisticated faculty might make to the internal dialogue within the academy on budgetary issues. In the present situation there is a kind of dialogue of the deaf, in which the administration (or the trustees) identify high-cost programs for possible elimination, while faculty defend the programs as essential for liberal education. There is a distant analogy here to the debate in the Pentagon before the introduction of systems analysis, when the military defined their needs for specific weapons and civilian managers set arbitrary budget ceilings, neither side directly addressing the relationships between weapons, dollars, and national security objectives.

The analogy is a distant one, particularly because the base cost of liberal education is so intractable. But it would no doubt be helpful, as the institution responds to tighter budgets, for those who are actually engaged in the work of liberal education to know what it costs to do each piece of work in the way it has been done up to now. Measuring cost does not measure value, but it fosters the search for new ways to accomplish old objectives. The fact that language departments have always been organized separately doesn't mean they can't be combined, and combining them might foster intellectual exchange as well as saving a little money. It also stimulates new thinking about alternative ways to measure costs: per degree granted, per credit hour, per student exposed to the discipline, and so forth.

Faculty consideration of budgetary issues can lead to faculty involvement in an explicit academic planning process, setting long- and short-term goals and allocating and reallocating resources. In a time of static or shrinking resources, planning can be a frustrating exercise; yet those elements of the institution that articulate plans for their future in ways that contribute to overall institutional goals will inevitably come off better than those elements that neglect this opportunity.

Does this mean that planning is a zero-sum game? Not necessarily. If liberal education is thought of as the business of a small group of departments within one division of the institution, then the game may be a cutthroat one, and liberal education's chances of winning are doubtful. But there are other options.

One option is to choose the St. John's model: simply to eliminate the competition by making liberal education the institution's only objective. One would not have to choose the same set of texts by dead white males as the whole curriculum, but within each institution there would have to be agreement on a single course of study, so that the faculty (and students) would not be tempted to pursue the false gods of professionalism and specialization. Requiring faculty to be prepared to teach any course in the curriculum would be another necessary deterrent to departure from the common path. Students could get an excellent education as much from each other as from their teachers, since they would all be sharing in the same intellectual experience.

The St. John's model might indeed be adapted for wider use, perhaps even as a separate program within an existing institution—a college within a college or university. But it would require a considerable leap of faith for entering students, although the record seems to show that St. John's students do at least as well as their peers in graduate and professional schools. The danger is that governing boards and higher education commissions might be tempted to use the creation of more St. John's–type colleges as an excuse to dump liberal arts out of the general undergraduate curriculum, reverting to Cardinal Newman's distinction between liberal and servile education, and reserving liberal education for those who choose to follow in the footsteps of Newman's liberally educated gentlemen of leisure.

Another option is to develop an institutional model that recognizes liberal education as an aspect of all undergraduate and graduate education—and which cuts across departmental and divisional boundaries to maintain liberal education's claim on scarce institutional resources. At the outset, there are two problems in developing such a model, one analytic and the other organizational.

The analytical one is familiar to students of public budgeting: How to identify the costs of a service that is not congruent with any one unit or group of units within the organization, but that draws on some of the resources of several units? The critical innovation here has been the application of systems analysis. The problem is complicated in higher education by the perennial difficulty of defining liberal education. We can no longer rely on Cardinal Newman's definition of "the subject matter of knowledge . . . intimately united in itself, as being the Great Creator and His work."[1]

Clearly, the content is in constant flux, and no matter what definition is adopted, constant reevaluation will be necessary. Even then, what emerges will be a rough approximation of an entity with fluid edges. Still, it should be possible to observe trends in the proportion of resources allocated to that entity, so that someone can decide what to do about them.

Then the critical question becomes who decides, both which expenditure should properly be considered dedicated to liberal education and whether the resulting distribution is the right one—and how often the balance should be reexamined.

Again, students of public budgeting will recognize the generic problem: allocations can be made as a result of bureaucratic infighting, executive fiat, or legislative action. Bureaucratic infighting is the standard model for allocations within the academy today, modified only by bursts of executive fiat from the administration or, occasionally, from governing boards or state commissions for higher education. Legislative action by the faculty as a deliberative body seems a more rational approach. Unlike other legislative bodies, a faculty consists of individuals actually involved in doing the work of the institution. One may regard Newman as unduly optimistic when he characterizes the faculty as "an assemblage of learned men [sic], zealous for their own sciences, and rivals of each other . . . brought by familiar intercourse and for the sake of intellectual peace, to adjust together the claims and relations of their respective subjects of investigation." But the dual role of faculty members may at least make them more realistic legislators.

At the same time, it might be useful to designate a senior administrative officer who would be responsible for the liberal education budget—say, a dean of liberal studies, or even a vice president for liberal studies. But whatever the title, the individual would not, and could not, exercise line authority over other people's budgets. As a staff person, her effectiveness would depend on whom she served. Whenever a chief executive takes the advice of staff over a line officer, there is a price to be paid. In the end, the welfare of liberal education will depend on the faculty committee, and the director or dean of liberal studies can only help by serving as attentive and diplomatic staff to the committee. Faculty judgments must be at the heart of the matter.

True, these decisions pit faculty members against each other in defense of their most fundamental interests. Can faculty be trusted to subordinate their individual interests to their common concern as educators? The short answer must be that if they can't, then the institution can't function as a community. The key ingredient here is leadership, and leadership within the faculties, both in the humanities and everywhere else (science, engineering, business, nursing), becomes as critical as leadership within the administration. The administration may insist that it has the ultimate responsibility for so fundamental a set of decisions. But on an issue that goes to the heart of the educational process, the faculty as a body must achieve a sense of ownership of the decisions.

This option differs from existing patterns of interaction between faculty and administration in at least four fundamental ways.

First, in faculty deliberations it relates program decisions directly to dollar expenditures. A program proposal must include a specific source of funding within a budget that is not likely to be increased significantly. Those funds may have to be taken from an existing program. How the proposal affects overall spending on liberal education, as well as how it reallocates dollars in the total, will be made explicit. It removes the dialogue from the realm of the abstract to the world of concrete and finite resources.

Second, it permits (indeed, it requires) faculty members to make judgments about the cost-effectiveness and relative value of each other's activities—judgments measured in dollars, a relentless medium of exchange. Faculty will be extraordinarily reluctant to make such judgments; their feet will have to be held to the fire. They will engage in the most blatant, the most elaborate, and sometimes the most short-sighted horse trading. But in the end they will have to accept the maxim that faculty so often attempts to deny: that to govern is to choose.

Third, it involves faculty members chosen from every department and division. Since the overall liberal education budget proposed here includes a part of the budget of every division, faculty members in each division must be prepared to defend that part of their budget as making a genuine contribution to liberal education.

Finally, it creates a new forum that may be able to reexamine fundamental questions of organization, almost never raised by administrations and governing boards, much less addressed by faculty. The kind of questions that may be provoked include these: What is a department? What should its responsibilities be? How should it interact with other departments, especially in the overlapping areas between disciplines and with professional schools? Who should teach statistics or expository writing to engineers and social workers? (This latter is a question inextricably entangled with questions about the liberal arts content of that teaching.) Does it still make sense (or did it ever?) to group chemistry students in an arts and sciences cluster and chemical engineering students in an engineering cluster? Is it appropriate for an undergraduate program to be organized so that any students will answer in the negative to the question, "Are you in liberal arts?"

Except in the smallest institutions, a faculty deliberative body must be representative rather than all-inclusive. There is a question whether it might be better to constitute a subordinate body—say, a committee of the faculty senate—charged with responsibility for the liberal education budget. This body would have to comprise representatives from the sciences and the social sciences, as well as the humanities, and from any professional schools or divisions, not overlooking the institution's outreach activities (a matter discussed more fully below). Its members would have to be chosen for their sympathetic understanding and commitment to liberal education. They would serve as critics of liberal education efforts and proposals of the several divisions, including arts and sciences. But they would also serve as advocates for liberal education within the faculty senate itself.

Of course, the structure could be perverted to serve as an instrument for downgrading liberal education. Instead of serving as an advocacy group, it could become a vehicle for transmitting all the outside pressures for more professional and vocational training to the faculty and administration. But perhaps there is reason to hope that the assemblage of faculty leaders—including humanists, scientists (of both hard and soft varieties), engineers, and accountants, all committed to the ideals of liberal education and well versed in budgetary numbers—could make the best use of shrinking resources and could even respond constructively to the expanding and accelerating expectations of students, parents, and other constituencies outside the institution, at least as well as any existing arrangements do.

We now turn to the impacts of these expectations.

Expanding Expectations

It is a paradox of the current labor market that as unemployment invades the professional and managerial ranks, the specialized skills required in college—skills that may give the graduate an advantage in competing for employment—obsolesce with increasing rapidity. There is a built-in conflict between teaching the generalizable skills and habits of mind that are an essential element of liberal education and teaching the specialized skills that may be a ticket to immediate employment. As the knowledge explosion increases the volume of specialized skills, the conflict becomes more acute. Hence, students may be likely to rank immediate skills above preparation for the uncertainties of lifelong employment. Student preference for immediate skill training is reinforced by the demands of corporate hiring officers, apparently still oblivious to the pronouncements of corporate CEOs on the long-term values of a liberal education.

At the same time, the growing privatization of the purposes of higher education makes it harder for the public values of liberal education—preparation for citizenship, perpetuation of tradition, pursuit of social justice—to compete with the private values of individual students. The increasingly prevalent characterization of students as "customers" underlines the shift in expectations. The rising tide of transfer students (as distinguished from first-time freshmen), particularly in the four-year public institutions, reduces the average length of stay in the institution and increases the sense of urgency about job preparation. The fact that the average undergraduate is older may also increase the sense of urgency, although one might hope that the more mature student would respond more positively to the larger appeal of liberal studies.

Finally, state officials exercising particular surveillance over public institutions of higher education, who are under increasing pressure from state legislators (and the legislators' constituents), are looking to projected manpower needs to shape the curriculum. These projections tend to be both specific and relatively short term. Needs that cannot be imagined cannot be projected, and the kind of liberal education that will prepare students for not-yet-imagined needs tends to get short shrift.

It would be futile to attempt to talk students and their parents out of their expectations of practical benefits from their education. The problem is rather to persuade them to include the objectives and benefits of liberal education within the ambit of their expectations. Four practical approaches suggest themselves.

First, the more students experience liberal education, the more they are likely to appreciate it. If liberal education methods are spread more widely and more explicitly across the curriculum, as proposed in the first part of this essay, they are more likely to be recognized and accepted by students and, through them, by other constituencies (parents, voters, and legislators).

Second, no matter how immediately career oriented they are, students respond to intellectual excitement. Two simple sources of intellectual excitement are honors programs and interdisciplinary studies programs. Honors programs challenge students to read more, to think more critically, to communicate more clearly. In the process, some of these students can't help becoming more interested in their education for its own sake. Interdisciplinary studies programs encourage students to make intellectual connections that might not otherwise have occurred to them. These students can't help becoming more aware of the unifying factors in the world of ideas. Both of these kinds of programs have to compete for students with programs that are more explicitly and narrowly career oriented. Some students are concerned that it may be harder, in honors programs, to get the A's they need for admission to medical school. Institutions have to find ways to give honors students and interdisciplinary studies programs more prestige and more esprit. Separate residential arrangements, special extracurricular opportunities (concerts, theater), opportunities to participate in faculty research, and even special financial incentives (non-need-based scholarships in lieu of outside employment?) can help to attract skeptics into the programs.

Third, students' choices within the curriculum are affected at least to some degree by academic advising—or else we are wasting a good deal of time and money. Academic advising was formerly the province of faculty members, but it has become more and more the responsibility of professionals without faculty status. Professional advisers perform a valuable service. On certain technical questions, such as admissions requirements for professional schools, they are indispensable. But they cannot be expected to have the same appreciation for the values of liberal education that their faculty colleagues have.

If the faculty were to reassume the primary responsibility for academic advising, they might be able to recapture student interest in liberal education, even in the face of competing demands for student attention.

Fourth, students are increasingly being involved as volunteers in outreach programs in schools and other community centers in nearby neighborhoods that their institutions have long ignored. Their work in these programs can be related to classroom instruction and reading on the underlying problems of these communities, as well as the broader issues of social justice and human nature. There is no reason why apprenticeship learning can't be part of liberal learning. Plato's fable of the cave may take on new meaning as students move back and forth between the classroom and community service. Students may discover goals and satisfactions beyond vocational preparation, which may help them relate more directly to the goals and satisfactions of liberal education.

Student enthusiasm for liberal education may be fostered in a number of ways, but the ultimate proof of its value is to be found in the lives of its graduates. Here the assessment movement has to be involved, and turned to a better use than the attempt to measure value added through standardized tests for all rising juniors. It may take graduates two or three years to gain a proper perspective on their undergraduate education, but that perspective will have unique value. Similarly, employers today go to great lengths to assess the performance of their employees, and they are generally alert to leadership potential. Research that relates the quality of undergraduate education to the development of leadership demonstrated in later life could be particularly useful in enforcing the still-tenuous connection between CEO platitudes and personnel office practices.

The climate of expanding expectations affects faculty not only indirectly, through the expectations of students, but directly, as governing boards, legislatures, and the general public look for more specific measures of faculty performance. It no longer suffices to describe faculty — in the image that the Harvard classicist John Finley proposed — as being like trees in the forest, whose only function was to exist. Institutions need to explain just what faculty do and why they do it. This justification has to be offered on two levels: that of the individual faculty member and that of the academic department.

For the individual faculty member, and especially for the faculty member in the liberal arts, there is a new and urgent need to explain all the ways in which time is spent productively to make up a working week — and a working year. This explanation must include the interrelationships of class presentation, preparation, research, and intellectual renewal. Here the task is primarily one of getting the facts out to the public. At the department level, the problem is a more difficult one. There is growing public concern about what are identified as "low-productivity departments"—those that produce less than a minimum number of graduates with degrees in their fields, averaged over several years. The argument is made that it is an inefficient use of resources to offer all the elements of an undergraduate major in, say, philosophy (or even physics) to a limited number of students. Why not get along with only one of each of these departments in the state or region, closing out the departments in the other institutions, while perhaps retaining one or two individual faculty to offer "service" courses in the subject? This argument is advanced most vigorously within state systems. The counterargument is that to attract and retain competent faculty members, the institution must offer them both the intellectual challenge of teaching majors and the colleagueship of peers in their discipline. The two arguments do not meet and are likely to result in a series of unsatisfactory compromises, little improved by offers of electronic equipment for interactive television instruction.

A more radical and perhaps more constructive solution would be to scrap the existing system of academic departments and reorganize around new units of instruction, each with a critical mass of faculty and students held together by a set of overlapping interests, and whose members would be free to shift their organizational alliances from time to time. This proposal has several advantages. It would permit the survival of high-quality instruction in an endangered discipline at the institution. It would give the faculty member in the endangered discipline a set of colleagues, not necessarily in the same discipline but with a similar set of interests. It would enable — indeed, empower — faculty members whose interests have broken out of the traditional mold of an established discipline to explore new fields, repairing some of the unhealthy disjunction between departmental and individual priorities. And it would foster new synergies across disciplinary lines. The most obvious arguments against the proposal are that it would threaten the intellectual integrity and rigor of the established disciplines, that it would impair the value of peer assessments, and that it would reduce the mobility of faculty members, particularly young teachers who were untenured or not yet on a tenure track. It might also be argued that the proposal could weaken or undermine the rights of tenured faculty where tenure is determined by departmental affiliation. Whatever the significance of current attacks on tenure across the board, there is no a priori reason why tenure must reside in a department, and the justification for tenure based on academic freedom is, if anything, more valid for free-floating academics.

The rebuttal to these arguments is simple: the proposal need only be tested where the alternative is the elimination of a department or departments and dismissal of faculty, even including tenured faculty — an alternative faced by some campuses today. If it works with endangered disciplines and in marginal situations, the lessons of the experience will be available for consideration of at least selective wider-scale application.

Broadly and superficially applied, the proposal could be destructive to liberal education, but as long as the reorganization can focus on continuing substantial intellectual interests, it should avoid debasing academic institutions into job shops or boutiques. Yet every institution must still face the increasing diversity of its student body in background and in interests.

Meeting the Needs of Diversity

The student body of the twenty-first century will be increasingly diverse, measured on any axis: age, ethnicity, preparation, and motivation. Consequently, fewer students may feel free to explore ideas for their own sake. Older students will hear time's winged chariot hurrying near. Students from minority and ethnic backgrounds will tend to react to the discontinuities between their own cultures and the plurality culture, either by seeking a lowest-common-denominator educational experience or, worse, by denigrating intellectual achievement as a betrayal of their ethnic identity. Students facing the undergraduate challenge with widely different degrees of preparation will find it harder to share their learning experiences with their fellow students, who, under better circumstances, should be an at least equal source of intellectual stimulation as their teachers. Nor does it encourage easy exchange of ideas that an increasing proportion of undergraduates are transfers, already out of step with entering freshmen. The differences in motivation derived from all these causes will inevitably result in enough frictional loss that the general level of motivation in the student body will decrease.

All these kinds of diversity strongly affect the undergraduate curriculum in a variety of ways. They also have a strong impact on the organization of undergraduate programs. Three facets of that impact are examined here: the allocation of responsibility for preparing students to enter regular academic programs, the allocation of responsibility for preparing teachers, and the role of academic majors in undergraduate instruction.

In earlier times, preparing students to participate in college-level education was the responsibility of the schools. Some of them (like those that produced half my own college class) were labeled "preparatory schools," while others had, and some still have, college preparatory departments. Preparation was supposed to prepare the entering freshman to move directly into college-level work. In my college yearbook, my classmates' names and addresses were supplemented by the information "prepared at [school]." Compare this attitude toward preparedness with that of my freshman advisee, who was pleased he could sign up for two courses that would duplicate (for credit) courses he had taken as a senior in high school.

The most prestigious high schools still pride themselves on their college admissions records. But the great bulk of entering undergraduates come from schools in which explicit college preparation has been minimal and where recognition of diversity may be emphasized more than achievement of common standards.

Colleges have been dealing with wider differences in levels of preparation by providing remedial instruction either formally (although grudgingly) in noncredit classes or sub rosa in introductory courses for credit. In the next phase of development it may be that the distinction between remedial and "college-level" work will be eroded, particularly if the distinction is based on content rather than on communication of basic skills. Even basic skills may have to be taught incidental to regular instruction.

This is not to underestimate the value of tutoring, particularly in the face of diversity in students' backgrounds. But tutoring need not take up significant amounts of faculty time and effort because it can be done by fellow students. Uri Treisman's research has demonstrated the effectiveness of undergraduate study groups, particularly with minority-group students, where the study-group members make up for each other's deficiencies. The only faculty effort required is for teachers to supply the initial impetus for the formation of the groups and for administrators to find physical locations where they can meet.

Even the simple task of orienting faculty toward organizing study groups suggests the need for some shift in emphasis in the preparation of faculty for their teaching responsibilities. The problem divides into two parts: how to educate new faculty, both in graduate school and during their initial term of appointment, and how to help established faculty adjust to increasing student diversity and accelerating expansion of the knowledge universe.

Graduate students preparing to enter the professoriate are essentially being prepared to teach subject matter and technique rather than to teach students. That kind of preparation may be enough at least to get them launched as teachers at institutions where students are uniformly or relatively well prepared. But when levels and quality of student preparation are increasingly diverse, new teachers need more help. This help will be difficult to come by in graduate schools, where instruction in pedagogy is regarded as rather infra dig and where the focus of intellectual vision is narrowing rather than broadening.

The graduate schools should still be pressed to take more responsibility for producing undergraduate teachers who can communicate their enthusiasm for the liberal arts. But as a practical matter, the institution where the new faculty member begins a teaching career will have to take primary responsibility. That means more than a few token lectures on teaching techniques. It may call for an intensive year-long seminar, with demonstrations and critiques of actual teaching, videotapes of classes, and discussion of special techniques for teaching to a wide range of student backgrounds and preparation. It will require sympathetic recognition of new faculty members' need for time and, where appropriate, facilities to satisfy their research interests and ambitions. If new faculty are frustrated researchers, they will be inattentive teachers. And what is done with new faculty must reflect a compatible set of values in the culture of established faculty.

New faculty are likely to approach their first teaching assignments with the enthusiasm that accompanies novelty. Established faculty may or may not attack their teaching with enthusiasm, depending in large part on the reward systems of the institution where they are teaching. Those reward systems (which include both material and psychic rewards) are manifestations of the culture of the institution, but the culture can also be modified through changes in the reward system. Established faculty will be less concerned than new faculty about maintaining their mobility by focusing on their research. Their difficulties in rising to the challenge of teaching a more diverse student body are more likely to be the result of habit or burnout. What is needed to stimulate their interest is first a demonstration that the institution cares about their performance and then an opportunity to be involved in a shared adventure with their colleagues.

The reward system ranges from released time or summer stipends for curriculum development to merit increments for teaching excellence and innovation. Shared adventures can include joint efforts to develop new courses or modify existing courses; faculty seminars on teaching a more diverse student body; work with staff members who manage internships and volunteer programs on closer integration of these programs with classroom teaching; and even "teaching tables" in the faculty dining room. Mutual support and stimulation are critical elements. Academic departments may provide the critical mass for these interactions. But when such interactions need to cross departmental boundaries — as is often the case — leadership from deans and provosts is essential, if only to validate the efforts of department chairs and individual faculty members. The role of academic departments in assimilating the more varied mix of students arriving on campus is crucial. Here the immediate interests of the departments and the students appear to coincide, but perhaps to the detriment of the longer range interests of both parties.

Students from diverse backgrounds, for whom the campus is not a traditional setting, tend to view their undergraduate education as a necessary means to a specific desired end. If you don't see yourself as heir to a tradition in which you and your peers spend this period of your lives as students, you are less likely to see your undergraduate years as an experience to be relished and more likely to see it as a stage to pass through as rapidly as possible. Of course, it is not always true that diversity increases alienation, and even when it is, the student who is less at home in the institution may be motivated to pursue his studies even more assiduously.

A natural instinct in this population of students who are likely to be strangers to each other is to identify themselves with a major as early as possible. For transfer students, who make up an increasing proportion of new entrants, the choice will be immediate. Academic departments—understandably anxious to latch onto new majors, especially in a world where numbers matter—will welcome early recruits. Administrations will be relieved to hand students over to the departments for rations and quarters.

But being a major in history or psychology or mechanical engineering is, in proper perspective, only one part of a liberal education. In the American Association of Colleges and Universities' classic catalog of the elements of a liberal education, the major comes last. Quite apart from the value of postponing career decisions as long as possible in order to permit mature consideration of this critical life choice, students who choose a major at the outset are narrowing the definition of their academic self. At the same time, they are cutting one of the ties that bind them to the mass of students from diverse backgrounds, who are pursuing still-undifferentiated goals within the universe of liberal education.

It is not easy to persuade undergraduates to put off the choice of a major. With engineering students, the requirements of ABET (the professional accreditation body) may make it almost impossible. If postponement adds an extra year to a bachelor's degree, the economic cost to the student could be substantial.

It should still be possible, however, to persuade some undergraduates to spend a year or even two in which they deliberately suspend the narrowing effects of choosing a major—a year or two that have the sole purpose of exploring the limits of a liberal education. For most students, the identification with a major will still come very early, especially as the idea of liberal education becomes less familiar to future student bodies. That makes it all the more important for the leadership of the institution to keep reminding students and faculty that their education—including the continuing education of the faculty—should not be confined within the boundaries of any one discipline or department.

Envoi: The Role of the Academic Administrator

The situation of the academic administrator today is not an enviable one, for all of the reasons just enumerated. Revenues are not keeping pace with costs, and there is no foreseeable prospect of relief. Faculty are feeling underappreciated as well as underpaid. Students, while no longer making nonnegotiable demands, are multiplying their short-term expectations. And the public is looking for objective proof of educational achievements that are particularly difficult to objectify. The basic units of instruction—the academic departments—are developing structural faults, and individual institutions are no longer seen as self-contained entities.

Administrators working under similarly trying conditions in other sectors of society have discovered that when one's responsibilities stretch the limits of one's authority, it is better to reach out to share responsibility than to push for more authority. This essay has suggested a number of ways in which academic administrators can share responsibility with faculty in allocating scarce resources; in responding to the enhanced expectations of students, public authorities, and the general public; and in coping with increased diversity. This is not to overlook the opportunities for sharing responsibilities with staff, particularly in service learning activities where student internship and volunteer work are organized to relate to classroom learning, and vice versa.

Long-established academic traditions hold that administrators should primarily be facilitators for faculty initiatives rather than executives deciding on the direction (and speed) of the academic enterprise. But the administrator should still feel free to exercise leadership, as distinguished from authority, and is particularly well positioned to do so. If where you stand depends on where you sit, the administrator sits where the view of liberal education can extend to the farthest horizon. The only limitations are in the administrator's own vision and in the ability to convey that vision to colleagues—and to all the diverse constituencies that now impinge on academia.

Note

1. John Henry Newman, *The Idea of the University* (Notre Dame, Ind: University of Notre Dame Press, 1982), p. 75.

10

The Student as Scholar

Ernest L. Boyer

While I thought about this conference, my mind drifted back to fall 1956, when I became academic dean at one of the world's smallest higher learning institutions, a tiny college of arts and sciences in southern California. During my first month on the job, the faculty curriculum committee met to review the college's requirements for graduation. In an act of unrestrained innocence, I asked why we had a "distribution requirement" for all students. A senior professor replied, "We borrowed it from Pomona College" (our prestigious neighbor down the road). I then asked where Pomona got it and was told, "From Harvard"—which gave me a basic lesson about higher education policymaking that's stood me in good stead for almost forty years.

Liberal education is one of the most enduring and widely shared visions in American higher learning. Almost everyone agrees that beyond acquiring competence in a special field, undergraduates must be broadly informed, discover relationships across the disciplines, form values, and advance the common good. It's also true, however, that this inspired vision of liberal learning, which is powerfully reaffirmed in almost all college mission statements, is under siege on many fronts.

The decline in the quality of the nation's schools surely has weakened liberal education, as has the growing emphasis on careerism and credentials. Also, the cultural fragmentation in America today makes it especially difficult for academics to bring to undergraduate education a sense of coherence and shared purpose. In 1920 Archibald MacLeish diagnosed the problem this way: "There can be no *educational* postulates so long as there are no generally accepted postulates of life itself."

Beyond all of these impediments, it is my own impression that the most serious challenge to liberal education on most campuses is the system of faculty rewards. And I remain convinced that liberal learning will be renewed only as faculty members who teach undergraduates and spend time with incoming students are rewarded for such efforts.

But before considering how this ambitious goal might be accomplished, I would like to take a backward glance and reflect on how priorities of the professoriate have changed through the years.

I

When little Harvard College was founded in 1636, the focus was on the student. Teaching in those days was a central, even sacred function, and the highest accolade a professor could receive was the famous one Chaucer extended to the clerk at Oxford when he said, "Gladly would he learn, and gladly teach."

Educating the whole person with a rigidly prescribed classical curriculum was at the very heart of the colonial college, and for a century and a half that's what scholarship in America was all about. Following the Revolution, teaching remained central, and the nation's colleges continued to define, with confidence, what all students ought to know. Even as late as 1869, Charles Eliot, in assuming the presidency of Harvard, declared that the primary business of the American professor must be "regular and assiduous class teaching."

But change was in the wind. And early in the nineteenth century, the focus of American higher education slowly began to shift from shaping young lives to building a nation. In 1824, Rensselaer Polytechnic Institute was founded in Troy, New York. According to historian Frederick Rudolph, RPI was a constant reminder that America needed railroad builders, bridge builders, builders of all kinds.

The famous Land Grant Act of 1862 linked higher learning to America's agricultural and technological revolution. And when social critic Lincoln Steffens visited Madison in 1909, he declared that "in Wisconsin the university is as close to the intelligent farmer as his pig pen or his toolhouse."

As the commitment extended from the campus to the state, higher education's commitment to liberal learning weakened. Driven both by new knowledge and by the new spirit of service, the undergraduate curriculum slowly shifted from an unwavering commitment to theology and the classics to a more open, less structured pattern of electives.

In 1869 in his inaugural speech, Harvard's President Eliot sounded the death knell of the mandatory classical curriculum. After surveying the rich menu of subjects to be studied, Eliot concluded, "We would have them all and at their best." Core courses began to disappear, and by 1895 the only remaining requirements at Harvard were two English courses and a foreign language course in the freshman year. For all practical purposes, the colonial college vision of liberal learning had faded.

At the turn of the century, utility was riding high in the saddle. David Starr Jordan, president of Stanford University, declared that the entire university movement in this country was toward "reality and practicality." Charles Eliot, still at Harvard, now defined "serviceability" as an essential mission of American higher education. Frankly, I find it quite amazing that just one hundred years ago the words "reality," "practicality," and "serviceability" were used by America's most distinguished academic leaders to describe the purposes of higher learning.

To put it simply, the scholarship of teaching had been joined by the scholarship of building.

Meanwhile, a third higher education tradition was emerging. American academics who had studied at the distinguished German universities of Göttingen, Heidelberg, and Humboldt were profoundly influenced by the scholarship of science. Inspired by the empiricism of the day, Daniel Coit Gilman, one of the most vigorous advocates of the German model, in 1876, became president of the Johns Hopkins University, which is often described as the first "true" university in the United States.

Woodrow Wilson, president of Princeton, spoke at Gilman's retirement twenty years later, and on this memorable occasion, Wilson described Johns Hopkins as the first university in America where the discovery of knowledge was judged superior to "mere teaching." Indeed, this may have been the precise moment when the teaching versus research debate actually began in America.

Thus, by the end of the twentieth century, American higher education had been profoundly shaped by three rich traditions—the colonial college, the land grant college, and the European university. Unfortunately, liberal learning's position in these cross-currents remained ambiguous at best.

II

Following World War II, America experienced a transformation in higher education. Thanks to the G. I. Bill, the country moved—almost overnight—from elite to mass higher education. Enrollments exploded, and campuses were built at the rate of one a week. The irony was that at the very moment the mission of higher learning was being broadened, the reward system of the professoriate was being narrowed.

Responding to explosive growth, a veritable army of newly minted Ph.D.s went to campuses from coast to coast, determined to recreate the academic climate they themselves had experienced in graduate school, and research, not teaching, became the primary criterion for success.

A core of baccalaureate colleges, including many represented at this conference, held firmly to the "collegiate tradition," with its strong connection to liberal learning, but in the academic culture overall, the reward system—in terms of salaries, mobility, and prestige—increasingly became skewed in favor of highly specialized research and publication, a shift that took its toll on liberal education. In the early 1960s, I was at the University of California, Santa Barbara, and I watched as a former teacher education and home economics institution was folded into the University of California system; faculty who had been hired to fulfill one mission suddenly were held accountable for another. I then went to the State University of New York, where we struggled to maintain separate missions among sixty-four institutions during a time of "upward drift," when campuses were rapidly becoming more imitative than creative.

Thus, by the late twentieth century, the land grant tradition had faded from the scene, and most campuses were caught in the conflict of the two other great traditions. On the one hand, there was the colonial college tradition, with its emphasis on the student, on general education, and on loyalty to the campus. On the other hand, there was the German university tradition, with its emphasis not on the student but on the professoriate; not on general but on specialized education; not on loyalty to the campus but on loyalty to the guild. And I've observed that almost all consequential debates on campus—including conflicts over the significance of liberal education—are really a struggle for the soul of the institution. Are we a colonial college, a European university, or a blend of the two?

When they are out recruiting students, most higher education institutions are collegiate to the core, describing themselves in viewbooks and videocassettes as places with lots of loving, tender care. But when students actually enroll, they frequently discover a campus sharply divided between the collegiate and university traditions—with liberal learning caught somewhere in the middle.

III

What are we to do about all of this? Is it possible to reorder the priorities of the professoriate and create a more supportive climate for the undergraduate experience, one in which the goals of liberal education are recognized as an authentic dimension of academic life?

Recently, at the Carnegie Foundation, we prepared a special report entitled *Scholarship Reconsidered*. In this small monograph, we propose a broader view of scholarship, one with four interlocking parts. This new paradigm acknowledges the full range of faculty work—teaching, research, and service—and it may provide a framework within which the purposes of liberal learning might be recognized and renewed.

The Scholarship of Discovery

Every member of the academy should demonstrate his or her ability to do research, and in our report we celebrate what we call the scholarship of discovery, insisting that higher education must continue to be the home of disciplined investigation.

Fifty years ago, Vannevar Bush of MIT said that universities are the wellsprings of human understanding and that as long as scholars are free to pursue truth wherever it may lead, there will continue to be a flow of new scientific knowledge. This vision of the pursuit of truth is surely the essence of what higher education is all about, and we urge that the scholarship of discovery be vigorously reaffirmed.

The Scholarship of Integration

Beyond discovery, we propose what we call the scholarship of integration. The tendency of the disciplines has been to isolate themselves from one another, with academic departments becoming political bases, not centers of intellectual quest. In such a climate, knowledge is fragmented and the integrative purposes of liberal learning are almost hopelessly obscured.

Geneticist Barbara McClintock, a Nobel laureate, on one occasion said, "Everything is one. There is no way to draw a line between things." Yet, to judge from the catalog, knowledge has been sliced up into little pieces. Frank Press, former president of the National Academy of Sciences, has suggested that the scientist is also, in some respects, an artist. He went on to observe that the magnificent double helix, which broke the genetic code, is not just rational but beautiful as well. Several years ago, when the world-renowned physicist Victor Weisskopf was asked, "What gives you hope in troubled times?" he replied, "Mozart and quantum mechanics." Yet where, in today's general education sequence, do undergraduates see connections such as these?

The good news is that the cognitive map is changing. Some of the most exciting work in the academy today is in what Michael Polanyi, of the University of Chicago, calls the "overlapping academic neighborhoods"—the new compound disciplines of psycholinguistics, bioengineering, molecular biology, and the like. Clifford Geertz, of the Institute for Advanced Study, in his fascinating essay "Blurred Genres," argues that a new paradigm of knowledge is beginning to emerge simply because the new questions don't fit in the old boxes.

In short, I'm convinced that prospects for liberal learning will surely be enhanced as colleges and universities affirm the scholarship of integration and encourage members of the professoriate to be more attentive to cross-disciplinary studies.

The Scholarship of Application

Beyond the discovery and integration of knowledge, we suggest, as a third priority of academic life, the scholarship of application.

Historically, higher learning in this country has been viewed as useful "in the nation's service," as Woodrow Wilson put it. Today, however, there's a growing feeling that higher education is a private benefit rather than a public good. Increasingly, the campus is viewed as a place where professors get tenured and students get credentialed, while the overall work of the academy seems irrelevant to the nation's most pressing social problems.

I'm convinced that higher education must respond to the educational and health and urban crises of our day, just as the land grant college responded to the needs of farmers a century ago—a commitment that can be viewed as a dimension of scholarship itself.

MIT professor Donald Schön, in his provocative book *The Reflective Practitioner*, argues that scholars move not only from theory to practice but also from practice back to theory, a point that is surely illustrated by placing students in classrooms, clinics, legal offices, architectural studios, or other locations where professional training can be remarkably enhanced.

When all is said and done, theory cannot be divorced from practice, and in developing new priorities for the professoriate, we simply must give new dignity and new status to the scholarship of application.

The Scholarship of Teaching

Finally, scholarship is, by definition, a communal act. Disseminating or sharing knowledge makes the work of academic life complete. Consider how we always say "research and publication," suggesting that scholarly investigation takes on meaning only when it is passed on to others, which might be considered an act of teaching. Surely teaching undergraduates can be an authentic form of scholarly work.

The simple truth is that almost all of us are where we are today because of the inspiration of an inspired teacher. Yet, on far too many campuses, it is deemed better for a professor to deliver a paper at the Hyatt in Chicago than to teach undergraduates back home. And it's really sad the way we speak of research "opportunities" and teaching "loads."

Giving teaching such a low priority has a profoundly negative influence on liberal learning. Young scholars often observe that, regardless of catalog commitment to general education, the reality is that too much time with students will, in fact, jeopardize their careers.

Robert Oppenheimer, speaking at the two hundredth anniversary of Columbia University, said, "It is proper to the role of the scientist that he not merely find new truth . . . but that he teach, that he try to bring the most honest and intelligible account of new knowledge to all who will try to learn." Great teachers keep the flame of scholarship alive, and surely that means teaching future scholars in the classroom.

I'm suggesting that the most imaginative and resourceful plans to revitalize liberal learning will get nowhere unless the priorities of the professoriate are redefined to include not only the scholarship of discovery but also the scholarship of integrating knowledge, the scholarship of applying knowledge, and the scholarship of teaching, including sharing knowledge with future scholars in the classroom.

To put it simply, liberal learning must be viewed not as a diversion but as an essential part of scholarship.

IV

This brings me to one final observation. Recently it occurred to me that this new paradigm of scholarship might be appropriate not only for the professoriate but also for the students. Would it be possible to break up the two-plus-two approach to the undergraduate experience (general education plus the major)? Could we better integrate these four years by defining discovery, integration, application, and the sharing of knowledge as the goals of collegiate education? Let me illustrate what I have in mind.

Consider first the discovery of knowledge. Currently, first- and second-year students often have limited contact with professors in their major field of interest until the junior year, and they have only the vaguest ideas of how professors spend their time. As an alternative, senior faculty could meet with incoming students in a new kind of first-year experience, one in which professors present a series of miniseminars that would give new students an overview of the disciplines, describe exciting research projects in the field, and, early on, help undergraduates sort out their own intellectual interests.

In this model of liberal learning, the academic major would run vertically, from the first to the last year. From the outset students would be introduced to an intellectual life that differs sharply from the high school culture. Further, every student, as a requirement for graduation, would complete a research project, working closely with a mentor. The goal would be to engage faculty *and* students in the scholarship of discovery.

The second purpose of liberal education—the integration of knowledge—would go beyond isolated facts and introduce all students to connections across disciplines. Almost every mission statement of liberal education cites integration as an essential goal. Yet on most campuses, general education is a grab bag of disconnected courses. Students pick and choose their way to a degree but often fail to gain a more integrated view of knowledge and a more coherent, more authentic view of life.

In searching for coherence, would it be possible to move beyond the distribution (which students try to get out of the way) and organize general education around a series of cross-disciplinary seminars on such topics as "great events that changed the course of history" or "the crisis in the city" or "art across cultures" or "the ethics of technology"?

Yet another approach would be to organize general education within a framework called the "Human Commonalities," a program Art Levine and I suggested many years ago in a monograph entitled *Quest for Common Learning.*

The larger purpose I have in mind is to replace the grab bag of isolated courses with cross-disciplinary seminars that could run vertically, from the first to the fourth years, would intersect the major, and would assure that all undergraduates are introduced to the scholarship of integration.

Fifty years ago, Mark Van Doren wrote, "The connectedness of things is what the educator contemplates to the limit of his capacity. . . . The student who can begin early in his life to think of things as connected . . . has begun the life of learning"—which is at the very heart of liberal education.

The application of knowledge also has meaning for liberal learning. Presently, undergraduates spend almost all of their time in classrooms, engaged in theory. Why not, as a third priority for liberal education, have all students participate in fieldwork or in community service that relates theory to real life?

We live in a society with a huge variety of social problems— neglected children, poor schools, and inner cities that are a maelstrom of joblessness, drug-related violence, and social disintegration. Beyond our borders, we confront a world still reeling and in disarray from the end of a forty-year-long Cold War and confronting monumental problems of overpopulation and environmental degradation. No definition of liberal education that is divorced from vigorous engagement is likely to be productive.

More than half a century ago, historian Oscar Handlin put the challenge this way: "Our troubled planet can no longer afford the luxury of pursuits confined to an ivory tower. Scholarship has to prove its worth, not on its own terms, but by service to the nation and the world."

Finally, liberal learning might be focused on the sharing of knowledge. Good communication is, in fact, at the very heart of liberal education. As a top priority, all students must become skilled in the written and the spoken word. Beginning in the first year, every undergraduate should complete a course on expository writing, and all students should write across the curriculum. And why not organize undergraduate classes so that students would be active learners and, at least occasionally, teachers as well?

Moreover, as a core component of liberal learning, we could ask undergraduates to write a senior thesis on a consequential topic and require them to take a seminar on the ethics of communication to help them become proficient in oral and written communication. They should thereby learn that honesty is the obligation we assume when we are empowered in the use of words.

I am suggesting that defining liberal learning as a scholarly endeavor would focus the work of undergraduates on four essential goals:

> First, all students would be introduced to the process of disciplined investigation and become proficient in gathering, analyzing, and evaluating information—the scholarship of discovery.
>
> Second, all students would become well informed in a core of general knowledge and begin to understand relationships and patterns across the separate fields of study—the scholarship of integration.
>
> Third, all students would relate learning to real life—the scholarship of application.
>
> Fourth, all students would learn to communicate effectively and ethically—the scholarship of teaching.

Defining liberal education this way would, I believe, create a sense of community on the campus. It would bring faculty and students together in shared intellectual quest and help close the gap between student and faculty cultures. In such a climate, incoming students would be viewed not as the great unwashed but as scholars in the making.

I am keenly aware of the limited impact people and their institutions seem to make these days on the events of our time. But it is my abiding hope that, with determination and effort, the undergraduate college can indeed make a difference in the intellectual and personal lives of its graduates, in the social and civic responsibilities they are willing to assume, and ultimately in their worldviews.

These scholarly intangibles, which reveal themselves in very real ways, are the characteristics by which, ultimately, the quality of liberal learning must be measured.

Appendix: Conference Statement

This statement was prepared by the participants in "Rethinking Liberal Education," a symposium held April 14–17, 1994, at the American Academy of Arts and Sciences, Cambridge, Massachusetts. It represents general agreement of those listed below. No one, however, was asked to sign it. Further, it should be understood that not everyone agreed with every part of the statement.

Our four-day conference of thirty-eight liberal arts college and university presidents, eleven chief academic officers, and twenty-nine educational association leaders, foundation officers, and scholars has represented an effort to look at the problems and opportunities for undergraduate education. We reaffirm the traditional values of liberal education, which have served us well over time. We recognize our success in graduating men and women prepared to contribute positively to our nation in the variety of leadership positions our society requires. At the same time, we acknowledge that we must improve our efforts to provide an education that is global and multicultural in context and both intellectual and developmental in its attempt to educate the whole person.

The task we have set ourselves here is to describe approaches to liberal arts education and to the organization of our institutions that we see as essential responses to our times.

As we look to the future, we see a new era dawning on the global horizon, a new cultural sensibility, and a new information age—all signals of immense possibility for humanity. We believe it is time to reexamine liberal education in the light of these changes, and we encourage institutions to articulate their own expectations and values with which to educate students for responsible citizenship in a democracy.

Specifically, we need to revisit the principles of liberal education in four distinct contexts:

First, we need to consider the world we are preparing our students to enter—a world increasingly defined by techno-logical change, shifting work patterns, cultural diversity, environmental fragility, and new global perspectives.

Second, we need to consider who our students are—the ways in which they learn, as well as their diverse backgrounds and preparations.

Third, we need to consider the setting of our educational enterprise: the explosion of knowledge, the proliferation of subject matter, and the development of new information technologies.

Fourth, we need to take into account the growing problem of educational costs and the difficulties this problem poses for many American families, and for educational institutions themselves.

Therefore, we propose that liberal arts institutions be strengthened in the following ways:

1. Liberal arts institutions should continue to implement al-ternatives to the traditional discipline-based major and dis-tribution requirements; they should expand collaborative learning, encourage interdisciplinary approaches, and sup-port faculty-student collaborative research. All of these efforts should be aimed at enhancing their students' understanding.

2. They should support comprehensive evaluations of all fac-ulty by students, peers, and administrators, including self-evaluations and periodic posttenure review.

3. They should increase the flexibility of their organizational structures, including academic departments.

4. They should include faculty, staff, and students in the pro-cess of developing institutional priorities and in linking those priorities to the budgetary process.

5. They should undertake systematic efforts to foster collab-oration among four-year colleges, schools, community col-leges, and graduate schools; to make the transition of their diverse student population from one level to another more efficient and effective; and to improve teaching at all levels.

6. They should explore and take advantage of the full potential of technology for teaching, learning, scholarship, creativity, and communication.

7. They should help new and established faculty improve their teaching throughout their careers.

8. They should encourage faculty to participate actively in student advising and helping students integrate what they have learned.
9. They should explore and develop alternatives to traditional student and faculty assessment techniques, and they should evaluate faculty teaching by reference to what students have learned.
10. They should assess students by a variety of methods through which students demonstrate their understanding of what they have learned.
11. They should encourage students to enhance their learning by involvement in their local and global communities through such activities as service learning, study abroad, and community internships. Faculty involvement should be encouraged in all learning activities both inside and outside the classroom.

Above all, we must continue to foster the life of the mind in devoting our resources to ensuring the primacy of the academic mission.

Participants

Nancy Y. Bekavac
President, Scripps College, California

Rita Bornstein
President, Rollins College, Florida

Leon Botstein
President, Bard College, New York

David W. Breneman
Dean, School of Education, University of Virginia

Paula Brownlee
President, Association of American Colleges and Universities, Washington, D.C.

Elizabeth Coleman
President, Bennington College, Vermont

Donald W. Crawford
Vice Chancellor, University of California–Santa Barbara, California

Barbara Doherty
President, St. Mary-of-the-Woods College, Indiana

Charles L. Duke
Dean of College, Grinnell College, Iowa

Nancy Dye
President, Oberlin College, Ohio

Harold Eickhoff
President, Trenton State College,
New Jersey

Alice T. Emerson
Vice President, Andrew W. Mellon
Foundation, New York

Nicholas H. Farnham
Director, Educational Leadership Program, New York

Andrew T. Ford
President, Wabash College,
Indiana

Mary Francilene
President, Madonna University,
Michigan

James Fries
President, College of Santa Fe,
New Mexico

Robert Gale
President Emeritus, Association of Governing Boards,
Washington, D.C.

Howard Gardner
Professor, Graduate School of
Education, Harvard University,
Massachusetts

Claire Gaudiani
President, Connecticut College,
Connecticut

Robert Gavin Jr.
President, Macalester College,
Minnesota

Gerald W. Gibson
President, Maryville College,
Tennessee

Hannah F. Goldberg
Provost, Wheaton College,
Massachusetts

Stephen R. Graubard
Editor, *Daedalus*, American
Academy of Arts and Sciences,
Massachusetts

Douglas Greenberg
President, Chicago Historical
Society, Illinois

Theodore L. Gross
President, Roosevelt University,
Illinois

Alfred J. Guillaume
Provost, Humboldt State University, California

John Hammer
Director, National Humanities
Alliance, Washington, D.C.

William H. Harris
President, Alabama State
University, Alabama

Donald W. Harward
President, Bates College, Maine

Richard H. Hersh
President, Hobart and William
Smith Colleges, New York

Barbara A. Hill
President, Sweet Briar College,
Virginia

Jerry Hudson
President, Willamette University, Oregon

Stanley Katz
President, American Council of
Learned Societies, New York

Randall Kennedy
  Professor of Law, Harvard
  University, Massachusetts

Julie Kidd
  President, Christian A. Johnson
  Endeavor Foundation, New York

Bruce Kimball
  Professor, Warner Graduate
  School of Education, University
  of Rochester, New York

Terrill Edward Lautz
  Vice President, Henry Luce
  Foundation, New York

Joab Lesesne
  President, Wofford College,
  South Carolina

Andrea Leskes
  Vice Provost, Northeastern
  University, Massachusetts

Arthur Levine
  President, Teachers College,
  New York

Peter Lyman
  Librarian, University of
  California at Berkeley

Tamar March
  Vice President for Academic
  Affairs, New England College,
  New Hampshire

Roger H. Martin
  President, Moravian College,
  Pennsylvania

Mary Andrew Matesich
  President, Ohio Dominican
  College, Ohio

Curtis L. McCray
  President, Millikin University,
  Illinois

Elizabeth McKinsey
  Dean of the College, Carleton
  College, Minnesota

Julia M. McNamara
  President, Albertus Magnus
  College, Connecticut

John Meisel
  President, The Royal Society
  of Canada, Ontario

Kathryn Mohrman
  President, Colorado College,
  Colorado

Richard Morrill
  President, University of
  Richmond, Virginia

James L. Muyskens
  Dean of Liberal Arts and
  Sciences, University of
  Kansas–Lawrence, Kansas

Robert Orrill
  Director, Office of Academic
  Affairs, College Board, New York

Lucius Outlaw
  Professor, Haverford College,
  Pennsylvania

Ladell Payne
  President, Randolph-Macon
  College, Virginia

Alfred Perkins
  Academic Vice President,
  Berea College, Kentucky

Richard Pfau
President, Illinois College,
Illinois

Susan Resneck Pierce
President, University of Puget
Sound, Washington

Gregory S. Prince Jr.
President, Hampshire College,
Massachusetts

Frank Reynolds
Professor, University of Chicago,
Illinois

William P. Robinson
President, Whitworth College,
Washington

Robert Rotberg
President, World Peace Foundation, Massachusetts

Thelma Roundtree
Executive Associate to the Presi-
dent, Saint Augustine's College,
North Carolina

Ruth Schmidt
President, Agnes Scott College,
Georgia

Talbert O. Shaw
President, Shaw University,
North Carolina

Joseph Short
President, Bradford College,
Massachusetts

James Shuart
President, Hofstra University,
New York

Allen P. Splete
President, Council of Independent Colleges, Washington, D.C.

Rebecca Stafford
President, Monmouth College,
New Jersey

John A. Synodinos
President, Lebanon Valley
College, Pennsylvania

Ronald D. Thorpe
Vice President, Cambridge
College, Massachusetts

Richard Warch
President, Lawrence University,
Wisconsin

Rudolph Weingartner
Professor, University of
Pittsburgh, Pennsylvania

John W. White Jr.
President, Nebraska Wesleyan
University

Harold R. Wilde
President, North Central
College, Illinois

James L. Wiser
Senior Vice President, Loyola
University of Chicago, Illinois

Frank Wong
Vice President for Academic
Affairs, University of Redlands,
California

Adam Yarmolinsky
Regents Professor, University of
Maryland System

Index

Confessing Our Faith

Confessing Our Faith

---

*An Interpretation of
the Statement of Faith of
the United Church of Christ*

Roger Lincoln Shinn

United Church Press
Cleveland, Ohio

Copyright © 1990 by The Pilgrim Press
All rights reserved

No part of this publication may be reproduced, stored in a retrieval
system, or transmitted in any form or by any means, electronic,
mechanical, photocopying, recording, or otherwise (brief quotations
used in magazines or newspaper reviews excepted) without prior
permission of the publisher.

Scripture quotations are from the New Revised Standard Version
Bible, copyright 1989, Division of Christian Education of the National
Council of the Churches of Christ in the United States of America,
and are used by permission.

Library of Congress Cataloging-in-Publication Data

Shinn, Roger Lincoln.
    Confessing our faith : an interpretation of the Statement of faith
of the United Church of Christ / Roger Lincoln Shinn.
        p.   cm.
    Includes bibliographical references.
    ISBN 0-8298-0866-3
    1. United Church of Christ.   Statement of faith (1959)   2. United
Church of Christ.   Statement of faith (1977)   3. United Church of
Christ. Statement of faith (1981)   4. United Church of Christ—
Creeds.   5. Congregationalist churches—United States—Creeds.
6. Reformed Church—United States—Creeds.   7. United churches—
United States—Creeds.   I. United Church of Christ. Statement of
faith (1959).   1990.   II. United Church of Christ. Statement of
faith (1977).   1990.   III. United Church of Christ. Statement of
faith (1981).   1990.   IV. Title.
BX9886.S45   1990
238'.5834—dc20   90-35445
                                                                    CIP

United Church Press, Cleveland, Ohio

To "the glorious company of the apostles . . . the goodly fellowship of the prophets . . . the noble army of martyrs,"

Who in times past have shown the meaning of Christian faith, and

Who in days to come will express new meanings of that faith as it enters its third millennium of history

Contents

Preface

This book is an interpretation of the Statement of Faith of the United Church of Christ. This statement exists in three versions: those of 1959, 1977, and 1981. All are recognized by the General Synod, all are printed in the *Book of Worship* of the United Church of Christ, and all are published in Braille by the Office of Church Life and Leadership. The principal purpose of this book is to interpret the common testimony shared by all three versions. Another purpose is to show why there are three versions, to explain their differences, and to point out the issues on which this church is still seeking a common mind.

I have written the book at the invitation of the Pilgrim Press. But that invitation does not make this an "official" book. The Statement of Faith is a public document that everyone is free to interpret. I have tried to interpret the Statement as an expression of the mind and faith of the church that has adopted it, but obviously my own convictions and ideas color this interpretation. Occasionally I use the personal pronoun, "I," as a reminder that this is one person's interpretation and as an encouragement to others to make their interpretations. More often I use the plural "we," because I am interpreting a shared document.

As a testimony of a church, the Statement rises out of the context of Christian history and the contemporary church. I try to show its relation to the Bible, to traditional belief, to Christian thinking in our time, and to the world in which we live. I point out where it takes clear stands and where it invites Christians to further thought and discussion about their faith.

In working on this book I have often remembered my great friend and colleague, Daniel Day Williams (1910–73). He and I cooperated in writing an earlier interpretation of the original Statement of Faith, *We Believe* (United Church Press, 1966). Now, when the insights of history and the two revisions of the Statement call for a reinterpretation, I can no longer call on his wisdom and collaboration. This book follows the same structure as the earlier book. In the chapters that I originally drafted, some parts are entirely new, while other parts echo or repeat the earlier book. In the chapters that he drafted, I have not been so bold as to guess what he would have repeated or changed. Instead I have taken responsibility for my own version, but with immense gratitude to Dan Williams.

So I submit this book, partly the work of one writer and partly the work of an American church of the twentieth century, as a contribution to the continuing Christian conversations and interfaith conversations of our time.

The three versions of the Statement of Faith immediately follow this introduction. The interpretations generally refer to the most recent version, with occasional comparisons with the earlier two.

STATEMENT OF FAITH

*The Revision of 1981: A Doxology**

We believe in you, O God, Eternal Spirit, God of our Savior
Jesus Christ and our God, and to your deeds we testify:
> You call the worlds into being,
>> create persons in your own image,
>> and set before each one the ways of life and death.
> You seek in holy love to save all people from aimlessness
>> and sin.
> You judge people and nations by your righteous will
>> declared through prophets and apostles.
> In Jesus Christ, the man of Nazareth, our crucified and
>> risen Savior,
>> you have come to us
>> and shared our common lot,
>> conquering sin and death
>> and reconciling the world to yourself.
> You bestow upon us your Holy Spirit,
>> creating and renewing the church of Jesus Christ,
>> binding in covenant faithful people of all ages,
>> tongues, and races.
> You call us into your church
>> to accept the cost and joy of discipleship,
>> to be your servants in the service of others,
>> to proclaim the gospel to all the world
>> and resist the powers of evil,
>> to share in Christ's baptism and eat at his table,
>> to join him in his passion and victory.
> You promise to all who trust you
>> forgiveness of sins and fullness of grace,
>> courage in the struggle for justice and peace,
>> your presence in trial and rejoicing,
>> and eternal life in your realm which has no end.
Blessing and honor, glory and power be unto you. Amen.

*Statement of Faith, Revised 1981 (in the form of a Doxology), affirmed
by the Fourteenth General Synod of the United Church of Christ.

xi

STATEMENT OF FAITH

*The Original Version, 1959**

We believe in God, the Eternal Spirit, Father of our Lord
Jesus Christ and our Father, and to his deeds we testify:
> He calls the worlds into being,
>> creates man in his own image
>> and sets before him the ways of life and death.
>
> He seeks in holy love to save all people from aimlessness
>> and sin.
>
> He judges men and nations by his righteous will
>> declared through prophets and apostles.
>
> In Jesus Christ, the man of Nazareth, our crucified and
>> risen Lord,
>> he has come to us
>> and shared our common lot,
>> conquering sin and death
>> and reconciling the world to himself.
>
> He bestows upon us his Holy Spirit,
>> creating and renewing the church of Jesus Christ,
>> binding in covenant faithful people of all ages,
>> tongues, and races.
>
> He calls us into his church
>> to accept the cost and joy of discipleship,
>> to be his servants in the service of men,
>> to proclaim the gospel to all the world
>> and resist the powers of evil,
>> to share in Christ's baptism and eat at his table,
>> to join him in his passion and victory.
>
> He promises to all who trust him
>> forgiveness of sins and fullness of grace,
>> courage in the struggle for justice and peace,
>> his presence in trial and rejoicing,
>> and eternal life in his kingdom which has no end.

Blessing and honor, glory and power be unto him. Amen.

---

*Statement of Faith, approved by the Second General Synod of the
United Church of Christ, 1959.

STATEMENT OF FAITH

*The Revision of 1977**

We believe in God, the Eternal Spirit, who is made known
to us in Jesus our brother, and to whose deeds we testify:
> God calls the worlds into being,
>> creates humankind in the divine image,
>> and sets before us the ways of life and death.
>
> God seeks in holy love to save all people from aimlessness
>> and sin.
>
> God judges all humanity and all nations by that will of
>> righteousness declared through prophets and apostles.
>
> In Jesus Christ, the man of Nazareth, our crucified and
>> risen Lord,
>> God has come to us
>> and shared our common lot,
>> conquering sin and death
>> and reconciling the whole creation to its Creator.
>
> God bestows upon us the Holy Spirit,
>> creating and renewing the church of Jesus Christ,
>> binding in covenant faithful people of all ages,
>>> tongues, and races.
>
> God calls us into the church
>> to accept the cost and joy of discipleship,
>> to be servants in the service of the whole human family,
>> to proclaim the gospel to all the world
>>> and resist the powers of evil,
>> to share in Christ's baptism and eat at his table,
>> to join him in his passion and victory.
>
> God promises to all who trust in the gospel
>> forgiveness of sins and fullness of grace,
>> courage in the struggle for justice and peace,
>> the presence of the Holy Spirit in trial and rejoicing,
>> and eternal life in that kingdom which has no end.

Blessing and honor, glory and power be unto God. Amen.

---

*Statement of Faith, revised by Robert V. Moss, Jr., president of the
United Church of Christ, 1969–76, and recommended for use by the
Eleventh General Synod, 1977.

PART ONE

The Great Story and a Lesser Story

All Christian faith arises out of two stories, the Great Story and a lesser story.

The Great Story is the story of God, creation, human history, and human hope and expectation, as Christians understand this story in faith. It begins, as the Bible begins, "In the beginning." It continues with the story of humanity, of a covenant people within humanity, of the coming of Christ Jesus, of a renewed covenant, of the pain and splendor of human life, of a hope that extends to the ultimate eternal reign of God. The Great Story is told in the Bible, partly as narrative of the past, partly as ever present encounter with God in the midst of life, partly as imaginative depiction of a future.

This book will often echo the Bible, as any Christian testimony does. But I will not try to settle arguments with biblical proof texts. I assume that all reading of the Bible involves interpretation, that Christian faith is the response *in faith* to the Great Story told in the Bible.

The lesser story is the more immediate story of one or another Christian community that, in particular times and places, tries to understand, declare, and enact its faith. To call a story lesser is not to demean it. Quite the opposite: the lesser story has its own glory. But its glory derives from the Great Story.

The United Church of Christ draws its faith and life primarily from the Great Story. It does so within the context of its own lesser story, the story of a church with a short history but with roots that go far back in time. Its faith is not simply the faith of an American church, formally organized as recently as June 25, 1957. It is a faith shared with prophets and

3

apostles throughout the ages. But it is that faith as understood in our time and place by a community of Christians
who believe that we have something to contribute to, and
much to learn from, the older and wider community of which
we are a part.

Faith and Its Testimony

People and communities express their faith in many ways.
A handclasp, a song, a gift, a helpful act, an outburst of
laughter or tears, a choice of vocation, a family budget, a
prayer, a rage against injustice or a deed of mercy, a confession of sin or an act of forgiveness, a sexual union, a
martyr's death— any of these may on a particular occasion
express faith. A profound faith is a matter of trust, of loyalty,
of belief that flows into all of life.

One expression of faith is talk. Often, we realize, talk is
cheap. A *statement of faith* is not the same as *faith.* Talk about
belief can be a cheap substitute or even an evasion of the trust
and commitment that belong to real faith. So no Christian
should exaggerate the value of confessions and creeds. Certainly nobody should assume that the faith of any church can
be fully expressed in its words.

But words are important. Particularly in biblical faith, the
Word of God—the Word communicated in words, the Word
made flesh—has decisive power. That is why Christians have
regarded language as a gift of God, why they have treasured a
written Bible and translated it into many languages (rather
lately, as such things go, into English), why they constantly try
to express their faith in language, knowing that faith can
never be reduced to language.

Ever since Jesus of Nazareth called his first disciples, those
touched by Jesus have sought for ways to confess their faith.
They wanted to put their faith into words, both to clarify
their own convictions and to tell others what had happened to
them and what they believed.

The first great Christian confessional statement ever recorded came from Peter, who said to Jesus, "You are the Messiah [Mark 8:29]." The New Testament includes other short declarations of faith—for example, "Jesus is Lord [1 Cor. 12:3]," and "Jesus is the Son of God [1 John 4:15]."

Such directness and brevity was sometimes enough—especially if people knew who Jesus was, what he had done, and what he had asked others to do. Those short confessions were often decisive, often costly. The words could rock an empire. In fact, the words and the community that said them did outlast the Roman Empire, which liked to think of itself as *Roma aeterna*, "eternal Rome."

But often more had to be said. Believers wanted to tell the Story, the good news (gospel), of Jesus and to explain what the Story meant to them.

If individual Christians needed to declare their faith, the church had even stronger reasons to express the common faith that united its members. This church wanted to identify itself and to tell its message to the world. Frequently it sought precision of language, in order to prevent misinterpretations that might fragment the church or confuse its beliefs with various rival beliefs. Hence the church—including many groups within it—has often through the centuries expressed its convictions in testimonies of faith.

Sometimes it exaggerated the importance of its formulations. It forgot that Jesus gave his followers not a creed but a prayer.[1] But even the prayer verbalized beliefs. And often the church had to attend to its beliefs.

The two communions who formed the United Church of Christ both had rich inheritances of confessional documents. Like all Christians, they were the heirs of the ancient creeds imbedded in scripture and developed in the early centuries of the church. The Evangelical and Reformed Church cherished the confessions of the Reformation. The Congregational Christian Churches treasured the documents of

English Puritanism and the many covenants and doctrinal statements of American Congregationalism. When these two traditions came together in the United Church of Christ, the occasion of union—an act of faith and not just a functional merger of organizations—became an opportunity for rethinking the meaning of their faith. In 1959, a year before adopting a constitution, the General Synod discussed at length and approved a Statement of Faith.

The General Synod and the many local churches that studied and adopted the Statement of Faith knew everything that can be said about the unimportance of mere words. But they also knew that one responsibility of a church is to search its mind and declare its convictions. A belief that is unspoken is incomplete, and a belief that is well spoken becomes a power for life and action. Therefore the process of thinking that led to the Statement of Faith and the continuing use of that Statement have become one part of the life of the United Church of Christ. And the Statement is part of that church's contribution to the life of the wider church in which it seeks to play a responsible part.

Statements and Creeds

Creeds often have a bad reputation in our world. The words *creedal* and *creedalism* are likely to sound reactionary. They may be associated with rigid orthodoxies, with unwillingness to face new evidence, with static traditionalism instead of living encounter with the present.

Actually *creed* is simply the noun that comes from the verb *credo*, which means "I believe." We expect people to have beliefs. We respect those who have the courage of their convictions—and we hope that the convictions are worthy of courage. So in the most basic sense of all, Christian faith has a creedal element.

But the history of creeds has its painful side. Arrogant

people have slaughtered their neighbors on creedal grounds. Sometimes thoughtful persons have been barred from the church because they questioned its creeds, while lethargic folk went on reciting the creeds without any trouble. Servants of Christ, living in his spirit, have suffered persecution by spiteful people who fanatically held to every article in an inherited creed.

The United Church of Christ, aware of this history, chose to develop a Statement of Faith rather than a creed. In the most literal sense, perhaps there is no difference between the two. But "statement of faith" suggests a less rigid, less authoritarian document than "creed." Perhaps it suggests also a more modest attempt to say what it is that contemporary Christians believe.

In any event, the Statement of Faith is not a standard of objective authority in the United Church. Whatever authority it has is the authority of an honest testimony whose persuasiveness depends on its contents. Long before its adoption the decision had been made that this Statement would be "a testimony, and not a test, of faith."[2]

In the usage of the United Church, "testimony" represents both less and more than a test. It is less in terms of a legal standard. The Statement of Faith is not a basis for heresy trials. No one is excluded from the church or denied ordination because of disagreement with it.

In a shrewd theological observation Ogden Nash once wrote:

> There are too many people who think that
>   just because they have parishes or dioceses
> It imparts infallibility to all their biases.

The United Church makes no claims to infallibility. It makes no pretense that it has discovered once and for all the right way to state the core of Christian belief. "All language is to some extent a groping for clarity," says Gustavo Gutiérrez, the Latin American theologian of liberation.[3] A testimony, compared to an examination in a school, is less than a test.

Yet a testimony is also far more than a test. A testimony involves a commitment. Many people who could pass a test in doctrine cannot make a testimony of faith, because they lack the courage and the joy of faith. The Statement of Faith is an effort to find a language appropriate for Christian testimony.

Consistent with this whole conception, the Statement of Faith has no legal status in the United Church. The General Synod "approved" it and "submitted" it to the conferences, associations, and local churches of the United Church, not for their ratification but for their approval and use. The General Synod further "encouraged" use of the Statement "in congregational worship, in private devotions, and for purposes of study." But the United Church of Christ nowhere requires its use.

A testimony, someone has observed, is in the last analysis inevitably a test. Perhaps this is so—in the sense that every day and every activity of life tests faith, love, and purposes. A church in declaring and living by its faith is putting itself to the test. But the Statement of Faith, as a testimony of Christian conviction, is adding to life no test that is not inherent in Christian existence.

William Temple, the great archbishop of Canterbury of the generation just past, once wrote: "I do not believe in any creed, but I use certain creeds to express, to conserve, and to deepen my belief in God."[4] The language of belief is important. But the belief is not in the language; the belief is in God.

Tradition and Contemporaneity

The Great Story, by which the Christian community lives, includes the memory of the past and an expectation of the future. As told in the Bible, it extends from the Creation to the Last Judgment and the Heavenly City. The present, the time of our responsibility, gets its meaning from a heritage of past history and a promise of history yet to come. Built into the meaning of the church are a faithfulness to its inheritance and a conviction of a mission that is uncompleted. Therefore the church by its very nature maintains a sensitivity to a tradition that has made it and a contemporary task that is still making it. If separated from its roots or its present-future mission, the church withers and dies.

The United Church of Christ, even before writing its Statement of Faith, had considered with some care the meaning for faith of the tug of tradition and the tug of contemporaneity. The uniting communions had already put it in these words:

> The faith which unites us and to which we bear witness is that faith in God which the Scriptures of the Old and New Testaments set forth, which the ancient church expressed in the ecumenical creeds, to which our own spiritual fathers gave utterance in the evangelical confessions of the Reformation, and which we are in duty bound to express in the words of our time as God himself gives us light.[5]

Since the interplay of tradition and contemporaneity is so important to Christian faith, let us look at each of these forces in turn.

Christian faith comes to us through a tradition. This faith arose almost twenty centuries ago in response to historical events centering in Jesus of Nazareth, whom some people acknowledged as the Christ (meaning "Messiah" or "Lord"). That history is recorded in a Bible, written long ago. Nobody, reading the Bible, would mistake it for the writing of twentieth-century reporters, historians, or theologians. It clearly comes out of the past.

The process of formulating Christian beliefs began in the Bible and continued in the life of the church. In its first five centuries the church developed several declarations of its faith. These grew out of a combination of informal and formal processes, as Christians searched for their identity or responded to challenges from outside the church and to debates within the church.

The most famous of the ancient confessions of faith is called the Apostles' Creed. It developed gradually in the Western church, taking preliminary form in the third century and its present form by about A.D. 600. Other creeds are associated with councils where Christians argued the meaning of their faith and carefully hammered out formulas to declare and guard its substance. The most important of these councils were the Council of Nicaea, A.D. 325,* and the Council of Chalcedon, A.D. 451.

This process continued through the centuries with many variations in different parts of the church. Through it all we see the working of tradition. It may happen that tradition becomes a dead weight from the past, stifling the present. But in its original meaning, tradition (rooted in the Latin verb *tradere*) is the activity that passed on the experiences and insights of the past to the present and future.

The Christian church does not originate a new faith in each generation. It confesses the faith of prophets, apostles, and martyrs. (Those three terms come from an ancient prayer, the *Te Deum*, quoted in the dedication at the front of this book.) Repeatedly, in times of persecution and temptations, loyalty to a living tradition has saved the church from cheap compromises and apostasy. Yet adherence to the past cannot shield people from the demands of life in the present. Therefore the church must constantly think about the relation between tradition and contemporaneity.

Christian faith is contemporary. It arose among those who

---

*The creed that is usually called the Nicene Creed and that is often used in Christian worship is not actually the creed that came out of the Council of Nicaea. It is a later, more comprehensive creed that includes some phrases from the Council of Nicaea. In this book, following common practice, I call it the Nicene Creed.

responded to Jesus of Nazareth, who refused to be imprisoned by any past, and whose followers often had to break with the past. This faith recognized that the Word of God, so powerfully set forth in books, could not be confined to unchanging words. This Word "became flesh and lived among us . . . full of grace and truth [John 1:14]." It was—and is— "living and active, sharper than any two-edged sword [Heb. 4:12]."

In the record of the Gospel According to John, Jesus told his disciples that the Holy Spirit would *both* recall to them what he (Jesus) had taught *and* teach them all things (John 14:26). Similarly Jesus said that his followers would *both* do what he had done *and* go on to greater works (John 14:12). Loyalty to that tradition, far from freezing us in the past, requires that we live, think, and act in the present, with a direction toward the future.

As we look at the creeds of the past, whether those in the Bible or those written in later times, we find always an interaction of the traditional and the contemporary. The declarations tell of something *given*, something that has happened, something that is not the achievement of the persons who report it. But the thought and language of the declarations are the work of Christians living in their own present, using the language and concepts of their time, yet challenging their own time.

What they did, we now must continue to do. The restatement of Christian faith is a task and opportunity for every generation. We are "in duty bound" to exercise that privilege today.

Tradition and contemporaneity often exist in some tension. Today especially we are likely to feel that tension. A scientific age understands—often misunderstands but often understands accurately—some things as no past age did. Our picture of the world, our concepts, some of our mental processes often are different from those of the writers of the Bible.

Christian thinking demands effort and imagination, as it seeks both to appreciate an ancient or alien insight and yet to be honest in its modern apprehension of things. Sometimes the church seems to be torn between a backward pull of the Bible and a forward pull of history, forced to make an unhappy choice or an equally unhappy compromise between the two.

The Statement of Faith sometimes shows the tension between the tug of tradition and the tug of contemporaneity. It has prompted many a discussion between those especially sensitive to the Christian heritage and those especially responsive to our time. The commentary on various declarations in the Statement, part two of this book, will touch on some of the issues at stake.

Yet for the most part the Statement has not led to a clash between "that faith in God which the Scriptures of the Old and New Testaments set forth" and "the words of our time." The reason lies in a discovery—perhaps the right word is revelation—that has come into the experience of Christians repeatedly in history, never more remarkably than in our own time. It is the experience of a scripture that does not pull them to the past but drives them into the midst of life today. When Christians get closer to the great scriptural declarations, they get closer to themselves. The Word of God, addressing them through the Bible, breaks through the hardened religious formulas and patterns of past and present alike. In the words of the Puritan Pastor John Robinson, so often remembered in the United Church of Christ, "The Lord has yet more light and truth to break forth from his holy Word."

This claim for a kinship between tradition and contemporaneity might be an example of pious hope and wishful thinking. But its genuine meaning becomes clearer in one specific characteristic of the Statement—its structuring around the deeds of God.

The Deeds of God

A first look at the Statement of Faith shows one difference from most of the classical creeds—a difference in the way it is structured and printed. It begins with a confession of belief and ends with a traditional doxology. Between beginning and ending come seven declarations, each telling of an activity of God.

By contrast, most of the traditional confessions of the church are organized in a triadic form derived from the doctrine of the Trinity. They contain three declarations of paragraphs concerning Father, Son, and Holy Spirit. Statements about the church, the Christian life, and other aspects of faith are either associated with the third article or are grouped in a fourth.

This time-honored form of testimony is one way of stating the Christian faith. It has been used long enough and effectively enough that it does not have to be defended. But it is not the only way. And it is not the characteristic way of the Bible. While the New Testament clearly tells of the Father, the Son, and the Holy Spirit—occasionally joining the three in a single phrase—it never states the content of faith in a three-point summary.

The Bible itself is primarily a narrative—a telling of the Great Story. It is a record of the deeds of God and the history of a people, beginning with the Creation, running through centuries of history, and pointing toward a future. Law, prophecy, doctrine, and devotional writings are incorporated within the historical narrative.

The Great Story of the Bible is distinctive—startlingly so. It is not the story that might be told by an astronomer, a geologist, a military historian, a political or economic historian, or an epic poet. All those stories have their validity, and the Bible shows an awareness of the realities they tell about. But the Bible is different. It is a meaning-drenched Story, the

Story of a people who in their history kept meeting God. Whether in gratitude or anger, in obedience or defiance, they met the God who would not let them escape the divine presence.

The Bible includes great variety. It describes God in figures of speech, dazzling in their diversity. God is known in darkness, in thunderstorms, in light unapproachable. God is a king enthroned in heaven, a warrior mighty in battle, a peacemaker, a lawgiver and judge, a shield and fortress, a deliverer of the weak and afflicted, a destroyer of evil, a shepherd, a householder and husband, a tent dweller, a commander of thunderbolts and chariots, a slayer of the wicked and the children of the wicked, a healer of the brokenhearted. God is like a refiner's fire, like a bird with protective wings. God is known for anger, for steadfast love, for mercy.

Within the same chapter (Rev. 5) Jesus is represented as both a conquering lion and a lamb. Elsewhere the devil also is likened to a lion—but never to a lamb.

The ethical directions within the Bible are likewise diverse. They exhort people to slaughter their enemies (assumed to be God's enemies) and to forgive them. They commend monogamy, polygamy, celibacy. Some writers tell us that all is vanity; others, that all is a gift of God.

The Bible *proves* nothing. That is why I said earlier that I would not try to settle arguments by proof texts. Every quotation from the Bible is a choice to use that one rather than another, and every understanding of the Bible is an interpretation.

Yet the interpretation of the Bible is not sheer caprice. The Bible is not a verbal smorgasbord, not a Bartlett's *Familiar Quotations* from which we select according to convenience—although some preachers have used it as such. The Great Story itself displays dominant and subordinate themes. It gives its own clues for apprehending its dissonances and harmonies. These never relieve us of the responsibility for our own interpretation, but they point to ways of a disciplined interpretation.

Within the Bible are several confessional statements that declare the biblical faith in brief, concentrated ways. They help us discover the core of the Story, to recognize what in the Bible to accent and what to subordinate. Biblical scholars have located these and have shown their importance in the structure of the Bible. They are among the earliest biblical passages. They took their form in the setting of acts of worship or in the communications that told people about the faith of Israel and of the early church. Then in the course of years, other elements of the Bible—memories, traditions, moral laws, collections of sayings, rituals, and prayers—were gathered around the basic declarations and were written down. The unique quality of the core confessional statements is that they, like the Bible as a whole, are testimonies to what has happened. They take a narrative form. They are recitals of the deeds of God.

In the Old Testament perhaps the most ancient and important of these confessional liturgies is found in Deuteronomy 26:5–10. As Gerhard von Rad has shown, it probably goes back to a time before David, perhaps even to the time of Joshua, long before the writing of the book of Deuteronomy, in which it is now included. It is the confession of faith made by the worshiper who presents the first fruits of the harvest.

A wandering Aramean was my ancestor; he went down into Egypt and lived there, as an alien few in number, and there he became a great nation, mighty and populous. When the Egyptians treated us harshly and afflicted us, by imposing hard labor on us, we cried to the LORD the God of our ancestors; the LORD heard our voice and saw our affliction, our toil, and our oppression. The LORD brought us out of Egypt with a mighty hand and an outstretched arm, with a terrifying display of power, and with signs and wonders;

and he brought us into this place and gave us this land, a
land flowing with milk and honey. So now I bring the first of
the fruit of the ground that you, O LORD, have given me.

A comparable confession in Deuteronomy 6:21–25 is given
as a way of telling children why their parents keep certain
commandments. The explanation is a testimony, telling what
God has done. The shortest of these Old Testament confessions is in Joshua 24:17–18, where again the content is a
recital of God's deeds.

Those statements of faith are vivid, immediate, in some
ways naive. They are concerned with the experience of a
people and their ancestors. Those who repeated the testimonies were not greatly concerned about some wider questions—the relation of their God to the Egyptians and the
many other peoples of the earth, the creation of the world,
the broader issues of justice and mercy. Eventually a mature
faith would have to be more comprehensive in its scope. But
already, in this very early declaration, the basic pattern of
scriptural testimony was set. The confession told what had
happened. It described the doings of God in the history of a
people.

If we turn to the New Testament, we find that the first four
books are called Gospels. These were not the first books to be
written down—the letters of Paul came earlier—but they
rightly became the opening books of the New Testament. A
gospel is a news report. The four Gospels and the Acts of the
Apostles, which together make up more than half of the New
Testament, are a record of events—events centering in the
life of Jesus Christ and the early years of the Christian
church. They tell what God was doing in the world and
among a people of faith.

Within the New Testament, as within the Old, are some
core declarations of faith. Their content is called, in the
technical language of biblical scholars, the kerygma. That

Greek word originally referred to the cry of a herald. It came to stand for preaching, not in the sense of a Sunday morning activity behind a pulpit but in the sense of the telling of the Christian message. The kerygma is stated in some of the passages in the book of Acts. Good examples are the sermons of Peter in Acts 2:14–36 and 3:12–26 and of Stephen in Acts 7:2–53. Again the message is a testimony about events, about the acts of God among a people who respond in faith. H. Richard Niebuhr, an eminent theologian of the United Church of Christ, put it this way: "The preaching of the early Christian church . . . was primarily a simple recital of the great events connected with the historical appearance of Jesus Christ and a confession of what had happened to the community of disciples."6 The kerygma is not history in the textbook sense of a record, pretending to objectivity, of dates and dynasties; it is history as remembered by a people who found God meeting them there. This kerygma, New Testament scholars widely hold, became the center for the writing of the Gospels.

The United Church Statement of Faith, in its basic structure, follows the lead of the biblical declarations, rather than of the typical creeds of later Christian history. It abandons the triadic form (although keeping the testimony to Father, Son, and Holy Spirit) and returns to the kerygmatic account of the deeds of God.

Thus the accented words in the Statement are the verbs that tell of God's deeds. The Statement addresses the God who *creates, seeks, judges, has come and shared, bestows, calls, promises.* In this respect the Statement is akin both to the Bible, with its emphasis on history and divine activity, and to contemporary affirmations of venture and activity. Perhaps the modern mind, taught by science that the real nature of matter is kinetic (or dynamic) rather than static, is more attuned than the mind of some past ages to the dynamism of scripture.

In another respect the Statement of Faith suggests an affinity between biblical and contemporary thinking. The Bible, although its language is often symbolic and poetic, is not a highly speculative book. It tells the Great Story—and, of course, the meaning of the Story for faith. It does not try to fill out a whole metaphysics or picture of the universe, as some Christian theologies have done. Although the classical creeds (especially of Nicaea and Chalcedon) do not indulge in elaborate speculations, they reflect theologies that did. The Statement of Faith, as physicist Harold K. Schilling once put it, shows the tendency "to return . . . to the more primitive confessional affirmations of the early church, and thus to focus attention upon the basic Christian creed, and to eliminate from it as much as possible the philosophical, metaphysical, theoretical constructions that do not belong there."[7]

Certainly the Statement, by its affirmation of belief in a God who acts, is aiming to describe reality—and that is the aim of metaphysics. Furthermore, the Statement in no sense forbids metaphysical thinking, an almost ineradicable characteristic of the human mind; and it has implications for a metaphysics that gives an important place to movement and activity. But it makes a few affirmations and leaves many questions open for further thought. Like the Bible, it reports—and lets the Story speak.

Declaration and Conversation

Whenever a church tries to put its faith into words, it says some things and leaves others unsaid. Every church is always deciding, day by day and century by century, what to say and what to omit. As it decides, it faces two issues.

The first is that Christian faith is far too rich, subtle, and many-faceted to be communicated in any one way. It can never be reduced entirely to words; and of those aspects that can be verbalized, only some can be stated on any single occasion. When the occasion calls for a short statement that can be said aloud by a worshiping congregation, the limitations are stringent. The question becomes, What in this faith is so fundamental that it must be said when all the rest is left out?

The second issue is that the faith of a church is different in some ways from the faith of an individual. A church includes persons with many opinions, even about matters of belief. A church decides to speak forthrightly on some questions; on others it keeps open the conversation among its members. The New Testament itself is both a declaration of faith and a conversation among differing understandings of that faith.

If a church declares and prescribes too much, it becomes unduly dogmatic. If it leaves too much open, it waffles on important issues. All of us have important testimonies and ideas that we cannot impose on the church. We appreciate diversity of ideas, even while we look for unity in our shared faith. When the church declares its faith, its seeks to find not the least common denominator of the beliefs within it but the heartbeat of conviction that unifies the church at its best.

So the Statement of Faith is both a declaration and an invitation to conversation. It says some things, leaves others unsaid. Its form determines, in part, its content. Since it takes the form of a declaration of the deeds of God, it does not include a confession of sin, because sin is a human act; it does include the declaration that God both judges sin and seeks to save us from our sin. On every subject that comes into the Statement, the accent is on what Christian faith understands God to be doing.

There is another obvious contrast between this Statement and the classical creeds. The latter center entirely on doctrine. This Statement, affirming the major Christian doctrines, gives an equal emphasis to God's demands and promises in regard to the Christian life. In this respect, as in its structure, the Statement is akin to scripture, which in both

Old and New Testaments gives great attention to faithful living. In view of this notable emphasis of the Bible, whether in the law and the prophets or in the teachings of Jesus and the apostles, it is surprising that the classical confessions have said so little.

Certainly any confession of faith that speaks to our time must look to the expression of faith in the practical decisions of personal and social life. Throughout the history of the church, the powerful confessions of faith have usually arisen out of situations of conflict and crisis. The ancient ecumenical creeds came out of struggles against heresies that distorted the faith. Today, we may judge, the temptations that most threaten the church are such modern heresies as nationalism, racism, the worship of mammon (yes, money), and complacent culture-religion. Hence it becomes important that the church, confessing its faith, recover the biblical emphasis upon faithful living.

The accent on ethics is not a separate item or an addendum to the Statement. As in scripture, it is an integral part of the meaning of faith. Thus the Statement declares that God seeks in holy love to save *all* people, that the Holy Spirit binds in covenant people of *all* races. It declares the judgment of God's righteous will. It reminds the church that God calls us to human service, that the sacraments are indissolubly related to costly commitment, that courage in the struggle for peace and justice is as truly God's gift as is eternal life. Faith and works are not opposed, but the meaning of obedience is stated in the context of the gospel of grace and forgiveness. In this respect, as in the structure of its recital, the Statement seeks to maintain its kinship to both its biblical sources and contemporary responsibility.

One further quality of the Statement is its ecumenical purpose. It does not intend to state the peculiar faith of the people who came together in the United Church of Christ; it aims to state the Christian faith as this church, in conversation with other groups of Christians, apprehends that faith. Yet those who use it know that it has the limitations of the historical experiences of a small segment of God's people in our specific time. It is one way—we hope an authentic and helpful way—but certainly not the only way to declare the Christian faith.

The General Synod, in approving the Statement, said that it was to be "understood as a testimony of the United Church of Christ to the faith commonly held among us in the words of our time and not as a substitute for or revision of the ecumenical creeds and the confessions, platforms, and covenants of the communions joined in the United Church of Christ." This church was not so foolish as to try to "patch up" or modernize the traditional creeds. Because those older statements still stand and speak with power, this church decided not to imitate them but to state the traditional faith freshly. The church could risk a different style of declaration because it knew that its limitations would be corrected by the continuing power of tradition, by conversations with other contemporary Christians, and by insights of future generations of Christians.

The Development of the Statement and Its Uses

If the Statement of Faith is an interpretation of the Great Story, the development of the Statement is part of the lesser story of the United Church of Christ. It is an example of the way in which a church enters into theological discussion in order to find its common mind.

In the long negotiations leading up to the union that formed the United Church of Christ, the uniting bodies had agreed that the new church would draw up a Statement of faith. The basic purpose of that Statement, as set forth in the *Basis of Union,* has been described on page 9. The Uniting General Synod, meeting in Cleveland in 1957, elected a commission of thirty men and women to prepare the Statement. The commission, drawn equally from the two denominations, included biblical scholars, theologians, pastors, and lay people from various walks of life.*

This commission inherited the two-year work of a sixteen-member committee of theologians appointed "to study basic Christian doctrine." The earlier committee had explored the theological traditions of the ancient ecumenical church, the uniting denominations, and twentieth-century churches around the world. Some of its members continued on the new commission, with the effect that the combined efforts of the committee and commission involved four years of work.

The commission began its task with discussion of its aims and hopes, the expectations of the church, and the issues that it thought most important. As a next step it invited each member to write a statement of faith. The twenty-three resulting statements, unidentified as to authorship, were circulated among the commission. Some members tested some of the statements in local churches or conferred with other church people about them.

At the next meeting of the commission the officers presented a composite statement drawn from the documents that had been circulated. The commission worked over this statement in detail. It was obvious that this method would not

---

*Congregational Christian members were: John C. Bennett, Grace Buckham, Loring D. Chase (co-secretary), Nels F. S. Ferré, L. K. Hall, Roger Hazelton, Douglas Horton (vice-chair), Walter M. Horton, Ralph Hyslop, Mary Ely Lyman, Edward F. Manthei, Richard R. Niebuhr, Oliver Powell, Helen Huntington Smith, Daniel Day Williams. Evangelical and Reformed members were: Elmer J. F. Arndt (chair), Edward W. Brueseke, Bernice A. Buehler, Alfred L. Creager, John P. Dillenberger, Louis H. Gunnemann, Robert G. Herrmann, Frederick L. Herzog, Beatrice Weaver McConnell, Allen O. Miller, Robert V. Moss, Jr. (co-secretary), John L. Schmidt, Roger L. Shinn, Morris D. Slifer, Bela Vassady. The co-presidents of the United Church, Fred Hoskins and James Wagner, were ex-officio members. Two fraternal observers participated in the meetings: Walter Sikes of the Christian Church (Disciples of Christ) and Otis A. Maxwell of the Council of Community Churches.

produce a statement with appropriate unity and style, but it led to a thorough airing of issues. After this discussion and study, four members of the commission were asked again to write statements, this time seeking to express the common mind of the commission. The officers, working primarily on the basis of one of these statements, again presented a draft to the commission. In detailed discussion the commission went over the draft, line by line, word by word. After thorough consideration, further work by a drafting committee, then still further revision by the whole commission, the draft document was released to the church and the public. The Statement was printed in the *United Church Herald,* the *Christian Century,* the *New York Times,* and other news media several months before the next General Synod. One result was wide public discussion. The commission collected suggestions and criticism from many sources, mainly in the United States but also overseas.

The commission made some revisions in the light of the wider discussions, then presented the Statement to the Second General Synod at Oberlin, Ohio, on July 6, 1959. The commission itself realized that its work was incomplete in the sense that attempts to state the Christian faith are always incomplete, but it doubted that it would do better by taking more time. At the same time it was prepared to do further work if the General Synod so desired.

The mood of the General Synod favored action on the report. Some of the delegates had hoped to adopt a constitution for the United Church. When they realized that the intricate work of completing a constitution would have to be delayed until an adjourned session a year later, they became the more eager to adopt a Statement of Faith. Some were pleased that agreement on faith should precede agreement on the constitution. Discussion, debate, and questioning on the Statement came from the floor of the Synod. On one evening, following a session of the Synod, the commission held an open hearing extending late into the night, to give opportunity for more discussion by delegates. Informal discussion continued in the dormitories of Oberlin College, where delegates slept. There was obvious desire to talk about the Statement, and the commission took the comments seriously.

The commission continued its meetings during the Synod, considering both the judgments of the delegates and the many other comments that had been received. One session was given to friendly criticisms that had come from the Evangelical Church of the Union in Germany, where a committee had translated the Statement into New Testament Greek and studied it.

Perhaps no theological statement of a church in modern times has had such extensive discussion by Christians at large before its adoption. In the time of the ancient creedal controversies, one participant complained that he could not visit a barber or merchant without getting an argument on the relation of the Son to the Father. The contemporary church cannot rival that. But in the ancient church, the bishops made the decisions. In the United Church of Christ a very wide body of people actually contributed to the document.

In the final meetings of the commission, during the General Synod, the discussion was spirited, and the commission made revisions in the light of opinions expressed at the Synod. But there were no factions committed to fixed positions. Specifically there was never an issue on which denominational divisions occurred; every question that divided the group also divided the two denominational contingents. Where opinions differed, the usual procedure was to work toward a consensus. On a few occasions, a matter came to a vote. More remarkable was the common mind that emerged and the final unanimous vote recommending the Statement to the General Synod.

On July 8 the commission brought back to the General

Synod a Statement revised at three points from its report of two days earlier. After further discussion from the floor, the Synod voted approval of the Statement of Faith in the terms described on page 21. The minutes of the General Synod report: "The delegates responded to the agreement on the Statement of Faith by standing and joining voices in the singing of the Doxology. Chairman Elmer Arndt was called to lead in a unison reading of the Statement." Louis Gunnemann, commenting on the "unanimous vote," has written: "This enthusiastic response presaged widespread acceptance not only in the United Church but also in other denominations."[8]

In the following years the Statement has been used in many ways. The General Synod, we have seen, submitted it to conferences, associations, and churches "for their approval and use." Subsequent approval was sometimes by recorded votes, sometimes by informal acceptance and use.

The United Church of Christ nowhere prescribes use of the Statement. It is, in fact, used frequently in services of worship of the General Synod and other assemblies of the church. Many local churches use it, either regularly or on occasion (sometimes during Lent or on communion Sundays). Other churches prefer to use classical creeds; still others use no confessional statements in worship. The United Church of Christ, encouraging freedom of practice, would not have it otherwise.

The Statement has been used in interdenominational college worship. The World Council of Churches has included it in a collection of resources for worship, and various denominations have used it occasionally. In German and Spanish versions it has been an act of worship in Europe and in Latin America.

Adult and youth groups in local churches or summer camps have studied the Statement. Ministers have used it in preaching and in confirmation classes. An adult course in the

United Church Curriculum, *Classical Creeds and Living Faith,* studied the Statement along with traditional creeds. A youth course, *Journey into Faith,* included study of the Statement and encouraged young people to write their own statements of faith.

The Statement has been set to music and sung by vested choirs with organ and by people gathered around a piano in the evening. It has been adapted as a hymn. It has been made into choral readings and incorporated in written dialogues. It formed the structure of *The Hymnal of the United Church of Christ* (1984).

Such varied uses are consistent with the purpose of the Statement: to be a testimony of faith in words of our time. It is one way of confessing Christian faith. No one assumes that it was written for eternity. In time to come Christians will again and again state their faith in words of their time as God gives them light. In fact, within the United Church of Christ the statement has already twice been revised. That requires attention to another aspect of it.

The Language of the Statement

Christian faith, I said earlier, knows both the importance and unimportance of words. Talk without deeds is empty, but words may tell of deeds and lead to deeds. Sometimes a word—a word of courage or of sympathy—is a deed. The experience of speaking and hearing permeates the Bible. Hence the language of a Statement of Faith matters.

There can be no one taste, no absolute accuracy in language, because words say different things to different people. Yet the choice of words is important. Mark Twain once said that the difference between the right word and the almost right word is the difference between lightning and a lightning bug.

The judgment as to how well the Statement of Faith found

the right words must depend on the test of continuous usage. All that can be said for certain is that every word in it represents a decision to use that word rather than alternatives. Many of the words were chosen after hours of thought and discussion, sometimes after debate on the floor of the General Synod.

Comments on the Statement have described it as both poetic and prosaic. The theologian Gabriel Fackre finds in it biblical and lyric cadences; others find commonplace language. Although it is printed in a semipoetic style, this serves to indicate its structure rather than to make claims for its literary form. Insofar as its words and rhythms resemble poetry, its style is free and contemporary rather than traditional. Occasionally the commission, choosing between various phrasings, read them in unison, and that unison reading led to a clear choice.

Four characteristics of the language deserve some comment here.

First, the language is simple. In that respect, it recalls the New Testament, written in Koine Greek—the language of ordinary people, not of Plato and the tragedians. The language of faith, even when it is most profound, grows out of the Great Story, which can be told in declarative sentences. The seven declarations, the subject of part two of this book, all have the same structure: a subject—God or a pronoun for God—and a verb, telling of an activity of God. The words are usually clear and plain. As the statement was taking form, James Wagner, one of the co-presidents of the United Church, got the idea of making a word count; he reported 159 words of one syllable, 56 words of two syllables, 15 words of three syllables, and 2 words of four syllables.

Second, the language includes symbolic expressions. Faith often uses words of ordinary experience to point to extraordinary experience, words of sensory impressions to describe realities that transcend the senses. The Statement represents an effort to speak directly and honestly—to avoid declaring beliefs that people do not really hold. But inevitably, like the Bible, it uses symbolic language. When it says that God "calls the worlds into being" and "calls us," it makes human speech a metaphor for a divine activity that is in many ways quite unlike human talk.

Third, the language is contemporary. It avoids Latinisms and Elizabethan forms that are no longer current. At the same time, because it is the document of a church, it seeks to avoid any vocabulary that is specifically associated with particular theologians or schools of thought. Hence most of the words are fairly common words in contemporary speech. Some, like "aimlessness," are plain and prosaic because they refer to plain and prosaic facts.

Fourth, the language often comes directly from the Bible. Biblical and contemporary expressions sometimes coincide, sometimes do not. The Statement uses "reconciling," which is both biblical and contemporary, rather than "atoning," which is biblical but more rarely contemporary (except in theology). Every sentence recalls the thought and language of the Bible. The Statement begins with phrases from the first book in the Bible and ends with phrases from the last book. The opening confession recalls the "Spirit" of God that moved over the face of the waters at Creation, and the first declaration takes over language from Genesis 1. The concluding words of praise come from Revelation.

One further characteristic of the language raises problems so important that it calls for special discussion.

Why Three Versions?

In the years since 1959 the American public, along with much of the world, has experienced a great change in gender consciousness. The original version of the Statement of Faith was loaded with words of masculine gender, most notably the repeated use of the pronoun *he* to refer to God and the use three times of "man" or "men" to refer to all people. Today those terms leap out at those who read the Statement.

Given our present awareness, it is hard to believe that the issue scarcely arose in the original development of the Statement. One man on the commission raised the question, and the women responded that they saw no problem. There is no available evidence that the issue was raised in the many published comments on the initial draft, in the letters received by the commission, or in the discussions at the General Synod that approved the Statement. But the winds of change were soon to blow through society and the church.

Their impact upon the General Synod can be dated. As late as 1971, the Eighth General Synod, giving attention to the "faith crisis," called on the United Church to "celebrate the Statement of Faith." But by 1975 the Office for Church Life and Leadership (OCLL) responded to a request from the Executive Council to begin a study to decide whether a new statement was desirable. In 1976 OCLL asked local churches to take part in the study. Then in October of that year Robert Moss, president of the United Church of Christ and co-secretary of the original commission, hospitalized with a terminal illness, wrote a revision of the Statement, intending it to contribute to further discussion. This was circulated widely and used in many churches. The Eleventh General Synod in 1977 commended that version to the church for study, use, and response through OCLL. The revision by President Moss is printed in the front of this book as the version of 1977.

As OCLL continued its work, a member of the original commission, who had been discussing the Statement with women in a seminary course, suggested that the Statement be recast as a doxology addressed to God. Behind this proposal was the awareness that most biblical psalms and most Christian hymns are addressed to God. As for gender, the pronoun *you* is neither masculine nor feminine.

The Thirteenth General Synod (1981) called for two actions. First, it recognized that the Executive Council had already "requested the President of the Church, through the Consultation on Church Union and other world communions to explore the joint development of new Statement of Faith." Endorsing this process, it asked that the "collaborative" work be done "as expeditiously as possible" with the aim of producing "a theologically sound and inclusive expression of our faith today." Second, it asked the Executive Council in cooperation with OCLL to "identify an interim version" of the Statement in time for the twenty-fifth anniversary of the United Church of Christ in 1982.

It was the second request that called for the most prompt action. The Executive Council responded by approving a doxological version, addressed to God, on October 31, 1981. (See the version of 1981, printed in the front of this book.) The Fourteenth General Synod in 1983 affirmed both the original Statement of 1959 and the new revision "until such time as a new statement of faith is received." Some have wondered why the Synod did not approve the new Statement *as a replacement* for the original Statement. The reasons probably lie in some theological differences that will become evident later in this book.

The same General Synod further recommended that the forthcoming "new" statement "affirm the triune nature of God, calling forth images to express the inclusiveness of our faith."

Progress toward the new collaborative statement has been slow, because it depends on processes involving other churches. Several of those processes are important. One is the partnership of the United Church of Christ with the Evangelical Synod of the Union in Germany (both East and West Germany). After twenty years of fraternal relationship, these two churches entered into full communion in 1980 and 1981. A second is the "ecumenical partnership" with the

Christian Church (Disciples of Christ), ratified in 1985 and extended to "full communion" in 1989. A third is the Consultation on Church Union (COCU) among nine denominations; its theological consensus was approved by the General Synod of 1989. A fourth is the effort, initiated by the World Council of Churches, "Toward the Common Expression of the Apostolic Faith Today." This process has produced a document, *Baptism, Eucharist and Ministry (BEM)*, unanimously adopted by the Faith and Order Commission of the World Council of Churches in Lima, Peru, in 1982 as a result of consultations among Roman Catholic, Orthodox, and Protestant Christians. It represents a "theological convergence" far greater than seemed conceivable in 1959, when the United Church of Christ adopted its Statement of Faith. But its Catholic and Orthodox strains make some problems for Protestants.

Only a very brave or a very foolish person would predict what may some day emerge from the "collaborative" effort endorsed by the General Synod. My guess is that the effort will disclose some tension between the attraction of unitive movements such as *BEM* (calling the church closer to "the apostolic faith" in resistance to many of the lures of the contemporary world) and those present-day impulses to put greater trust in contemporary experience than in inherited patterns of faith. There are some expressed concerns that the United Church of Christ, glorying in its freedom and independence, may become a "sect," incapable of further church union. That could be an ironic destiny for a church that began with the intention to be a "united and uniting" church—an intention reaffirmed by the Fifteenth General Synod in 1985. But to express the concern is not to make a prediction; it is to locate an issue that calls for attention.

Meanwhile the United Church of Christ has its Statement of Faith in three versions for the "interim." How long that interim will be, nobody knows. An interim is sometimes as short as the time between the present and next month's paycheck. In theological language it is the time between Christ's first coming and the ultimate coming of the kingdom of God in its fullness. When the General Synod spoke of an interim, it meant something more than the shortest and less than the longest interims.

The Statement of Faith was never meant to be everlasting. But in this interim it is a point of reference, perhaps a banner as the United Church of Christ guides its own life and enters into ecumenical conversations, looking for more light to break forth from God's holy Word.

PART TWO

The Deeds of God

The Confession of Faith

We believe in you, O God, Eternal Spirit,
God of our Savior Jesus Christ and our God,
and to your deeds we testify.

The Statement of Faith begins by confessing belief in God. Most classical Christian creeds begin, "We [or I] believe in God." In using those familiar words, the United Church of Christ places itself clearly within the great tradition of the church.

But to affirm a belief in God may mean very little or may mean a decisive act. Sometimes the cost of such a declaration has been martyrdom. Today in some places it means acceptance of social disadvantage, suspicion, and physical risk. But often the words flow easily with no cost at all. When the Gallup poll asks Americans whether they believe in God, the vast majority say yes. That is the conventional thing to do. But, as Daniel Day Williams wrote, "The Bible never speaks of God's presence as something to be taken for granted, but always as a truth to be confessed and a wonder to be celebrated."[1] For us today, belief in God, if we understand it in depth, is still a perpetual surprise, a continuing occasion for awe and delight. What it means depends on the meaning of "belief" and the meaning of "God."

Martin Luther stated the issue in a way that resounds across the centuries. In his *Large Catechism* he wrote: "What your heart clings to and relies upon, that, I say, is really your God." Luther was describing the nature of belief or faith. (In his

German language one word, *Glaube,* stands for both.) To say, "I believe in you," is far more than to say, "I believe that you exist." It is a testimony of trust and confidence. To say, "we believe in you, O God," is far more than to say, "we believe you are there."

In that spirit the Statement of Faith uses the word *believe* only once: "We believe in you, O God." The Statement goes on to affirm other beliefs: in creation, in the church, in the forgiveness of sin, in Christian callings, in eternal life. In everyday language we might say that we believe in all these. But the Statement, taking the word *believe* in its most profound sense, reserves the word for God.

That requires us to ask what we mean by the word *God.* Walter Marshall Horton, a member of the commission that prepared the Statement of Faith, once began a book about God[2] with a chapter, "Gods Many and Lords Many." He showed that, through the ages and today, people have put many meanings into the word *God.* He knew, with Luther, that they have trusted in and relied upon objects or illusions that are far less than the God of Christian faith. Indeed, Luther often pointed out that people trust gods of their own creation—wealth, status, military power—that is, idols. To say, "We believe in you, O God," is to say almost nothing unless we say something about the God in whom we believe. Who is this God?

An ancient Christian tradition says that nobody can define God. To *define* is to make *finite;* both words have the same root. God is not finite. God is the *mysterium tremendum,* the "tremendous mystery," the source and end of our lives and the universe. As Augustine put it, if you claim to define God, what you have defined is surely less than God. Calvin, overwhelmed by the mystery of God, wrote that the most we can say of God is something about God's relation to us.

But to believe in God is to identify, in some way, the God in whom we believe. The Statement of Faith does so, initially, in two ways. Our God is "Eternal Spirit" and "God of our Savior Jesus Christ and our God."

Eternal Spirit

To identify God as Spirit is to recall the second verse of the Bible, where the Spirit of God is the creative power and energizer of creation. It is to recall the words of Jesus, quoting from Isaiah, in the synagogue at Nazareth, "The Spirit of the Lord is upon me [Luke 4:18; Isa. 61:1]." It is to anticipate what the Statement will say later about the gift of the Holy Spirit at Pentecost.

By "Eternal Spirit" we mean a reality not of our own creation, a reality prior to ourselves, our solar system, our galaxy. To return to Luther's theme, if money is our idol, we have made it so. Human societies have fabricated it and learned to manipulate it, and some people have divinized it. We do not fabricate and manipulate or confer deity upon God.

God is not a human projection but the power who has given life and imagination to human beings. Granted, any conception of God has something of projection, something of human imagination in it. We need not regret that, provided we recognize that God is the Eternal Spirit to whom we respond in awed imagination. God creates us; we do not create God.

God of Our Savior Jesus Christ and Our God

If "Eternal Spirit" is general and universal, the reference to Jesus Christ is historical and specific. The Great Story is a universal story; yet it is also a historical story, related to specific times and places. That the ultimate power and mystery giving rise to all creation is also the God of Jesus Christ, the God who enters into personal relations with us—this magnifies the mystery. The Bible tells the story with an awareness that it is almost—almost, but not quite—unbelievable. Yet the belief has survived attacks and persecutions. It has outlasted many beliefs that, in their time, were to most people more persuasive.

This belief in God requires the denial of many other gods. Part of Christian faith is the denial of idols. In the ancient Roman Empire, Christians were called atheists, because they denied the gods of popular religion. In the contemporary world, Christians are more likely to look at atheists as outsiders. We may be wise to recognize that we share with atheists many of their denials. We need to ask whether we have sometimes so trivialized God as to promote atheism. But Christian faith remains primarily an affirmation. It testifies to the deeds of God.

Before examining that testimony of the Statement of Faith, we should notice four other issues in the opening confession.

1. We believe. The Apostles' Creed begins, "I believe"; the Nicene Creed, "We believe." An argument can be made for either. Something in every faith is personal; something is shared. The Statement of Faith is cast in the plural, partly because it is intended to express the faith of a church, not just of the various individuals who belong to the church. Still more profoundly, the Christian faith could not possibly be conjured up by an individual in contemporary times. We could not have this faith if it were not for a long succession of people who lived in a covenant community, who wrote the Bible, who lived by this faith and communicated it across the centuries.

One powerful symbol of the social nature of Christian faith is the Lord's Prayer. It is a "we-prayer" and an "us-prayer," not an "I-prayer" and a "me-prayer." There is no Christian life without personal prayer and faith, but the favorite prayer of the church is a social prayer. For the same reason the Statement is a communal one.

2. Symbolic language. The original Statement of Faith identified God as "Father of our Lord Jesus Christ and our Father." The revisions of 1977 and 1981 omit the word *Father.* The reason is the desire to correct a bias, the representation of God as male.

Some corrections of that bias are easy. They require only a sensitivity to language, an alertness to overcome the laziness of habit. Changing pronouns, for example, is fairly easy. But other corrections are more difficult. Some raise questions about the substance of belief.

We start with the realization that every term for God is inadequate. Speaking of God, we must use symbols. These are necessary and helpful, but they may be deceptive. In the Bible, God is frequently described as a rock; for example, "the rock of our salvation [Ps. 95:1]." In many ways a rock, an inert object, is an extraordinarily bad symbol for God; but in certain contexts it is a helpful symbol. Christians still sing, "Rock of ages, cleft for me, / Let me hide myself in thee."

When we use personal language of God, as surely we must, we need to avoid ascribing a gender to God. The biblical symbols are usually masculine, sometimes feminine. To take a feminine example that most Christians rarely think about, a biblical prophet hears God saying: "I will cry out like a woman in travail, I will gasp and pant [Isa. 42:14]." That symbol, like any other, can be carried too far, but it shows that female images of God are as valid as male images. We can expect that the church will learn to cultivate those images that it often suppressed in the past.

The word *Father,* like any term for God, has difficulties. For women it may represent male authority. For men it may evoke the Oedipal complexes so emphasized by Freudian psychology. Many children know only a vindictive father or no father at all.

Yet the word *Father* has an importance not easy to erase from Christian faith. Jesus taught his disciples to pray, "Our

Father." Can the church avoid or revise the Lord's Prayer? Some worshiping communities are doing so, and others regard such acts as near blasphemies.

When Jesus addressed God as *Abba,* he used the most intimate of Aramaic words for "father." The German biblical scholar Joachim Jeremias has shown that Jesus was an innovator in this respect; he characteristically and uniquely prayed to God as *Abba.* Rarely do we know the exact language that Jesus used. His Aramaic words come to us in Greek, later in English translations. Even the Lord's Prayer comes in different versions in Matthew and Luke. But, Jeremias concludes after extensive research, that in *Abba* we have the exact language, the *ipsissima vox* of Jesus.[3] But Jeremias also shows that in ancient Oriental usage, "the word 'father,' as applied to God" includes "something of what the word 'mother' signifies among us."[4] This suggests that the church might more regularly cultivate feminine, as well as masculine, symbols for God. Some have suggested that the contemporary church might learn to address God as *Abba,* thus preserving the meaning of its heritage without the bias that surrounds it. If this suggestion is too "far out" for consideration, it shows the depths of the issue of gender that the church faces in our time.*

3. Another issue of language. Where the Statement of 1959 refers to "our Lord Jesus Christ," the revision of 1981 changes the language to "our Savior Jesus Christ." Both

---

*In this book, I intend to use gender-inclusive language, except when referring to particular persons, male or female. When I quote others, including the Bible, I do not change the quoted language. I am grateful for the New Revised Standard Version of the Bible and for other translations that avoid the male bias imposed on the Bible by past translations. But I agree with the biblical scholar Phyllis Bird that translators should aim for historical accuracy rather than for revision of the original texts in the light of postbiblical sensitivities. The task of interpretation remains ours. See Bird, "Translating Sexist Language as a Theological and Cultural Problem," *Union Seminary Quarterly Review* 42:Nos. 1–2 (1988), pp. 89–95.

phrases are familiar in Christian history. But "Lord" is masculine and "Savior" is gender-neutral. In that respect the change is clear and simple.

But the same change involves other theological issues. The term *Lord* involves an acknowledgment of sovereignty, of a claim that Christ exerts upon the church and even, in a different sense, on humankind. A *Savior* is one who has done something crucially important for us but whom we do not necessarily acknowledge as sovereign. In the New Testament, "Lord" is by far the more frequent designation of Christ, but both terms are used. Both appear often in Christian tradition. The Constitution of the United Church of Christ, describing the basis of the local church, refers to "Jesus Christ as Lord and Savior." But some discussion in the United Church is now asking whether the change from "Lord" to "Savior" means a theological change, deliberate or inadvertent, in the Statement of Faith.

Historically "Savior" has been the favored designation of pietistic versions of faith. Pietism, contrary to some prejudices, is not a bad word. It represents the emphasis on the inward, highly personal experience of Christ. It is an important accent in Christian faith. But pietism has tended to neglect human political involvement in obedience to Christ.

"Lord" has been the favored designation of those forms of faith that emphasize Christ's claim upon us, especially in public life. When the early Christians, in perhaps their first creedal declaration, said, "Jesus is Lord," they were also saying, "Caesar is not Lord." That led to social and political acts that had a transforming effect on history.

W. A. Visser 't Hooft, the first general secretary of the World Council of Churches, has shown how "the Lordship of Christ" became the banner under which Christians defied Hitler in the Nazi era. Some Christians could retreat into a privatistic religion, as though Nazism were irrelevant to their faith. But to others the "Lordship of Christ" became the "dynamic truth" that governed them "in decisions of life and death."[5]

When the General Synod adopted the Statement of 1959, the memory of the struggle of the German church was still vivid. The Lordship of Christ seemed an obviously important affirmation. Today, when many people seek a more privatized faith, there are still strong reasons to declare the claims of Christ upon us as public citizens. The church is struggling to find a fitting language.

4. The Trinity. I have already said (in part one) that the Statement of Faith is organized not in the traditional triadic structure but as a declaration of the deeds of God. Occasionally people have asked, Is it trinitarian? The most frequent answer has been, It is at least as trinitarian as the Bible. Now some questioners are asking whether the version of 1981 is less trinitarian than the original.

The original Statement, in its opening sentence, speaks of Father, Christ, and Spirit. It goes on to tell of the One God who comes to us in Jesus Christ and bestows upon us the Holy Spirit. Thus the whole Statement expresses the experience that led, during the first three centuries of church history, to the formal doctrine of the Trinity. But it does not go on to enter into the debates that have surrounded that doctrine.

To sense the meaning of the issue, it is helpful to distinguish two themes within the doctrine of the Trinity, a word that is an abbreviation of Tri-unity. One theme, emphasizing the unity of God, recognizes that this one God is known in three kinds of relationship to us. The other theme, putting a little more accent on the "Tri-", affirms that something of community—akin to a familial relationship—is part of the one God. To oversimplify a complex history, the Western churches have tended to emphasize Tri-*unity;* the Eastern churches, *Tri*-unity.

To many sincere believers, these distinctions are too subtle to worry about. But for two reasons they matter.

The first reason is that the General Synod of 1981 asked that the new "collaborative" statement "affirm the triune nature of God." That insistence is important to many members of the United Church of Christ, and it is important for ecumenical relations, both with other Protestant churches and with Roman Catholicism and Orthodoxy. Protestants do not always realize, for example, that Catholics regard a Protestant baptism as entirely valid, provided it is done "in the name of the Father and the Son and the Holy Spirit (or Holy Ghost)." A change in that language would create a major barrier to ecumenical conversations now in progress.

The second reason comes out of contemporary feminist theologies, among others. Barbara Brown Zikmund, while finding difficulty in the traditionally masculine formulations, sees important meaning in "the trinitarian truth that there is one God *existing* in community." The triune God "embodies the very nature of reality as relational or communal."[6] Other writers have said that the traditional language of Father, Son, and Holy Spirit expresses a communal or familial relation within the unity of God—a relationship that may be lost in such revisions as "Creator, Christ, and Holy Spirit."

It is evident that important conversations lie ahead in the "collaborative" effort to rethink and restate the basic Christian testimony.

THE FIRST DECLARATION

God Creates

You call the worlds into being,
   create persons in your own image,
   and set before each one the ways of life and death.

God the Creator

The Great Story, as told in the Bible, begins: "In the beginning God created the heavens and the earth." This is the bold declaration that this whole universe is the work of one Creator Spirit.

The Statement of Faith, addressing the Creator, says: "You call the worlds into being." Here is an echo of the words of Genesis: "God said, 'Let there be light'; and there was light." It is an echo also of other sayings of scripture: "By the word of the LORD the heavens were made [Ps. 33:6]"; "In the beginning was the Word [John 1:1]"; "By faith we understand that the worlds were prepared by the word of God [Heb. 11:3]."

Why this language of speech and word? It suggests that creation is not solely an act of power; it is also an act of communication, an act of meaning.

In the opening verses of the Bible, it seems as though the Creation was an effortless act. God spoke, and something tremendous happened. But a little later we read that on the seventh day God "rested" from the "work" of creation (Gen. 2:2). Even for God, creation requires an effort and earns a rest.

Once again we must realize that language about God is symbolic. To say that God "breathed" into Adam "the breath of life [Gen. 2:7]" or made the heavens "by the breath of his mouth [Ps. 33:6]" is not to say that God has a body, a metabolism, lungs and a mouth, a gender like ours. The creation story takes the form of "myth"—using the term not as a fanciful and unreal tale but as a story that touches on profound themes that human language can only suggest. Like a poem or a hymn, the words of immediate experience here point to meanings that cannot be stated literally. We are not dealing with a scientific account from which we can calculate the age of rocks and skeletons of dinosaurs. We are facing mysteries that have concerned the wisest of people over the ages.

The Christian doctrine of creation denies that the world or any object in it is God. This belief rejects pantheism—the belief, pervasive in many religions, that nature is God or the veil of the one spirit who is all that is truly real. It rejects the worship of sacred objects—the sun, animals, people (often emperors). Any of these may tell the glory of God (in the language of Psalm 19:1). But they are not God.

But though the world is not God, it is not alien to God. The belief in creation is a rejection of all bias against material reality. That bias has often crept into Christianity. It crept in from the philosophy of Plato and from other religions that teach the goodness of spirit and the evil of matter. But the scriptures remind Christians that dualisms of matter and spirit are misleading, that the material world is the creation of God. In the repeated words of Genesis, God saw that the creation was "good"—yes, "very good."

This is not to say that the entire creation is friendly to human beings. A modern astrophysicist, Sir James Jeans, has called it "the mysterious universe." Its dimensions in time and space, its awesome power, its creative and destructive power—these are overwhelming. Why, if it is "very good," does it include so much that is hostile to human life and purpose? Is it related to "the power and weakness of God,"[1] to use the title of a famous sermon by Reinhold Niebuhr—a theme that we must come back to later when we look at the Statement's declaration about Christ? Is it because the tremendous vitalities of nature are in some ways akin to the freedom that we know in ourselves? Does creativity—in physical nature as in human life—always mean the risk of destructiveness? We have every right to think about these questions. What we know is that Christian faith dares to call the whole creation a consequence of God's activity.

Modern science has expanded our conception of the universe to include many galaxies and aeons of time. Where the Apostles' Creed calls God "the creator of heaven and earth," the Statement of Faith says that God calls "the worlds" into being. That recognition of many worlds is a modification of some traditional beliefs, yet is suggested by the biblical declaration that God created "the heavens and the earth." The biblical writers marveled at the God who made the Pleiades and Orion (Amos 5:8), who made the hippopotamus and the crocodile and the mountain goat, who laid the foundation of the earth "when the morning stars sang together [Job 38:7]." Surely this stupendous creation is not all for human convenience. Yet humankind has an honored place within it.

The years since the first adoption of the Statement of Faith have brought some changes in the winds of theological discussion. One change was the flowering of theologies of secularization. These pointed out that the Christian belief in creation "de-divinized" nature. By insisting that nature is not God and is not filled with divine spirits, it achieved "the removal of traditional religious restraints to scientific and technological change." It meant, said some, that human "freedom to master and shape, to create and explore now reaches out to the ends of the earth and beyond."[2]

That assertion exaggerated one note in the complex chord of historical and theological insight. It soon had to meet the new recognition of the rash destructiveness of human actions that threaten the ecological health of the planet and human life itself. In recent years we have learned to appreciate again the insight of the eighteenth-century theologian Jonathan Edwards: "perhaps there is not one leaf of a tree, nor a spire of grass, but what produces effects all over the universe and will produce them to the end of eternity."[3] The World Council of Churches and many of its member churches have come to a new appreciation of "the integrity of creation"; and Pope John Paul II, in his New Year's message for 1990, warned against ecological collapse and called for "Peace with All of Creation."

To say that God calls the worlds into being is to say that the world is not God; it is less than God. Yet it has a secondary glory as God's "handiwork"—to use another symbolic term from Psalm 19.

The Creation of Humankind

Within the whole of creation, God's human creatures have a place of special significance and responsibility. As the Bible tells the Great Story, we are created in God's image.

In the second account of creation we are made of "dust of the ground [Gen. 2:7]," the common stuff of the world—a reason for some modesty about our status. Yet our life comes from the breath of God—a reason for thanksgiving and wonder at the marvel of our existence.

Christian faith has a deep suspicion of images. The Ten Commandments warn against graven images as occasions for idolatry. So it is the more remarkable that the first chapter of the Bible describes us—human beings—as created in the image, after the likeness, of God. "Image," in the context of creation, clearly does not mean a graven object or a reflection in a mirror. The divine image is a capacity to respond, a gift of freedom, a sharing in God's creativity and love.

The New Testament goes on to say that the image and likeness of God, in us, is incomplete. In Jesus Christ we see "the image of God [2 Cor. 4:4]." That tells us something about human possibility. "All of us, with unveiled faces, seeing the glory of the Lord . . . are being transformed into the same image from one degree of glory to another [2 Cor. 3:18]." That comes later in the Great Story, but already the first stage of the story points toward it. Our creation is incomplete; it is directed toward a future.

The liberal theology of the early twentieth century often spoke of people as "co-creators" with God. The terrible and humbling events of the mid-century made that language unbearably pretentious. Now in the late decades of the century it is returning. It has a valid meaning. God has given us creativity, has offered us a "dominion"—a word usually used in the Bible of God, rarely also of human beings (Gen. 1:26, Ps. 8:6)—over some of the created world. But if we are cocreators, we are decidedly junior partners. Again we think of the question Job heard from God: "Where were you when I laid the foundation of the earth?" We did not create the sun, the Pleiades and Orion, the birds and fish and animals. We did not create ourselves. Yet God grants us a share in the divine creative work.

One sentence in the record of Genesis (1:27) has awakened new appreciation in our own time. "So God created man in his own image, in the image of God created he him; male and female he created them." Dietrich Bonhoeffer pointed out that the image of God is here integrally related to the creation of "male and female."[4] It is as though that language had slumbered through the centuries to erupt with power in our own time. An isolated person is incomplete. Mutuality—here represented by sexual mutuality—is essential to selfhood.

And if the image of God is so related to "male and female" humanity, then something like what we recognize as male and female must belong, in some profound sense, to God.

The Ways of Life and Death

Human freedom means the capability for decisions, good and bad. The Statement of Faith joins to the story of creation the later words of Moses to the people of Israel: "See, I have set before you today life and prosperity, death and adversity [Deut. 30:15]."

Those words tell us of the importance of human decision. God has given us a portentous responsibility. We are meant to create; we can also destroy. It is easier to destroy than to create. Tiny children discover that when they build a house of blocks and knock it over or when they jostle a vase onto the floor. Adults discover it repeatedly in social life.

Today that power of decision is more frightening than ever before. Human creativity and destructiveness are magnified far beyond possibilities of the past. The radically secular French existentialist Jean-Paul Sartre echoed a Christian insight when he said that we are condemned to be free. Christians see freedom primarily as opportunity, but they know it is also a destiny that humankind cannot escape.

Looking at the words of Moses, we might ask: But why would anybody, given the choice between life and death, choose death? Perhaps because of the subtlety of temptation, perhaps because of arrogance that blinds us to our true good. We must look later at the place of sin in human life. But the obvious fact is that people often do choose death: they choose it in yielding to drug addiction, in despising their sisters and brothers in the human family, in choosing death for their enemies and thereby choosing it for themselves. The United Church of Christ, adopting the Statement of Faith in 1959, could not know that the peace movement of later decades would often use the words from Deuteronomy and call on humanity to "choose life." The unprecedented choices of our own time dramatize the choice that is inherent in human life.

One turn of phrase in the Statement of 1981 has caused surprise and discussion. The Statement of 1959 said that God "sets before him [man] the ways of life and death." Robert Moss, in the version of 1977, modified the masculine gender by changing "him" to "us." The version of 1981, instead of "him" or "us," says "each one." The intended change to a more inclusive language led to another change, intended or inadvertent, to a more individualistic conception of human nature.

The original word, "man," had to go, for the reasons stated earlier. But in its original usage it had the deliberately double meaning: it could represent both an individual and the collective human race. The change to "us" preserved the double meaning; it could refer to "us" both as a collection of individuals and as an organic human society, including the total society of humankind. The change to "each one" means a loss of the double meaning and a choice for the individual rather than the social conception of selfhood. Some people, both inside and outside the United Church of Christ, have wondered whether a church, so known for its social consciousness, was choosing to take a more individualistic direction. This is the issue that I discussed earlier (Prologue to "The Deeds of God") in the case of the words *Lord* and *Savior*. As we shall see later, there is no abandonment in the revision of the social mission of the church; the point involved is the sense of selfhood.

Is there an unreal and unbiblical individualism in the emphasis on "each one"? Is not the choice between "ways of life and death" often a choice of national, racial, and economic groups? Can we say that the infant, born with a drug addiction or malnourishment or syphilis, has chosen the way of death? The Ten Commandments say that the sins and the blessings of the parents are visited on the children. Christians have often disliked that insight, but they have usually recognized the truth in it. We—all of us—are bound up with others in the web of life.

The revision of 1981 forcefully reminds us of our personal responsibility. Perhaps that is the needed emphasis in a time when individuals have so often evaded moral responsibility by blaming their choices on "the system"—the corporation or the government or climate of the culture. But perhaps this is also a time to remember Isaiah's confession, "I am a man of unclean lips, and I dwell in the midst of a people of unclean lips [Isa. 6:5]." The boundary between the self and the social groups that form the self is not always clear and distinct. For Isaiah, that was not a reason to avoid personal responsibility; it was an occasion to take a bold, personal action.

Christian faith calls for personal response. It also calls for social response in the community of faith and the community of humankind. We can expect continued discussion on the relation of the self to the communities in which it finds its life.

THE SECOND DECLARATION

God Seeks to Save

You seek in holy love to save all people from aimlessness and sin.

The Human Problem

Between our creation in God's image and our present existence, something has gone wrong. In the Great Story the problem is identified with "the fall." Christians, especially in the modern world, have sometimes rejected the story of the fall. If it means that all of us are in deep trouble because of acts not of our doing—mistakes of Adam and Eve long, long ago—the story strikes us as rationally ridiculous and morally offensive. But if we understand the fall, in a phrase of the psychotherapist Rollo May, as "a snapshot of personality," it may guide us to self-understanding. It tells us that we are created for love and that, when we fail to love or when we love possessively, we violate God's will and our own deepest selfhood. The Statement of Faith uses two words, among many possibilities, to describe this human problem.

One is the familiar word *sin.* We meet it directly in the Lord's Prayer: "Forgive us our sins," as Luke (11:4) reports it, using the most frequent of the Greek words for "sin" in the New Testament. Matthew's version (6:12) says, "Forgive us our debts," using a Greek word sometimes used quite literally in the New Testament for cash debts. In either case, we need forgiveness. "If we say that we have no sin, we deceive ourselves, and the truth is not in us. If we confess our sins, he

[God] who is faithful and just will forgive us our sins and cleanse us from all unrighteousness [1 John 1:8–9]."

All of us, at least part of the time, resent accusations of sin. Our present society has great discomfort with the idea of sin. People want self-esteem, self-fulfillment, the avoidance of guilt feelings, the excusing of wrongs. National leaders have been known to admit, "Mistakes were made"; it is much harder to say, "I made that mistake," and still harder to say, "I did wrong."

The valid note in this mood is that self-contempt is not healthy and a steam bath of remorse can be an evasion of the will to do right. But the dismissal of a sense of sin has gone so far that the psychotherapist Karl Menninger decided to write a book, *What Ever Happened to Sin?* It is a forthright advocacy of a strong doctrine of sin, bluntly defined as "transgression of the law of God; disobedience of the divine will; moral failure."[1] He gives particular attention to sin as "collective irresponsibility," a theme I have mentioned earlier. What does it mean that in our time a psychiatrist must remind church people that an acknowledgement of sin can be healthy? Menninger realizes that until we recognize sin, we are not able to take responsibility to correct it.

Obviously a lot is wrong in this twentieth-century world. We are familiar with war, with racial conflict, with greed, with crime, with drugs, with the suffering of the poor. Some of us can plead innocent to some of these sins. But if we look for their roots, we find that they are not just "out there." Sometimes we have to accept the famous words of Pogo, "We have met the enemy and he is us."

What, more specifically, is sin in the Christian vocabulary? What is the *sin* that underlies the many *sins* of our experience? It is estrangement from God, the irresponsible use of God's gifts of knowledge and freedom. Traditionally it takes several forms. It is *pride,* not in the sense of self-respect but pride as defined by Augustine: the situation of the self who turns away from God and becomes an end to itself. In Luther's description, it is the heart curved in upon itself rather than opening out to God and the world. Sin is *apathy*, the neglect of responsibility in laziness or frustration or defeatism. Sin is *sensuality*, not the sensuous joy in the delights of the created world but the sensual exploitation of objects or other people. Sin is all these and more. In its depths it is the loss or perversion of love.

The traditional doctrine of sin, so often assumed to be demeaning to human dignity, actually embodies a noble conception of selfhood. Sin is possible only for persons created in God's image, empowered with freedom. The doctrine of sin tells us that we are not basically animals, dragged down by predatory instincts, insufficiently humanized. That idea helps explain some things. But the Christian doctrine tells us that our deepest nature is love, and in sin we betray our true nature and destiny.

The biblical conception of sin also helps us understand a problem that we saw in the First Declaration: the choice between "the ways of life and death." Usually we do not clearly discern ways of life and death, of good and evil, then deliberately choose death and evil. We are not that stupid or perverse. Instead, such is the insidious nature of sin, we yield to temptation by misperceiving evil and calling it good. By grasping for a false kind of life, we choose death.

The Statement of Faith uses a second word to describe the human predicament: *aimlessness*. The word came out of long discussions in the formulation of the Statement. It expressed a sensitivity to a mood common in our culture. If sin is the perennial problem, acknowledged by the Bible and the long Christian tradition, perhaps aimlessness is a characteristic problem of our time.

This is not to say that aimlessness is brand new. One translation—an accurate translation but not the only one—of some of the Hebrew and Greek words for sin is "missing the mark."

That can be a comforting thought, sometimes too comforting. Missing the mark is an error of human finitude, not a crime. Nobody is so gifted as to hit the center of the target every time, to bat a thousand, to play an errorless season. But curiously the Bible sometimes calls for *forgiveness* for missing the mark. Maybe we miss the mark, not simply because of fallibility but because of a failure of effort or commitment, or because of a divided aim. Then, one stage further, we may miss the mark because we lack an aim. We may have no high desire, no soul-stirring vision, no loyalty that inspires courage and dedication.

The world today, notably the American society, knows well the affliction of aimlessness. Sometimes it is the aimlessness of affluence, the satiation with consumer goods that saps commitment. Sometimes it is the aimlessness of despair in a world that teaches many people that nothing they do can lift them out of an oppressed existence. In either case the ailment is both individual and social, a theme I have mentioned earlier.

Holy Love

The Christian faith is that God seeks to save us from aimlessness and sin. Why does God do so? The Statement ascribes to God a "holy love."

Of all sayings about God, none has been more cherished by Christians than the three-word, three-syllable sentence, "God is love." The words come to us from 1 John 4:8, but they come out of many testimonies of Jesus and the apostles. So highly do Christians esteem this faith in God's love that they sometimes make the mistake of contrasting the New Testament God of love to the Old Testament God of wrath. That error began in the ancient church. It was declared a heresy, but it has persisted through the centuries.

True, there is a fierceness in some Old Testament descriptions of God. But the Hebrew prophets brought to the world the insight—revelation is a better word—of God's love. Hosea in his life enacted the forgiving love of God who said that, despite the sins of the people, "I will love them freely [Hos. 14:4]." Jeremiah heard God's word to sinners, "I have loved you with an everlasting love [31:3]." Jesus appealed to this tradition when he told the parable of the prodigal son and the forgiving father, and the parable of the shepherd and the lost sheep.

Both Testaments tell also of God's severity toward sin. If God is sometimes depicted as a warrior in the Old Testament, the same is true of The Revelation to John in the New Testament. The love of God means the wrath of God against all that destroys love. The prophetic denunciations of injustice led to Jesus' condemnation of hypocrites and oppressors. In both cases the wrath of God is required by the love of God. A loving God cannot be indifferent to wrong.

The Statement speaks of God's "holy love." Divine love is not soft and sentimental. It is not amiable and easygoing. In our own time some adults, working with troubled young people, have coined the term *tough love.* Such love is no less loving for being tough. It knows that disturbed youth, experiencing a hostile world, need love—enduring love that outlasts anger, frustration, and defiance. But they do not need indulgence or indifference to destructive habits. They need to know that freedom must always relate itself to limits—to limits of possibility and to moral limits.

God's love is tough love. More than that, it is holy love. Love does not overcome the awesome majesty of God. Indeed, the mystery and holiness of God is the more overwhelming when it is recognized in divine love.

All People

The Statement affirms that God seeks to save *all* people. That was not an issue of controversy in the formulation of the Statement. But it led to considerable discussion. Many Christians across the ages have not believed this. Some saints of the church have taught that God predestines many to damnation, even that one of the joys of salvation is the knowledge that many are condemned.

The Great Story includes records of covenants between God and human communities. There was the covenant of Eden, the Noachic covenant (the renewed covenant with humankind represented by Noah), the covenant with Abraham, the covenant with Israel at Mount Sinai, the covenant in Jesus Christ. Some Christians have interpreted these to mean that people outside one or another of these covenants are excluded from God's love and concern.

Yet there are other strands in the Great Story that tell of God's love for all. The Word of God came to the prophet Ezekiel, saying: "As I live, says the Lord GOD, I have no pleasure in the death of the wicked, but that the wicked turn from their ways and live [Ezek. 33:11]." Jesus taught, "It is not the will of your Father in heaven that one of these little ones should be lost [Matt. 18:14]." One of the pastoral letters of the New Testament says that God "desires everyone to be saved" [1 Tim. 2:4]." The Statement of Faith, by deliberate choice, builds on these biblical themes.

Beyond this, the Statement does not go. It is aware of the seriousness of evil, as known in our experience and attested in scripture, and it does not affirm or deny universal salvation. There were differences of opinion in the original commission, as there are in the United Church of Christ today. Some believe that, if God seeks to save all, then God must save all, for God cannot fail. Others believe that God's gift of freedom means that some people may resist God forever. Still others, echoing Karl Barth, believe that in each of us there is that which God saves and that which must perish. The church, in its limited knowledge and wisdom, does not have to know everything. The Statement of Faith simply affirms God's love and refuses to set limits on its power and scope.

THE THIRD DECLARATION

God Judges

You judge people and nations by your righteous will
declared through prophets and apostles.

The Judgment of God

The God who seeks to save is our Judge. The sequence of
the deeds of God is itself important. The Statement of Faith
does not tell us that God first judges us, then seeks to save.
Rather, it is the saving God who judges.

Life, we all know, is full of judges and judgments. We judge
one another, fairly and unfairly. We judge ourselves, fairly
and unfairly. Society sets up judicial systems, designates
judges and juries. In all this activity there is a groping for
justice.

But we know, all too well, the fallibility of human judgment. In law we set up courts, then appeal their decisions to
higher courts, then to a Supreme Court, then sometimes
hope that a future Supreme Court will overrule this one. In
personal affairs we fly from judgments of adversaries to
judgments of friends; when friends turn against us, we seek
some wider vindication. Sometimes we appeal from the judgment of our contemporaries to the judgment of history. But
the judgments of history are constantly shifting. We crave—
and sometimes fear—a truly reliable judgment. A common
saying begins, "As God is my Judge . . ." Finally, a true judgment transcends the partial and prejudiced judgments of
human life and history.

God's judgment, says the Statement of Faith, is the judgment of a "righteous will." That righteous will is intimately related to the "holy love" that seeks to save us.

Lesser judgments rely on many criteria. Courts judge according to laws, whether the laws be just or unjust, and the testimony of fallible witnesses. Banks judge applicants for loans according to estimates of financial reliability. Schools judge by standards of scholarship, sports fans by statistical achievements and crowd appeal, stock markets by expectations of profits. God's judgment is an expression of justice, a justice that is both stern and compassionate.

God's judgment, says the Statement, is "declared through prophets and apostles." Our recognition of justice is not solely a matter of conscience. Human conscience is important. Sometimes we resist temptation by saying, "I have to live with myself." But conscience is fallible, shaped by the surrounding culture. It needs guidance. To say that God's righteous will is declared by prophets and apostles is to point to a message recorded in scripture. That scripture does not tell us what to do on all occasions. It has its inner tensions. It must be interpreted and can easily be misinterpreted, a point emphasized in part one. But there it is, a constant reminder of the Great Story, a constant voice recalling the church to its mission.

Out of the whole scriptural record, the Statement at this point selects the prophets and apostles for emphasis. The Hebrew prophets declared God's righteous will in ways that resound through the centuries. They told kings that their power was nothing as compared with God's. They told the people that trust in military power (in "men and horses") and wealth was no assurance of security. Above all, they condemned religion when it became a way to evade God's demands for justice. God's voice, as it came to the herdsman Amos, said:

"I hate, I despise your festivals,
and I take no delight in your solemn assemblies. . . .
Take away from me the noise of your songs;
I will not listen to the melody of your harps.
But let justice roll down like waters,
and righteousness like an everflowing stream."
—Amos 5:21, 23–24

If we turn from the thundering Amos to the loving Hosea, we find no softening on this issue:

"For I desire steadfast love and not sacrifice,
the knowledge of God, rather than burnt offerings."
—Hosea 6:6

The emphasis of the Statement on apostles reminds us that eventually, Christians believe, God's will is not only declared; it is embodied—enfleshed—in Jesus Christ, to whom the apostles testify. But in the Great Story that comes later.

People and Nations

God's judgment, says the Statement, falls on people and nations. Here is the correction of the individualism that I pointed out earlier in the First Declaration, the accent on "each one." God's judgment of individuals is utterly important. In this day of mass communications and vast organizations, when individuals often try to escape accountability, Christians affirm that each single person has a responsibility to God and neighbors. But shared responsibility in our institutional life is also important. We individuals participate in the wrongs of society.

In the days of slavery it was not enough to say that individual slaveholders were doing a wrong. Race prejudice, economic oppression, international imperialism, and war are social ills, often built into the structures of society. The Christian response is not solely to convert individuals, to "win them one by one." Sometimes the response is to correct institutions of injustice, to change laws, to redistribute power. God, we believe, judges "people and nations."

Recognizing God's Judgment

With God's judgment we come to an important, yet dangerous aspect of Christian belief. God's judgment is recognizable in experiences and history in a fragmentary way. The double accent is important: signs of judgment are both recognizable and fragmentary.

Judgment is recognizable because "the wages of sin is death," as the apostle Paul put it (Rom. 6:23). There are judgments on sin, punishments for sin in history. Sin is destructive, and it sometimes destroys itself. Good behavior often has its rewards. There are blessings in righteousness. Parents try to teach their children that good acts bring benefits and evil acts bring harm. Something in us wishes this were true more obviously and more generally.

The wish gives rise to an error, a false belief or heresy. It is the belief that God consistently punishes evil and rewards good in a visible way. If this heresy were true, we wouldn't even know what noble behavior is. The most selfish act, shrewdly aimed at securing rewards, would be indistinguishable from the truly generous act.

Parts of the Bible, taken in isolation, express or verge on this heresy. The prophets pointed to disasters in social life as signs of God's judgment. Jeremiah (44:2–3), for example, said that the desolation of Jerusalem was evidence of God's judgment against its wickedness. The "Deuteronomic view of history" shows how God rewards righteous behavior of kings and people with peace and prosperity, while punishing evil behavior with disaster.

The strain of truth in this belief is important. The prophets help us to realize that our defeats are often the consequences of our moral failures.

But the belief can lead to serious errors. It often doesn't fit the facts. When sin leads to disaster, the pain often hurts the victims as well as the doers of evil. Furthermore, the belief may lead to the "blame-the-victim" syndrome, in which we respond to the suffering of others by accusing them of wrong instead of helping them. It leads also to harmful self-condemnation (when suffering people assume that God is punishing them) and sanctimonious self-congratulation (when people assume that good fortune is God's reward for their virtue). The extreme expression of this belief appears in some Eastern religions, where human misfortunes—disease, catastrophe, low-caste status—are attributed to karma, a destiny that determines the status of people on the basis of their past conduct in this life or a prior incarnation.

The Bible frequently refutes such beliefs. The book of Job is a vindication of a good man against his "friends," who tell him that his agonies are God's punishment for his sins. Isaiah of the Exile tells the people that suffering can be an act of love and service, a redemptive opportunity. (See especially Isaiah 52:13—53:12.)

Jesus points out the double theme—the recognizable and the fragmentary character of God's judgment in our historical experience. Healing an invalid, Jesus says, "Your sins are forgiven you [Luke 5:20]." Some of our illnesses are the judgment on our own irresponsible behavior. But on another occasion, when the disciples ask, "Rabbi, who sinned, this man or his parents, that he was born blind?," Jesus gives an answer that upsets their question: "Neither this man nor his parents sinned; he was born blind so that God's works might be revealed in him [John 9:2–3]." This is not an intellectual explanation of the blindness; it is the shift of the situation from a matter of theory to an opportunity for helpfulness.

In the New Testament the fragmentary evidences of God's judgment are signs pointing to the reality of God's ultimate judgment, which confounds many of the judgments we human beings make of ourselves and one another. That point gets ringing emphasis in Jesus' parable of the Last Judgment (Matt. 25:31–46). It tells us that God is the ultimate judge over "all the nations." The divine judgment, coming from God's righteous will, is based on human care for people in need, for "the least of these." And God's judgment, so far from being predictable by conventional human standards, comes as a surprise to both the good and the guilty.

The further word on God's judgment is not another "teaching." It is Jesus himself. And that bring us to the next deed of God.

THE FOURTH DECLARATION

God Comes to Us in Christ

In Jesus Christ, the man of Nazareth, our crucified
>and risen Savior,
>you have come to us
>and shared our common lot,
>conquering sin and death
>>and reconciling the world to yourself.

In Jesus Christ

At the center of the Great Story, as Christians tell it, is the
coming of Christ. This is the distinctive note in Christian
faith. When we call ourselves Christians, we invoke the name
of Christ.

In the Statement of Faith this theme has been heralded
from the beginning. The confessional prologue identifies our
God as the God of Jesus Christ. All the deeds of God are
deeds of the God of Jesus Christ. But in the narration of the
Story, this deed follows a long history. Now it is stated explicitly.

The structure of the Statement marks the decisiveness of
this deed in two ways. First, it is placed in the center. Three
other statements lead to it; three follow from it. Second, a
change in wording takes place. In the other six declarations
the first word is God or the pronoun for God. In this declaration the subject of the sentence is still God. But the sentence
begins, "In Jesus Christ." We are here telling what God did,
quite specifically, in Jesus Christ.

But who is this Jesus? From the days when he walked the

hills of Galilee and the streets of Jerusalem, people have asked that question. What we know about Jesus, we know mostly from the Gospels of the New Testament. They give impressions and memories of him, in great variety, enriching and correcting one another. They include testimonies of Jesus' followers and accusations of his enemies. We have no "neutral" record from his times, no biography as a scholar might write it, no obituary as a newspaper might publish it. The opening words of Mark, usually regarded as the earliest of the Gospels, are: "The beginning of the gospel of Jesus Christ, the Son of God." Thus Mark immediately declares his faith, makes a claim for Jesus. All the New Testament is written as a testimony, as the validation and elaboration of a claim.

The Statement of Faith identifies Jesus in two phrases. The first is "the man of Nazareth." Jesus is a person, living in a particular place and time. He is a human being, not a mythical character, an angel, or one of the gods in a divine hierarchy. Jesus is a very specific human being, a Jew of Nazareth, born into a laborer's family. The infancy narratives locate his birth not in a palace or parsonage, not in a hospital, but in a stable. To many people Jesus appeared to be a quite ordinary person. They said of him, "Is not this Joseph's son [Luke 4:22]?" A more skeptical person, later a disciple, asked, "Can anything good come out of Nazareth [John 1:46]?"

The second phrase of identification in the Statement is "our crucified and risen Savior." Here the "ordinary" becomes the extraordinary. The culmination of the Gospels is the crucifixion and resurrection.

Why was Jesus crucified? The fact is that he died the death of a criminal. He was perceived as a dangerous character, a threat to those in power. Religion and government worked together to kill him. There have been many attempts to fix the blame—on religious leaders, on the state, on common people caught in a mob psychology. Perhaps the best answer is the words of the spiritual: "Were you there when they crucified my Lord? Sometimes it causes me to tremble!" It was sin that crucified the Lord. Knowing our share in sin, we tremble.

But the Gospels testify that the crucified Jesus is the risen Christ. He is living. He appeared to the women whose lives he had touched, to the disciples, to various others, to the apostle Paul. Centuries later Albert Schweitzer wrote, in words now famous, that Jesus still speaks to us: "'Follow thou me!' He commands. And to whose who obey Him, whether they be wise or simple, He will reveal Himself in the toils, the conflicts, the sufferings which they shall pass through in His fellowship, and, as an ineffable mystery, they shall learn in their own experience Who He is."[1]

If we examine the New Testament texts, we find two remarkable characteristics of the testimonies to the resurrection. The first appears in Peter's impromptu sermon at Pentecost. Peter tells a curious, conglomerate crowd: "God raised him [Jesus] up, having freed him from death, because it was impossible for him to be held in its power [Acts 2:24]." Notice the total confidence in that statement. Peter did not try to persuade a skeptical audience that, in spite of all experience to the contrary, a resurrection just might be possible. Turning the case around, he said that, to those who had experienced the resurrection, the triumph of death was impossible. That certitude was so powerful that men and women died for that faith.

But turn to a later testimony of Peter, as he tells the story of Jesus to the Roman centurion Cornelius. "They put him to death by hanging him on a tree; but God raised him on the third day and allowed him to appear, not to all the people but to us who were chosen by God as witnesses, and who ate and drank with him after he rose from the dead [Acts 10:39–41]." Those "chosen by God as witnesses," as all the records agree, were people who had known Jesus and come to trust him.

There was only one other, who had been much troubled by Jesus: Saul of Tarsus, to whom Jesus appeared later. Pontius Pilate was not a witness. Indifferent observers were never witnesses. There were no witnesses whose testimony would carry much weight in an "objective" court. The New Testament record makes this plain, not as an embarrassed admission but as an essential part of the record. Belief in the resurrection is available only to those with faith; to them, the triumph of death is impossible.

God Has Come to Us

The biblical records tell in various ways of God's deed in Christ. "The Word became flesh and lived among us [John 1:14]." "For God so loved the world that he gave his only Son [John 3:16]." "God has made him both Lord and Messiah, this Jesus whom you crucified [Peter, in Acts 2:36]." "When the fullness of time had come, God sent his Son, born of a woman [Gal. 4:4]." "In Christ God was reconciling the world to himself [2 Cor. 5:19]."

From the beginning the church sought ways to express its conviction. Its basic belief was that in the genuinely human being Jesus of Nazareth, believers had truly met God. Not simply an ambassador from God, but the true God, Creator and Judge of all. Looking at the cross of Christ, the community of faith identified the power of God not with government and its armies but with the suffering man. Somehow, hard though it was to comprehend, the Eternal Spirit and the crucified Jesus were one.

Christians, attempting to state this belief, sometimes made fumbling compromises. Sometimes they said that Jesus was God, pretending to be human. Or that Jesus was truly divine and *almost* human. Those beliefs were soon declared heretical (although they survive occasionally today). Sometimes Christians said that Jesus was really human and *almost* God. Or that

Jesus was an in-between being, *almost* divine and *almost* human. Those beliefs were soon ruled out.

The early church, living in a world filled with stories of gods masquerading as human beings, wanted to say that Jesus was genuinely a human person, one who prayed, "Abba, . . . not what I want, but what you want [Mark 14:36]," one who cried out from the cross, "My God, my God, why have you forsaken me [Mark 15:34]?" Yet it wanted to declare also that in Jesus—in his demands, his love, his judgment—it had met the demands, the love, the judgment of the one true God.

The classical creeds sought for ways to express this faith. The Apostles' Creed called Jesus the "only begotten Son" of "God the Father." If all of us are sons and daughters of God, Jesus is the only begotten Son. The Nicene Creed declared Jesus Christ to be "very God of very God," who for us "was made man." The Creed of Chalcedon described "our Lord Jesus Christ" as "of one substance with the Father in his deity, and of one substance with us in his humanity."

The Statement of Faith, in attempting to say what can be said in a sentence, goes behind the Greco-Roman formulations to the theme of Paul, quoted five paragraphs back: "In Christ God was reconciling the world to himself." This choice may be akin to Karl Barth's advice to his students: "Between Creator and creature there is a history and not a relationship as of two static substances."[2] It comes directly from the Great Story, not from Greek metaphysics. But the intent of the Statement is not to reject alternative ways. It is to find a way that is faithful both to the biblical testimony and to our contemporary awareness of the dynamic nature of human life, the universe, and God.

So the Statement says: "In Jesus Christ, the man of Nazareth, our crucified and risen Savior, you [God] have come to us." That is, in this person Jesus, a genuine human being, you, the true God, have entered into our midst. You have not simply sent a messenger, a representative, but you ("very God of very God") have entered the life of this person and through him the life of humankind.

What God Has Done

God, says the statement, has "shared our common lot." God did not in remote majesty utter a word or wave a scepter to relieve our misery and transform our lives. Rather, God shared (and shares) our common lot. The words are plain and prosaic. They tell us that life is not only a matter of grand struggles. It includes hunger and pain, friendships, joys and disappointments, good and bad weather, pleasant parties, the flu, boredom, accidents.

Traditional theology often insisted that God could not suffer, because suffering represented an imperfection, a defect, a vulnerability. The Statement of Faith, harking back to the Bible, says that God, entering our common life, accepts vulnerability. God, accepting the burdens of common life and the brunt of human sin, suffers.

At this point the prosaic character of "our common lot" leaps into high drama. Our common lot includes the consequences of sin. God, who "seeks in holy love to save all people from aimlessness and sin," now accepts the pain inflicted by sin. Christian faith has often related Jesus to the "suffering servant" of Isaiah of the Exile. "Surely he has borne our infirmities and carried our diseases; . . . the LORD has laid on him the iniquity of us all [Isa. 53:4, 6]." As Christians have appropriated those phrases, they have sometimes made God seem extremely unfair. It is as though God had to punish somebody for human sin. Wanting to be merciful to us, God laid the cost on Jesus, and we got off the hook. But if we understand that, in Jesus, God "shared our common lot," the meaning of the old words is transformed.

God does not inflict on Jesus, the innocent bystander, the cost of our human sin. God, entering into our lives in Jesus, shares our suffering, including the cost of our sin.

Again we come to the theme of "the power and the weakness" of God. (See the First Declaration above.) Dietrich Bonhoeffer, soon to be killed by the order of Adolf Hitler, wrote in his prison letters, "God lets himself be pushed out of the world on to the cross. He is weak and powerless in the world, and that is precisely the way, the only way, in which he is with us and helps us. . . . Only the suffering God can help."[3] Yet that weakness is its own kind of power. It is God's way of "conquering sin and death."

The biblical testimony is strong. Entering into human life, in Jesus Christ, God conquers sin and death. But obviously sin and death continue. They are not only facts of existence; they are often overwhelming, destructive facts. The gospel tells us that God, even in the weakness of the cross, defeats them. The power of sin and death was broken in the one life, death, and resurrection of Jesus. Their weakness has been exposed. Now we are invited to become "more than conquerors through him who loved us [Rom. 8:37]." Those words are almost too easy to write and to read. They can be hypocritical if said in untroubled comfort. Their real meaning comes out of the lives of some people who, in suffering, have conquered. Some hints of their meaning are available to us all.

This article of the Statement ends with one of the pivotal phrases of the New Testament, "reconciling the world to himself [yourself] [2 Cor. 5:19]." As Paul put it, in Christ God was reconciling the world *and* committing to us a "ministry of reconciliation [2 Cor. 5:18]."

Traditionally the doctrine of reconciliation has been called the doctrine of the atonement. If we spell it at-one-ment, we see the derivation of the word. Conflict is overcome in harmony. The historic creeds never defined the doctrine of the atonement, as they defined—though not always in the same way—the doctrine of Christ. But one thing was always clear: atonement was related to the cross. Harmony does not come by avoiding or evading conflict. Often confrontation is the only way to reconciliation. This is a warning to those who turn away from conflict; they may be suppressing hostility rather than overcoming it. This is equally a warning to those who delight in confrontation; the valid purpose of confrontation is reconciliation.

The Statement, using the language of the New Testament, says that God reconciles "the world" to God. The Greek word is *kosmos* (in English, cosmos). It means the entire universe, a theme that Orthodox Christianity has remembered when Western Catholicism and Protestantism often forgot it. Today that Eastern insight is reawakening Western sensitivities to physical nature in a time of ecological crises.

The cosmos obviously includes all people—a theme I have commented on earlier (the Second Declaration). The Christian faith does not say that God reconciles only Christians to God. Our Great Story centers in Jesus Christ. But the deed of God in Christ is for the sake of the whole creation. To repeat Paul's words, "In Christ God was reconciling the world [not just Christians] to himself." There are times when a rejection of Christ is a rejection of God. But what of the many people who do not know the story of Jesus or who have been repelled by it because Christians have embodied it in such inadequate, even perverse ways? What of people who tell their Great Story in the language of Asian, African, or native American religions? At a minimum we must refuse to impose limits on God's ability to reach those people with reconciling love. More positively, we can recognize that what God has done in Christ is a deed for the reconciliation of *the world*.

The Statement does not specifically mention Judaism, although it draws much of its content from the Hebrew Bible. Christians are becoming increasingly aware that our Great

Story relies on the Hebrew Story, that the Bible describes the covenant with Israel as an "everlasting covenant [Isa. 55:3; Jer. 32:40; Ps. 105:10]," that Paul wrote that "all Israel will be saved [Rom. 11:26]."

The Statement is silent about other religions or the ways in which God may be present in them. Christians are increasingly aware that we are a minority in the world, that world peace and justice require working sympathetically with people of many faiths and looking for the best in those faiths. Surely we can learn from the experience of people of many religions. We are still called to denounce idolatries, but we need to start with our own. Perhaps we should modify some traditional claims—should say not that only Christ saves but that only the God who has met *us* in Christ saves.

This is not to say that all religions are equally valid or that the best faith is a synthesis of various religions. It is to say that our Great Story, which centers in God's deed in Christ, is the story of a God whose reconciling action encompasses the world. We have a mission to tell that story and enact it in life. In so doing, we have no right to put boundaries on God's power and love.

Past and Present

The Great Story is a story of God's deeds, past and present. The Statement of Faith is written, for the most part, in the present tense. That was a deliberate decision, aimed to remind us of our present relationship to God. It would misrepresent Christian faith to say that God *sought* to save, that God *judged* people and nations—as though these acts were not going on now. In the case of God's creation, the present tense ("You call the worlds into being") is not a denial of an original creation but a recognition that God's creative acts continue in our time.

With the declaration on Christ, the Statement shifts tense.

"In Jesus Christ . . . you have come to us and shared our common lot." That is to recognize the historicity of Jesus and of Christian faith. Jesus, to repeat a point, lived in a particular time and place. The Gospels are filled with geographical locations, so much so that many a Bible is published with maps bound into the text. They are filled with the names of specific people—Herod, Pontius Pilate, and others who lived in a past historical era.

But then the question arises: What in this declaration is past and what is present? The very first version of the Statement, published for the sake of discussion before the General Synod considered the Statement, used this language: "In Jesus Christ . . . he [God] has come to us, shared our common lot, conquered sin and death, and reconciled the world to himself."

It was as though all this had happened. The Statement emphasized the historical character of Christian faith, the rootage in the biblical record of things said and done. It also drew on an old Christian belief, stated by Augustine in his controversy with those religions that saw history as a constant repetition with nothing ever decisive: "For 'Christ died once for all for our sins'; and 'in rising from the dead he is never to die again.'"[4]

That theme was getting great attention in the dominant theologies when the United Church of Christ was coming into existence. During World War II and in the aftermath, the churches had many reasons to emphasize the decisiveness of God's act in Christ. They had reasons to distrust innovations, which too often softened or warped the faith. Theologians were emphasizing the "once-for-allness" (the Germans said the *einmaligkeit*) of God's deed in Christ. The drafting commission saw the force of that strong historical accent.

But then the wider discussions raised questions. Are we being too blithe if, looking at the world with all its evils, we declare that God *has conquered*? In particular, how in the aftermath of the Nazi holocaust, can we say that God *has reconciled* the world? Often the questions came from lay people. The commission was persuaded. It modified the verbs. It kept the recognition of a decisive past history: God "has come to us and shared our common lot." That happened in Jesus, and nothing can undo it. But it changed "conquered" to "conquering" and "reconciled" to "reconciling." The total sentence then emphasized a past action still incomplete, still continuing in the present. When the commission presented and explained its revision to the General Synod, the Synod agreed. The modification continues in the revisions of 1977 and 1981.

THE FIFTH DECLARATION

God Bestows the Holy Spirit

You bestow upon us your Holy Spirit,
   creating and renewing the church of Jesus Christ,
   binding in covenant faithful people of all ages, tongues,
   and races.

The Holy Spirit and Pentecost

In the Great Story, Pentecost follows fifty days after Easter. It is described in the Acts of the Apostles, chapter 2. The followers of Jesus were gathered in a room. The day was a traditional midsummer Jewish harvest festival, the Feast of Weeks. Jesus was no longer with them—in anything like the sense that he had been in the days when they had known him in Galilee and around Jerusalem before the crucifixion and immediately after the resurrection. Then "suddenly," the record says, "like the rush of a mighty wind," the Holy Spirit came upon them. They experienced an explosive enthusiasm, a glowing power. It was as though "tongues of fire" were resting on each person. They "spoke with tongues"—a phenomenon of ecstatic expression known in Greek (and now in English) as glossolalia. Their fervor attracted a crowd, and Peter seized the opportunity to address the curious spectators. Many of them believed his message and were baptized. Pentecost became known as the birthday of the church.

Peter saw this event as the fulfillment of a prophecy in Joel, in which God had declared, "I will pour out my spirit on all flesh [Joel 2:28]." Believers came to understand it as the outcome of a promise of Jesus that, when he was gone, God would send "another Advocate"—the Spirit of truth, or the Holy Spirit (John 14:16, 26).

The experience of the Holy Spirit was decisive in the life of the early church. It was unpredictable. Nobody could set a timetable for the arrival of the Spirit. The usual expectation was that the Spirit would come upon believers at baptism; but some baptized persons did not immediately experience the Spirit (Acts 8:14–17, 19:1–7), and others were grasped by the Spirit before baptism (Acts 10:44–48). The church baptized "in the name of the Father and the Son and the Holy Spirit." People of faith looked to the Spirit for divine power and for guidance in making decisions.

The Eternal Spirit

When Peter related the Holy Spirit to Old Testament prophecy, he tapped into a rich tradition. (Here I return to a theme that I began in the discussion of the Eternal Spirit, Prologue to "The Deeds of God.") Jesus, speaking in his "hometown" synagogue at Nazareth, had read from the book of Isaiah:

"The Spirit of the Lord is upon me,
because he has anointed me to bring good news to the poor.
                                —Luke 4:18; see Isa. 61:1

The Gospel writers tell us that at the baptism of Jesus, the Holy Spirit descended upon him (Matt. 3:16; Luke 3:22), and soon after, Jesus went into the wilderness "full of the Holy Spirit [Luke 4:1]." So it is clear that, for the New Testament, the activity of the Spirit is not something entirely new at Pentecost.

Following the clue of Peter at Pentecost, we find that the Old Testament has many references to the Spirit. Several of the prophets wrote of the Spirit. (The Nicene Creed holds that the Holy Spirit "spoke through the prophets.") Job said, "The spirit of God has made me [Job 33:4]." One psalmist, recognizing that God is everywhere, asked: "Where can I go from your spirit [Ps. 139:7]?" Another prayed, "Do not take your holy spirit from me [Ps. 51:11]." Peter in the New Testament says that the Holy Spirit had spoken through David (Acts 1:16).

The Bible, not concerned about precise distinctions that sometimes interest modern Christians, uses interchangeably various phrases: spirit of God, spirit of Jesus, holy Spirit, Holy Spirit, the Spirit, the spirit. (The capitalizations are the work of modern English-language editors, interpreting Hebrew and Greek manuscripts.)

In a favorite text of many Christians, "God is spirit, and those who worship him must worship in spirit and truth [John 4:24]." The Holy Spirit is not someone other than God, not some deputy whom God sends when busy with other things. The Holy Spirit is God, the Spirit of God, the same Spirit who is mentioned in the second verse of the Bible. The Holy Spirit is "the Eternal Spirit," addressed in the prologue of the Statement of Faith.

Why then is there a special name for the Holy Spirit, different from the name for God? One reason is that the Holy Spirit represents the immediacy of God in human experience. Christians, like other people, sometimes feel the distance of God, the awesome majesty of the Creator of galaxies, the "Judge eternal, robed in splendor." The Holy Spirit is God experienced in intimacy, God's liberating presence in persons and communities, God in Pentecostal power. A second reason is related to Trinitarian belief. Do we emphasize the Tri-*unity* or the *Tri*-unity of God. (See the Prologue to "The Deeds of God" above.) On this issue Christians have a variety of beliefs, and the Statement of Faith does not choose any single one.

The Spirit and Freedom

The Holy Spirit represents a tremendous freedom and emotional power. That can be threatening to those who value order and decorum. God's presence is disturbing because it is out of our control. "The wind blows where it chooses [John 3:8]." In the Greek New Testament, the word here translated "wind" *(pneuma)* is the same word elsewhere translated "Spirit." In a managerial-minded society, where we have invented new disciplines of crisis management and risk management, it is uncomfortable to experience a Holy Spirit that we cannot manage.

The Holy Spirit is often associated with high emotion. Our American society, especially in its "respectable" forms, tends to distrust emotionalism, especially in religion. Sometimes we are so emotionally inhibited that we deprive ourselves of authentic human experience. We may crowd religious emotion out of our churches into "sects" and "cults" that do not fear it. We may then wonder why young people, emotionally starved in conventional churches, slip into these cults. Charismatic movements, cultivating the emotional life in specifically "Pentecostal" forms (e.g., glossolalia), then sometimes reenter the more conventional denominations.

Here, as in so much of life, we need to be honest with ourselves. We should not fake experiences that we do not have, and we should not strain for particular forms of emotional expression that have been characteristic of other times or other people. But if we fear and shun emotion, we deprive ourselves. We may be resisting God.

One characteristic of the Holy Spirit is a capacity to break through conventional boundaries of law and authority. People in the power of the Spirit have defied emperors, popes, parents, agencies of law and order, biblical authority. Such freedom can be creative: "for the letter kills, but the Spirit gives life [2 Cor. 3:6]." But undisciplined freedom can also be destructive. We have seen spectacular examples in our own time of vicious and self-serving actions, purportedly authorized by God. To those who claim to defy social norms by God's command, we must sometimes ask, "How do you know that God, not your own rebellious spirit, prompted those acts?"

The early church wrestled with such questions. The apostle Paul has told us of its struggles. Paul was able to "let go" in a way that many of us cannot, and he wrote candidly of his ecstatic experiences. But he was critical of any fervor that took the place of love or that spread confusion instead of clarity.

James Forbes, senior minister at The Riverside Church in New York City, a Pentecostal and Baptist pastor, has called on Christians to realize anew the meaning of the Holy Spirit. He sees accurately, "Many of us fear being grasped by an invisible presence we cannot control." He invites us to welcome that presence. And he also asks us to "discern between what is of the Spirit and what is not of the Spirit."[1]

Forbes is here echoing a double warning of the New Testament: "Do not quench the Spirit [1 Thess. 5:19]" and "Do not believe every spirit, but test the spirits to see whether they are from God [1 John 4:1]." How shall we know whether the spirit or spirits are of God? Sometimes, let us admit, we are perplexed. But, we know, "The fruit of the Spirit is love, joy, peace, patience, kindness, generosity, faithfulness, gentleness, and self-control [Gal. 5:22–23]."

The Holy Spirit and Humankind

Pentecost brings together the gift of the Holy Spirit and the birth of the Christian church. It also makes clear that the Spirit is not a possession of the church.

The Presbyterian theologian Henry P. Van Dusen criticized the Statement of Faith (before its final adoption) for tying the work of the Holy Spirit too closely to the church. He rightly said that the Holy Spirit often stirs the faith of creative rebels who are more sensitive than the church and who disturb the church.[2]

The criticism was an interesting example of the ecumenical discussions of the Statement. The commission working on the Statement agreed in taking Van Dusen's criticism seriously. It agreed that the activity of the Holy Spirit cannot be confined within any human boundaries, that Christians must be alert to the moving of the Spirit outside churches and even against them.

Nevertheless, the commission decided not to revise the Statement, at this point, before presenting it to the General Synod. Its reasoning was that the Statement in no way confines the activity of the Spirit to the church. In the sequence of the Great Story the bestowal of the Holy Spirit at Pentecost marks the birth of the Christian church. But all the acts of God recorded in the Statement are acts of the God who is Eternal Spirit, Holy Spirit. The Spirit that came at Pentecost is the Spirit active long before the coming of Jesus, as evidenced by the Old Testament.

But what are Christians to say of the activity of the Holy Spirit in the whole human race—among people untouched by any influence of the Bible or any knowledge of Christianity? The Statement has already said that God seeks to save *all* people. The New Testament maintains that among "all the nations" God "has not left himself without a witness [Acts 14:16–17]." These beliefs have led Christians from the earliest times to look for signs of the Holy Spirit among non-Christian people. Faith in God does not entitle people to limit the freedom of the Spirit to act "where it wills." It makes us grateful for signs of God's Spirit wherever we may find them.

At the same time we must realize that recognition of God's work "at large" does not relieve Christians of their specific responsibilities. God bestows the Holy Spirit, "creating and renewing the church of Jesus Christ."

The Spirit and the Church

The Statement of Faith gives no formal definition of the church. It prescribes no specific form of organization, no doctrine of the ordained ministry, no location of authority. Such questions have their importance, but they were never part of the kerygma, the core declaration of the Christian gospel. They are under continuous discussion in the United Church of Christ, as this church engages in conversation with other churches. It brings to those conversations several convictions that are implicit in the Statement of Faith.

First Conviction. It is God, the Holy Spirit, who creates the church. This church is not a creation of and not a possession of men and women.

At this point, appearances may be deceptive. In its institutional organization the church is a voluntary association, and United Church polity strongly affirms that concept. People join or leave it of their own free will. Its members determine its policies through congregational meetings and representative bodies. The members have, therefore, sometimes decided that they had the right to do with the church as they pleased. They have excluded others from "their" church, have avoided opportunities for service, have tried to make the church a congenial club of like-minded people.

But all this is to corrupt the meaning of the church. The Christian faith maintains that the Holy Spirit has created the church. In response to God, people gather for worship and expression of faith. God has given them freedom, by which they may defy God in the church as well as outside it. But when churches defy God, they falsify their nature and calling.

Second Conviction. The Holy Spirit ceaselessly works for the renewal of the church. In its human frailty the church errs, sins, drifts in inertia. Already in New Testament times an apostle declared, "The time has come for judgment to begin with the household of God [1 Pet. 4:17]." The church is always under judgment, always in need of renewal. And renewal goes on continually. A motto, much honored in the traditions of the Reformation, is *ecclesia reformata, semper reformanda*—"the church, reformed, always undergoing reformation."

Sometimes the renewal of the church goes on in especially notable and invigorating movements. We may think of Saint Francis of Assisi, of the Protestant Reformation, of the confessional church defying the idolatry of Hitler at Barmen, of Pope John XXIII and the Second Vatican Council, of liberation movements in Africa and Latin America, of current local and international ferments that shake the church out of stodgy habits and invigorate it to meet the special challenges of the contemporary world.

Churches can be guilty of all the sin and mediocrity that abound in human nature. But God's church, in a distinctive way, lives under the mandate for renewal and acknowledges the renewing power of the Holy Spirit.

Third Conviction. The church is a covenant people. The meaning of the covenant has special importance in the United Church of Christ, because many of its local churches were established by Christians coming together and entering into a covenant, declaring their purposes and accepting their responsibilities. Behind this practice lies the far older meaning of "covenant," which is shared throughout the ecumenical church.

The significance of the covenant is rooted deep in the Old Testament, which tells of God's covenants, noted in the Second Declaration above, with Noah, with Abraham, with Moses and the children of Israel. The prophets repeatedly called on the people to be true to the covenant. Jeremiah prophesied the day of a covenant written on human hearts, a covenant rising out of God's forgiveness (31:31–34). And, as the apostle Paul tells us, "the Lord Jesus on the night when he was betrayed" said: "This cup is the new covenant in my blood [1 Cor. 11:23, 25]." Actually the phrases "Old Testament" and "New Testament" might more accurately be translated "Old Covenant" and "New Covenant"—and both covenants (as we have seen in the Fourth Declaration) are inviolably important.

Since public law often describes legal contracts as covenants—sometimes real estate covenants that express human prejudice—it is important for the church to remember the nature of its belief about the covenant. The Christian covenant is not simply an agreement between consenting people, who are free to break it by mutual agreement. It is a covenant between people of faith and God, the Creator and Renewer of the church.

Fourth Conviction. The church, which often needs to be reminded of its contemporary responsibilities, needs to remember also that it is not merely contemporary. It includes— today—the great cloud of witnesses (Heb. 12:1) who stretch back through the centuries. The covenant is far older than the United States of America or the British Empire—it is older than any nation. "Faithful people of all ages" constitute the church. We today must live in our time, as people of the past have lived in theirs. But we are what we are because we stand in this long succession. The United Church of Christ does not have a doctrine of apostolic succession in the sense of an ordained hierarchy stretching back through the ages; it recognizes a profound apostolic succession of all Christians.

Likewise the church includes people of all tongues and races. On Pentecost, it is recorded, the Holy Spirit enabled people of different languages to understand one another. Ever since, the Holy Spirit has continued that work. Today, despite the remarkable techniques of linguistic science and simultaneous translation, languages separate people—sometimes by barriers that can be overcome only by the Holy Spirit.

Early in its history the church welcomed into its membership Jews and Greeks, Romans and Ethiopians, slaves and free folk of many nations. The Revelation to John foresaw the church as "a great multitude that no one could count, from every nation, from all tribes and peoples and languages [Rev. 7:9]." That vision is still unfulfilled; yet it has in significant degree been realized. The church, which to its shame has sometimes heightened human hostilities, has also reconciled people across national and racial antagonisms. Today, in the midst of racial strife and wars hot or cold, Christians pray for those who differ with them. They recognize their unity in Christ as they strive for reconciliation.

It is a strange heresy that rejects racial equality—or that regards it as a peculiar concern of "social action" that stands apart from prayer and faith. Christians are bound by a covenant with God to brothers and sisters in the faith, regardless of race, tongue, or nation. To raise barriers between people, because of differences that are part of God's creation, is to violate the covenant.

The church, to repeat a point, is not the possession of its members. It is created and renewed by God's Holy Spirit.

THE SIXTH DECLARATION

God Calls to Discipleship

> You call us into your church
>> to accept the cost and joy of discipleship,
>> to be your servants in the service of others,
>> to proclaim the gospel to all the world
>>> and resist the powers of evil,
>> to share in Christ's baptism and eat at his table,
>> to join him in his passion and victory.

The Call

God calls the church to a mission in the world. The covenant community is a missionary community. The word *mission* comes from a Latin verb that means "send." To have a mission is to be sent.

The church is a called-and-sent community. God creates the church by gathering and binding in covenant those who respond to God's work in Christ. God sends the church on a mission.

The mission of the church—this is the remarkable fact that must cause the church always to wonder—is the mission of Christ. The church, of course, is subordinate to Christ; its mission is one of discipleship. But that mission is a participation in Christ's mission.

We have (in the Fourth Declaration) looked at Paul's description of this mission. "In Christ God was reconciling the world to himself." And, says Paul, God through Christ "has given us the ministry of reconciliation [2 Cor. 5:18]." The church exists to celebrate and carry on the activity of Christ.

85

In another phrase from the New Testament, the church is "the body of Christ" in the world today. Like any collection of human beings, it is many other things as well—an organization with buildings, treasuries, rules and procedures, officers, human rivalries, status symbols—and some of these sadly interfere with its mission. Yet the very criticisms that we make of the church come from the recognition of its high calling.

Cost and Joy

The call to discipleship reminds us of Jesus, who called the first disciples in the neighborhood of the Sea of Galilee. The records of those calls are tantalizingly brief. Sometimes the Gospels report only that Jesus said, "Follow me [Mark 2:14]" or "Follow me and I will make you fish for people [Mark 1:17]." A few people heard that call and followed. We might like more details, but in the cryptic record one thing is unmistakable. The disciples were a called-and-sent group. They gathered around Jesus. In shared experiences they came to know and trust him. But they were not permitted to remain basking in the warm glow of friendship and the ecstasy of religious experience—although on at least one occasion they wanted to do just that (Mark 9:5). They were called to a mission.

It was a costly mission. Jesus lured nobody with promises of prestige or affluent living. At least once he rebuffed an enthusiast who thought he wanted to follow Jesus but did not realize what a radical venture he was about to walk into. Discipleship meant discipline, commitment, and danger. According to tradition, the first twelve disciples (excepting only Judas Iscariot) became martyrs for Christ. Centuries later another Christian, Dietrich Bonhoeffer, after writing a book called *The Cost of Discipleship,* found that the cost for him was a concentration camp and death by hanging.

But God calls us "to accept the cost *and joy* of discipleship."

Jesus led his disciples in a life not of grim duty but of eager opportunity. He came that we might "have life, and have it abundantly [John 10:10]."

In the Beatitudes at the beginning of the Sermon on the Mount, Jesus expresses the joy of the life into which he calls us (Matt. 5:3–11). Blessed, he says, are the poor in spirit, the merciful, the pure in heart, the peacemakers. Blessed are those who hunger for righteousness and are persecuted for righteousness' sake. Our English translation, "blessed," sounds more pious than the Greek word in the New Testament. The Gospels, reporting Jesus' sayings, use the Greek word for "exuberant joy."

In a society where church membership is often a convenient habit, the Statement of Faith reminds us that God calls us into the church "to accept the cost and joy of discipleship." Those who are called are also sent. A disciple (a learner) is an apostle (messenger). God today calls disciples and apostles. All Christ's followers live in an "apostolic succession" (see the Fifth Declaration), called to be disciples and apostles in a mission that is both costly and joyful.

Servants in Service

"Servant" is not the most attractive of words. A servant is somebody who does a job for somebody else. In biblical times a servant might be either a slave or a hired worker—and the language of the time does not always distinguish between the two. But biblical writers, starting in the Old Testament and continuing in the New, gave the common word a special meaning.

We have already looked at the theme of the Suffering Servant expressed in several poems in the book of Isaiah.[1] We have seen that God's Suffering Servant has a healing and saving vocation for humankind. It may be that Jesus, who knew the book of Isaiah well, consciously conceived his ministry in the light of the Suffering Servant. What is sure is that Jesus' followers found these poems helpful in their understanding of him. They had hailed Jesus as Messiah (Christ). The Messiah was expected to be a heroic king, a conqueror, a ruler who would establish justice. Jesus, contrary to messianic expectations, died on a cross. His followers might have decided that he was not really the Messiah they looked for. Instead, they transformed their idea of a Messiah into that of a Suffering Servant who is yet Lord. One of the earliest Christian liturgies, included in the letter to the Philippians (2:7–8) says that Christ Jesus, "taking the form of a slave . . . humbled himself and became obedient to the point of death—even death on a cross."

In recent years emerging theologies of liberation—whether feminist, black, or Latin American—have protested against a misuse of the theme of the Suffering Servant. They have shown forcefully how people in power have commended the life of the Suffering Servant to oppressed people. Sometimes the oppressed have thought it their duty to accept injustice as though it were somehow God's will for them.

The liberationists are surely right in saying that Christian faith should not justify acquiescence in injustice. In the original biblical poems, the prophet hears God say of the servant:

> "I have put my spirit upon him,
> he will bring forth justice to the nations."
> —Isaiah 42:1

The Statement of Faith declares that we, following Christ, are called to be God's servants in the service of others. The mission of the church is not to seek honor and authority for itself; it is to enter into the suffering of human life, to work for justice among the nations, to bring healing and forgiveness to a sinful humankind.

"Service" has become a common word in the life of the twentieth century. Business and professional people belong to service clubs; we take our cars regularly to service stations; we read advertisements that promise superior service. The American economy, we sometimes hear, is shifting from an industrial to a service economy. We should not disdain this ordinary, even commercialized use of the word. It reminds us that in ordinary human life we depend upon one another and we need mutual service. The routines of making a living, as Jesus sometimes showed, may be parables of human life.

But the parable should lead us to the deeper reality. Jesus Christ was a servant who loved, shared, and suffered. God calls the church to participate in Christ's mission, to be servants in the service of others.

Proclaiming the Gospel

An integral part of the reconciling ministry is the telling of the good news of Christ to the world. By placing the proclamation of the gospel in the midst of the description of the Christian mission, the Statement of Faith suggests its significance. It is not the whole mission of the church, yet it is essential to that mission.

There are times when "service of others" means that works of justice and love are more important than any talk about faith. There are other times when the telling of the gospel is more important than any good works. No doubt there are Christians who in the diversity of gifts are especially effective in one task or the other. But the Christian mission is incomplete without both.

On the one hand, some Christians occasionally talk as though the aim of missionary activity were simply to spread the message of Christ, and the effectiveness of missions were to be measured by the number of converts. But the New Testament and the teaching of Jesus do not support this judgment. On the other hand, the church is not solely a social service agency, aiming to help people but indifferent to their beliefs. Rather the church has heard the words, "Go therefore and make disciples of all nations [Matt. 28:19]."

Through the centuries the church has spread the news of Christ with remarkable results. A vast part of humankind has heard the message. Many have believed and have become part of the church. The entire church in Europe, the Americas, Africa, and most of Asia is the result of missionary activity. Today most Christians who value their life in the covenant community owe gratitude to missionaries past or present.

The missionary story at its best has been a stirring epic. Christians—people of genius and very ordinary people— have felt stirred by God to spread the news of Christ. With no incentive of profit and no expectation of personal gain, they have accepted hardship, danger, and death. In their reconciling ministry they have taken educational activities, agricultural skills, and the arts of medicine with the gospel.

There have been many other factors in the spread of Christianity, some of them quite alien to the spirit of Christ. Kings have marched armies through rivers in mass baptisms. Political, commercial, and military forces have hopelessly confused Christianity with imperial aims. Some persons and societies have accepted Christianity as the religion of a more advanced or more powerful culture—a familiar phenomenon in the history of many religions.

Today that situation is passing. Increasingly the world resents imperialism. Many societies are discovering that they can import Western technology and weapons without importing Western religion.

The church can, for the most part, be grateful for this change. Christians will not agree with the naive faith that technology and weapons will solve all human problems. But they can welcome a situation in which people can make their own response to the Christian message, freed from economic, political, or cultural pressures.

Christians will continue to proclaim the gospel, because they believe it is truly good news. There is no reason—certainly no biblical reason—to expect all the world to accept it. In addition to the natural human resistance to God—a resistance that Christians know in themselves as well as outside themselves—there are two main reasons why many people do not find the Christian message convincing.

The first is that Christians are often such poor representatives of the gospel. A message of reconciliation, unconnected with deeds of reconciliation, is not convincing. Christians have, to their shame, made Christ a symbol to many people of white supremacy, of outside domination, even of persecution. Often when people reject Christ, they are really rejecting his messengers. Before criticizing those who reject Christ, Christians need always to ask, "Is it our fault?"

A second reason is that many people in all parts of the world find strength and meaning in other faiths—a theme I have touched on earlier (the Fourth and Fifth Declarations). These may be ancient faiths, embodying wisdom and insights of centuries of experience, or they may be modern faiths in their great variety. The Christian mission in such cases is not to argue for the superiority of "our" religion as against "theirs." We want people everywhere to hear the story and make their own free responses. If the influence of Christ makes Hindus more critical of the inequalities of caste, without converting them to Christianity, that too is a work of the ministry of reconciliation.

Christians will continue to tell the world of Christ. The aim will not be to pressure the world or to argue it into agreement. But the church cannot be silent about its faith. In gratitude to God, Christians will tell the news of God's deed in Christ and will carry on the reconciling ministry. Others, hearing and seeing, may make their own decisions.

The Statement of Faith at this point joins closely two phrases: "to proclaim the gospel to all the world and resist the powers of evil." That juxtaposition, which has seemed strange to some, comes directly from the work of Jesus. He sent out the twelve "to proclaim the message" and "to cast out demons [Mark 3:14–15]." The telling of the gospel inevitably means conflict with the demonic forces of our experience.

The Statement carefully avoids any suggestion that the world, as such, is evil. It particularly rejects any theme of struggle between the church (good) and the world (bad). It has earlier affirmed that this world is God's creation, that God loves the world, that God seeks to reconcile the cosmos to God. But it has also recognized the reality of sin.

But the Statement recognizes that the proclamation of the gospel meets antagonism. Not always. Sometimes the response is approval; sometimes, indifference; sometimes, opposition.

In this twentieth century the opposition has often been spectacular. Under the Nazi regime and in some other situations of racial strife (particularly in the United States and South Africa) the declaration of the gospel has been costly and dangerous for faithful Christians. The church has learned that the age of the martyrs is not restricted to ancient history. Communism, particularly in its Leninist-Stalinist mode, has repressed Christian (and other kinds of) freedom. In many less conspicuous situations, too, the Christian mission has encountered opposition from those who feel threatened by its call for justice and love. In the language of traditional doctrine, this is the age of the church militant, not the church triumphant.

Perhaps the most common response of "the powers of evil," particularly in our time, is not to oppose the Christian message but to seduce or corrupt it. People claim the gospel for their own unholy purposes, change it into an ideology supporting their partisan interests, build religious institutions that shield them from the demands of God. Christians who tell the good news of Christ must resist the powers of evil that operate at large and that tempt them from within.

To Share in Christ's Passion and Victory

Sharing in Christ's passion and victory is a bold claim, too bold, some have said. I shall come to that issue soon. But immediately the Statement of Faith relates that claim to the sacraments. God calls us "to share in Christ's baptism and eat at his table, to join him in his passion and victory." The sacraments are not the only way of sharing with Christ. They may even be a sinful evasion of more demanding ways. But they are one way, a real way and a profoundly symbolic way.

Baptism and the Lord's Supper, going back to Jesus himself, have always been major celebrations of faith and marks of the church. Curiously the classical creeds have given them little attention. The Apostles' Creed does not mention either. The Nicene Creed refers to "one baptism for the remission of sins" but says nothing about the Holy Communion. But in Christian history, baptism and the Lord's Supper have been central acts of worship throughout the ages.

The Statement of Faith does not develop a specific doctrine of the sacraments. That is an issue which the church continues to discuss—recently in the *BEM* document, mentioned in part one of this book. But the Statement puts the sacraments in a context—a context important in the Bible and church history but strange to many modern Christians.

In the practice of recent centuries the church has often assigned the sacraments to the inner (almost the introspective) or the institutional life of the church, as contrasted with the outward reach of the Christian mission. Sometimes the church has found within itself cults of sacramentalists, who like ceremonial worship, and activists, who want to change the world. The Statement of Faith includes the sacraments within the article on God's call to mission. It relates them closely to life in the world—as does the New Testament.

The sacraments are the acts—rather, some of the acts—in which Christians join themselves to Christ "in his passion and victory." But is it pretentious, or even irreverent, to say that we share in Christ's baptism? Is Christ's baptism something quite different from ours?

Let us notice immediately that the Statement does not say that every ceremony of baptism is a sharing in Christ's baptism. It says instead that God "calls us . . . to share in Christ's baptism." From this point we can go on to investigate three themes in the discussion of baptism in the New Testament.

The first theme is the baptism of Jesus himself by John the Baptist (Matt. 3:13–17; Mark 1:9–11; and Luke 3:21–22). This baptism bothered some of the early Christians. Baptism, they thought, was for ordinary mortals; Jesus had no need of baptism. Mark and Luke do not raise this issue, but Matthew does. He reports that John the Baptist protested that Jesus should not be baptized by John, but Jesus insisted on the act in order "to fulfill all righteousness." Here it seems clear that Jesus, as a genuine human being, shared with other human beings in baptism.

The second theme arose when James and John made their foolish request for an honored place in glory. Jesus asked them whether they could be baptized with his baptism. They replied, again too brashly, that they could. Jesus answered: "With the baptism with which I am baptized, you will be baptized; but to sit at my right hand or at my left is not mine to grant [Mark 10:39–40]." The church has usually taken this to mean that these disciples, despite their present stupidity and naiveté, would share in a baptism of suffering yet to come.

The third theme was developed by Paul, who understood baptism as the symbol of our death and resurrection with Christ. "We have been buried with him by baptism into death, so that, just as Christ was raised from the dead by the glory of the Father, so we too might walk in newness of life [Rom. 6:4; see also Gal. 2:20]."

In each of these cases the belief is that Jesus shares in human baptism and that we share in his baptism. This discussion all centers on one major point. Baptism, as a sacramental and ceremonial act, is the symbol of something far more than ceremonial—the entrance into the missionary community that continues Christ's reconciling ministry and shares in his death and resurrection. Far from being an exclusively "religious" act, baptism sends the Christian into the life of the world.

Much the same may be said of the Lord's Supper. It began with the last meal of Jesus with his disciples the night before his crucifixion. Throughout the centuries of history new generations of disciples have repeated that act. It is known also as the Holy Communion, the Eucharist ("thanksgiving"), and the Mass (a word related to "mission"). These names have valid and important meanings, but they have sometimes helped people to forget that the Lord's Supper is a shared meal. Our forms of celebrating it also tend to hide any resemblance to a common supper. But it is important to realize that the central sacrament of Christian faith is a meal—as "worldly" an act as anything that people do.

At the General Synod that adopted the Statement of Faith, a delegate asked whether so common a word as "eat" was appropriate in the Statement. Might not "commune" be an improvement? But Jesus, according to the scriptural record, used the common word. "Take, eat," he said (Matt. 26:26). So the act of eating becomes one sign of the Christian's recognition of the cost and joy of discipleship.

Believing in God, I have said earlier, is an act of faith. Now I should add that celebration of the sacraments is also an act of faith. Protestants and Catholics, who used to differ on that issue, increasingly agree. Although Hans Küng is not the most orthodox of Roman Catholic theologians, he speaks for a growing consensus when he writes: "Neither the word nor the sacrament work automatically; if they find no faith they cannot function."[2] In infant baptism the emphasis is on the faith of the church, the faith that God loves the infant before the infant is capable of loving God. In adult baptism and the Lord's Supper, the emphasis is on the faith of both the church and the individual in their response to Christ.

Baptism and the Lord's Supper are thus memorials and living symbols of Christ's passion and victory, in which the Christian is called to join. If the last few paragraphs have emphasized the passion, the next ones will emphasize the victory.

THE SEVENTH DECLARATION

God Promises

You promise to all who trust you
    forgiveness of sins and fullness of grace,
    courage in the struggle for justice and peace,
    your presence in trial and rejoicing,
    and eternal life in your realm which has no end.

A God Who Promises

What does it mean to believe in a God who promises? That is not an easy idea for us to wrap our minds around. Yet the Bible is filled with statements about the promises of God— promises to Noah, to Abraham, and to many another. We read that God's promises prove true, that God never lies. This language comes out of a world different from our own, where we often demand that promises be signed in triplicate, witnessed, notarized, and enforceable in court.

The promises of God meet none of those requirements. We may wonder how men and women of the Bible *knew* and *verified* that God had made promises. If we try to enter their world, we realize that they did not have our scientific picture of things. But they surely reflected upon their experience as intensely as we do on ours. When they talked of God's promises, they were less inhibited in their imagination than we. Usually they took their visions and dreams more seriously than we. Even so, they knew that imagination, visions, and dreams are often deceptive. Like us, they had to sort out truth from illusion.

The prophets criticized vain imagination and wishful thinking about God. The people they addressed had to check out their beliefs about God with their daily experience, to sift the many mistaken religious ideas from the few that held good. So when biblical writers expressed trust in the promises of God, they were not simply taking the word of some seer. They knew that the seers were wrong as often as they were right.

Trust in God's promises, then as now, required some confirmation in experience. Some claims for God's promises were shattered by events. Some held up for a long time, then collapsed. When people believed, as some of them clearly did, that God guaranteed victory in battle, prosperity to the righteous, long life to the faithful, those beliefs smashed against grim realities. But some beliefs stood the test of long experience in good times and bad.

We might make a comparison with astronauts, who trust that their spaceships will stay in orbit and will not capriciously hurtle out into interplanetary space. They know that accidents can happen, but some guarantees of nature are reliable. We can quickly see the difference between the astronauts' trust in nature and the biblical prophets' trust in God. The former can be tested by measurements and experiments that are publicly verifiable; the latter, even though the experience of a community and not merely of individuals, is not testable by the same devices. But in both cases there is an assurance that, though never totally proved, is validated in experience.

The biblical faith in God's promises does not depend on the reports of any individuals about what God secretly told them. It depends upon the conviction of a community of faith about the character of God. To say that God keeps promises is to say that God is faithful and reliable, that God's character as revealed to the faithful is constant, that God can be trusted. That is why Paul can write to his friends at Corinth that "God is faithful [2 Cor. 1:18]" and "every one of God's promises is a 'Yes'" in Christ (1:20). That is why contemporary Christians, no less than the people of the Bible, can talk of the promises of God. We do not simply take on authority words out of the past. We have the same responsibility as people of old to sift out truth from error.

Hence we can quickly say that God does *not* promise us freedom from suffering. We know that, both from the story of Jesus and from our experience of the world. God does not promise us triumph over our enemies. God does not promise "success" to the virtuous. God does not promise immunity to disease. God does not even promise—a new lesson that this generation has learned for the first time—that human beings will not destroy their world with weapons of their own invention. We have today a jarring awareness of the radical freedom God has given us.

Four Promises of God

Yet the Statement of Faith confesses a belief in the promises of God. It affirms four of these.

1. Forgiveness and grace. In affirming forgiveness and grace the Statement builds upon its earlier declarations. Addressing God, it has said, "You seek in holy love to save all people from aimlessness and sin," and "in Jesus Christ you have come to us, . . . conquering sin and death and reconciling the world to yourself." Now it continues, "You promise to all who trust you forgiveness of sins and fullness of grace."

Forgiveness comes close to the center of the gospel. We have already looked at the Christian understanding of sin (the Second Declaration). As Christians, we seek forgiveness.

In the Lord's Prayer, as reported by Luke, Jesus tells us to say: "Forgive us our sins, for we ourselves forgive everyone indebted to us [Luke 11:4]." That version requires us to make a claim that for most of us would be arrogant and untrue:

"We ourselves forgive everyone who is indebted to us." Matthew is not much gentler: "Forgive us our debts, as we also have forgiven our debtors [Matt. 6:12]."

Usually we ask for something more than that. We should like God to forgive us before checking to be sure that we have forgiven all who have offended us. Indeed, part of the very sin that we need to be forgiven is our inability to forgive others.

God, who has come to us in Christ, does even that. As Jesus said, "I have come to call not the righteous but sinners [Matt. 9:13]." Forgiveness extends to the prodigal son, to the guilty tax collector whose only prayer was "God, be merciful to me, a sinner!," to the repentant thief on the cross.

In our modern sophistication we often seek to get rid of "guilt complexes"—an idea with some merit, no doubt. But often it is easier to get rid of the complex than of the guilt. We may evade guilt with an "innocence complex." The good news is that God offers forgiveness.

In recent years many Christians have learned to sing an old hymn that begins, "Amazing grace, how sweet the sound, that saved a wretch like me." That song had long been out of style when the Statement of Faith was first adopted in 1959. Then it leapt back into prominence, as though speaking to a long-suppressed need. It is not the whole of Christian faith. No one song is. We are not solely wretches, but if we cannot acknowledge the wretchedness in us, we do not understand ourselves. The song is too individualistic in its concentration on inner experience and its neglect of everything else. And it may be too complacent, as though salvation were so completely accomplished that no struggle is left. And yet it makes the testimony often neglected by modern Christians. We are saved by grace, by God's amazing grace.

"Grace," like a few other words in the Christian vocabulary, has a meaning and tone that cannot be entirely translated into any secular language. But, again like other words of faith, this one has roots in an ordinary, everyday meaning. We see it in the trio of words: *grace, gracious,* and *graceful.* A gracious act is done generously, magnanimously, with good will. A graceful act is beautiful, poised, and free. Painstakingly to live up to the letter of an agreement or to do a good deed grudgingly may sometimes be our duty, but it is neither gracious nor graceful. An act of grace goes beyond any requirements; it is done freely and in good spirit for the sake of another.

God's love, in the Great Story, is outgoing love—love beyond our deserving, love freely given, love that is concerned for our good rather than for the prerogatives of God. It is not sentimental love that protects us from hardships: it is constant love in the midst of prosperity or hardship. The Christian faith is that God extends such love to us, that God confers such love upon us so that we can ourselves act graciously.

In the Christian tradition, grace is understood in three ways: as common grace, as forgiveness, and as illumination and power. Common grace, a term used by Calvin, is the grace that sustains the whole creation, the grace that day in, day out supports us and our planet and our universe, whether we acknowledge it or not. It is the grace evident in plants and animals, in human athletes and artists, in family love, in scientific genius and human heroism wherever we find these. It is evident also in the daily lives of many ordinary people.

Grace as forgiveness is the "amazing grace" we have just been thinking about. In the language of the Statement, it saves us from aimlessness and sin. It does not relieve us of responsibility. Our sins are costly—to those we have harmed, to ourselves, and to God. But in the assurance of forgiveness, we find ourselves more ready to forgive others. In the healing of forgiveness, we are better able to live in thanksgiving, better able to be God's "servants in the service of others."

Grace as illumination and power is partly experience,

partly hope. In our confused and struggling world, "The light shines in the darkness, and the darkness did not overcome it [John 1:5]." Even as we tremble in darkness, we recognize the light and its power. Even as we struggle with sin, we recognize the power of love.

Life knows enough of grace to justify trust in God's promise of fullness of grace. The church remembers this whenever it hears the familiar benediction of Paul: "The grace of the Lord Jesus Christ, the love of God, and the communion of the Holy Spirit be with all of you [2 Cor. 13:13]."

2. Courage in struggle. Another of God's promises is "courage in the struggle for justice and peace." Underlying this belief is the confidence in the *ultimate* victory of justice and peace. But human history as we know it shows many partial victories and many partial defeats in struggles for justice and peace. We have no promise of victory in every struggle. What God promises is courage in the struggle.

There is a tension in the language of "struggle" for "peace." In the ecumenical discussions of the Statement of Faith, prior to its adoption by the General Synod, the commission received one friendly criticism of the Statement from Christians in Germany. Their point was that "peace" is a gift of God, not an attainment of human struggle. That led to discussions within the United Church of Christ about the character of peace, a word with rich meanings in the Bible.

The critics made an important point. There is in Christian experience a peace, an inner serenity, that comes from trust in God. It is a peace that endures in the midst of outer conflict and peril. It is "the peace of God, which surpasses all understanding [Phil. 4:7]," "the peace of Christ" that may rule in human hearts (Col. 3:15). This peace is not attained through struggle. It is a gift of grace—although like all gifts of grace it requires a response from us.

There is another important meaning of peace—peace

among the nations and among the people within the nations. It is a peace based on justice. It is the peace of the prophecy:

> They shall beat their swords into plowshares,
>   and their spears into pruning hooks;
> nation shall not lift up sword against nation,
>   neither shall they learn war any more.
>   —Isaiah 2:4; Micah 4:3

This peace is also a gift. It is not a packaged gift that we find under the Christmas tree. As the prophets describe it, it shall come to pass "in days to come." It stands on the horizon of our history, never entirely realized, luring us forward and influencing our conduct now.

At just this point, human efforts make a difference. There are policies that make for injustice and war, and policies that make for justice and peace. A great and prosperous nation can support justice or inflict justice in far parts of the world. It can help to spare people from starvation, can improve educational opportunities, can sponsor medical programs, can offer to settle disputes through international organizations rather than through threats and warfare. None of these policies can guarantee world peace. But they can make a difference. The Jesus who said, "Peace I leave with you; my peace I give to you [John 14:27]," also said, "Blessed are the peacemakers [Matt. 5:9]." That gives us a responsibility. We are called to enter into "the struggle for justice and peace." Our prayers for peace will not be for some divine intervention that will end war apart from our acts; they will include prayers for courage and wisdom in the struggle for peace.

We have been considering justice and peace together, because ultimately, if not at every hour of history, they belong together. As Augustine wrote in *The City of God*, an unjust peace is not truly peace. It is a spurious imitation of peace. Hence we return to the prophetic demand that we have seen earlier. The prophets knew that no evasions and no pious ceremonies could satisfy God's requirement of justice.

> He has told you, O mortal, what is good:
> and what does the LORD require of you
> but to do justice, and to love kindness,
> and to walk humbly with your God?
> —Micah 6:8

Jesus continued this prophetic heritage. He criticized the religious leaders who performed their ceremonial duties with meticulous care but "neglected the weightier matters of the law: justice and mercy and faith [Matt. 23:23]." He brought "good news to the poor" and "let the oppressed go free [Luke 4:18]."

If the church is faithful to Christ, it will take up the cause of those who suffer from poverty, racial discrimination, and oppression. Sometimes the church does that. Too often it forgets. Over the course of time the church has become one of the established institutions of society. It is made up largely, in North America and many other parts of the world, of people who have a fairly good position in their society and are therefore content with things as they are. They tend to resent any change—even a change for justice—that disturbs the social order or threatens their privileges.

Karl Marx maintained that every group's outlook upon the world, including its ideas of right and wrong, is determined largely by economic interests. It is easier to argue with Marx than to demonstrate by actions that he is wrong. Christians refute Marx when they think and act for justice, even though that justice will be costly to themselves.

It is easy for even well-meaning people to deceive themselves on issues like this. For example, white people may theoretically favor racial justice even at the cost of their privileged position in society. But in a time of social change, which is almost always a time of confusion and conflict, they are likely to value peace, even unjust peace, above justice. Prosperous people may theoretically favor justice for the poor, but easily find objections to all specific antipoverty programs. The American society with its wealth and power may still believe in "liberty and justice for all"; but we have trouble understanding the hopes of people who are more eager for justice than for a stable world.

The theologians of liberation that have flourished since the formulation of the Statement of Faith often emphasize the importance of seeing history "from the underside." Long ago some Hebrew slaves in Egypt saw the world as the pharaoh was incapable of seeing it. Those who suffer injustice today have experiences of the world that are hidden from those who are comfortable. The church cannot always be a mediating force between groups in conflict; sometimes it is called to follow God by entering into the struggle on the side of the oppressed.

Peace, detached from justice, easily becomes the ideology of the comfortable. Christians have special reason to be on their guard against this temptation. Long ago Jeremiah heard God's warning against the prophets and priests of that time:

> They have treated the wound of my people carelessly,
>   saying "Peace, peace,"
>   when there is no peace.
>
> —Jeremiah 6:14

The Prince of Peace actually brought disruption into the world. On one occasion Jesus said: "Do not think that I have come to bring peace to the earth; I have not come to bring peace, but a sword [Matt. 10:34]."

That last statement, of course, has been taken out of context to justify all kinds of hostility, including destruction of enemies with no aim of reconciliation. The point is that justice and peace alike belong in a context that includes both.

We may have deep perplexities about the way to relate the two in many specific situations. We may not know precisely when peace means the end of struggle and when justice requires a struggle. But we cannot evade the issue. The ministry of reconciliation, as the life of Jesus shows, sometimes brings disturbance and strife into society. Yet its purpose remains, in the most profound sense, peace.

So Christians are called to act for justice and peace. *Courage in the Struggle for Justice and Peace* has become the title of a monthly publication within the United Church of Christ. The struggle continues. Evil is persistent in our world. God promises not easy victories, but courage in the struggle.

3. God's presence. The third promise is God's presence "in trial and rejoicing." Life knows both. In a precarious existence we never know what tomorrow will bring.

It is strange that Christians have sometimes expected that their faith and obedience would spare them from trials. Ordinary experience tells us that human life is uncertain, sometimes painful, and always mortal. In pain and death we learn what it is to be creatures and not gods. Even more, when we look at Christ, we know that the most faithful may endure agonizing pain, that faithful living may lead us into suffering.

The Christian life may, in fact, avoid some of the sufferings that can be called "the wages of sin." The Christian virtues include prudential virtues that make life move more smoothly, and many of us try to teach our children ways of staying out of trouble. But the Christian life also includes responsibilities and risks that a shrewd self-interest can easily avoid. As Jesus walked knowingly into life's trials, his followers will do the same.

The influence of Christianity upon the world has brought relief to some sufferings. Medical missions, education, and the spread of a humanitarian spirit have lifted burdens from humankind. Yet the twentieth century has brought intense suffering to millions of people, often without regard to their religious faith. Sometimes they have suffered specifically because of their faith.

Christians in countries of relative freedom and security know that they are bound in the covenant community with Christians who have maintained their faith through persecution. The fortunate need to remember their sisters and brothers in peril, but they need to remember also the trials of prosperity. Some years ago, at a tense time in the Cold War, an American at an ecumenical gathering said something about praying for the church behind the "iron curtain." The reply came gently but pointedly: "We want your prayers, if you want ours." Suddenly the Americans realized with new force the trials of life in an affluent society where the church may be corrupted by ease rather than battered by persecution.

Life, which has its trials, both of hardship and prosperity, has also its occasions of authentic rejoicing. It is a mistake so to emphasize God's support in suffering as to forget God in the exultancy of life. "Joy" and "rejoicing" are frequent words of scripture. Believers naturally call upon God at weddings as truly as at funerals—not only because of the solemnity of the marriage vows but also because of the sheer joy of marital love.

When we ask God's presence, whether in trial or rejoicing, God will be there. Indeed, God will be there, whether or not we ask. Often it is easy to forget, convenient to ignore God. But wanted or not, God is with us in trial and rejoicing.

4. Eternal life. The culminating promise of God in the Statement of Faith is eternal life. In the versions of 1959 and 1977, that life is located in God's "kingdom which has no end." The revision of 1981 changes the wording to the "realm which has no end." That change is consistent with the desire for a gender-inclusive language. Some have objected to any change in a phrase so important to the New Testament as "the kingdom of God." But a generation ago the much admired translation of the Bible by James Moffatt (final revision, 1935) used "realm" or "reign" instead of "kingdom" throughout the Gospels. The Statement of 1981 is not changing the New Testament; it reflects the kind of judgment that translators are always making.

The important affirmation here is that the God of Creation is the God of our final destiny. The God who gave us life will not desert us at the end. This has been the faith of Christians ever since the first of them told the world that Christ had risen from the dead.

The way in which Christians have visualized and conceptualized their final destiny—the doctrine of "last things," or eschatology—has varied. One theologian has observed that the Statement of Faith includes some equivalent for all the major affirmations of the Apostles' Creed, except possibly one: "He ascended into heaven, and sitteth on the right hand of God the Father Almighty; from thence he shall come to judge the quick and the dead." The Statement affirms that God is the ultimate Judge of people and nations (the Third Declaration) and that God's promises include eternal life. It gives no details about the end of the world, the return of Christ in judgment, and the nature of heaven and hell.

One reason is that our imaginative depictions of the ultimate future are likely to be more restrained than those of past centuries. Just how much they have changed is hard to say. Perhaps some Christians took quite literally that statement in the Apostles' Creed; possibly a few took literally even the biblical descriptions of the New Jerusalem with its gates of pearl and streets of gold. Even today some try to predict Middle Eastern politics and wars, even recommend American foreign policy in that region, from biblical prophecies. Most do not.

A literal understanding of the statement in the Apostles' Creed would mean that God had a body with a right arm and a left. One of the great Christian thinkers of the past, Augustine, for a time thought that he could not accept Christian faith because he could not believe that God had a body. When he realized that the Bible taught that God is Spirit and that he did not have to take literally language about God's "right hand," a block to his conversion was removed.

Today we are likely to be skeptical of traditional attempts to describe the outcome of life and history. We reject the three-story picture of the universe with heaven above, hell below, and the earth between. We may do this too smugly; the past was probably wiser than we think, and there is no reason to assume that our generation is the arbiter of truth for all time. But we are true to the gospel if we realize that our trust in God does not depend upon specific pictures of the future that were prominent long ago.

The Bible itself is more restrained in its affirmations than many later believers have been. Jesus refused to elaborate on the future. His major statement about the future judgment is cast in the form of a parable (Matt. 25:31–46). It is meant very seriously, but the language of the throne and the sheep and the goats is a reminder not to take it too literally. On another occasion, when questioned about the future, Jesus candidly acknowledged the limitations of his knowledge and said that only the Father knew (Matt. 24:36). More important than any conjectures is the trust with which Jesus met life and death. In both his acceptance of limitations and his assurance he can be our guide.

The Christian confidence is that our destiny is in the care of the eternal God, whose steadfast love is not defeated by our sin or our death. In Jesus Christ, God has won a victory over both sin and death. Those who trust God have already begun to experience eternal life: for "this is eternal life, that they know you, the only true God, and Jesus Christ whom you have sent [John 17:3]."

Day in and day out, year in and year out, the church prays in the prayer of Jesus: "Your kingdom [or reign, or realm] come." The prayer reminds us of an older prayer: "Your kingdom is an everlasting kingdom [Ps. 145:13]." In Christ we are assured that we have a place in that realm. What more do we need to know?

If some Christians want to say more than the Statement says about eternal life, that is entirely appropriate. Presumably most Christians want to say more than this brief Statement says about other subjects as well. It is good to say more—but with one warning: no elaboration of belief, whether in terms of traditional doctrine or contemporary conjecture, can take the place of the trust in God that is the basis of Christian hope. A frantic effort to peer into the future is an evasion of the real issue: the trust in God that sustains life now and gives us confidence for our future.

With this trust we can say with the apostle Paul: "I am convinced that neither death, nor life, nor angels, nor rulers, nor things present, nor things to come, nor powers, nor height, nor depth, nor anything else in all creation, will be able to separate us from the love of God in Christ Jesus our Lord [Rom. 8:38–39]."

Then we may want to go on to look for the day when, as an imaginative writer put it, voices in heaven will say: "The kingdom of the world has become the kingdom of our Lord and of his Messiah, and he will reign forever and ever [Rev. 11:15]."

The Concluding Doxology

Blessing and honor, glory and power be unto you. Amen.

Following the seven declarations, the Statement of Faith ends with a doxology. In keeping with the Great Story, the final words come from the final book of the Bible.

In the first formulations of the Statement, people quickly recognized that the doxology came from Revelation. Yet nobody could find precisely those words in the Authorized (King James) Version, the Revised Standard Version, or any other translation of the Bible. They came close to Revelation 5:13 but were not quite the same. Yet the words were more hauntingly familiar than any of the recognized translations.

Repeating the words, some people began to hum them. Then they realized that the language comes from the English version of Handel's *Messiah*. Melody and words belong to the memories of countless Christians. Coming at the end of the Statement of Faith, they are a reminder of the comment of John Calvin (and many another after him) that a creed should be sung rather than said. Whether we say or sing it, a confession of faith is an act of worship—a testimony rather than a test of faith.

111

Notes

Part One: The Great Story and a Lesser Story

1. More than a generation ago the New Testament scholar E. F. Scott made this point in his book *The Lord's Prayer* (New York: Charles Scribner's Sons, 1951), p. 55.

2. The phraseology comes from the *Basis of Union of the Congregational Christian Churches and the Evangelical and Reformed Church with the Interpretations,* Article II. Faith, n. 3 and Article IV. Section F found in *The Shaping of the United Church of Christ,* by Louis H. Gunnemann (New York: United Church Press, 1977), pp. 208, 211.

3. Gustavo Gutiérrez, *A Theology of Liberation* (Maryknoll, N.Y.: Orbis Books, 15th anniversary ed., 1988), p. xviii.

4. William Temple, *Nature, Man and God* (London: Macmillan, 1934), p. 322.

5. *Basis of Union,* p. 4.

6. H. Richard Niebuhr, *The Meaning of Revelation* (New York: Macmillan, 1946), p. 43.

7. Harold K. Schilling, *Science and Religion* (New York: Charles Scribner's Sons, 1962), p. 135.

8. Louis H. Gunnemann, *The Shaping of the United Church of Christ* (New York: United Church Press, 1989), p. 70. The official record of the development and adoption of the Statement is in the Minutes of the Second General Synod, pp. 7–8, 27–30. 111–17. A more detailed and colorful account, written by Loring D. Chase, one of the co-secretaries of the commission, appeared in the *United Church Herald* of 26 March, 1959, reprinted in *Classical Christian Creeds* by Paul F. Mehl (Philadelphia: United Church Press, 1964). See also Harold E. Fey's news report in the *Christian Century,* 22 July 1959.

Part Two: The Deeds of God

PROLOGUE: The Confession of Faith

1. Roger L. Shinn and Daniel Day Williams, *We Believe* (Philadelphia: United Church Press, 1966), p. 36.

2. Walter Marshall Horton, *God* (New York: Association Press, a Hazen Book, 1937).

3. Joachim Jeremias, *The Central Message of the New Testament* (New York: Charles Scribner's Sons, 1965), ch. 1, "Abba." The Roman Catholic Edward Schillebeeckx has similarly emphasized the exceptional way in which Jesus addressed God as Abba.

4. *Ibid.,* p. 10.

5. W. A. Visser 't Hooft, *The Kingship of Christ* (New York: Harper & Brothers, 1948), p. 46. The title, with its word *Kingship,* involves the same gender problems that concern the church today.

6. Barbara Brown Zikmund, "The Trinity and Women's Experience," *Christian Century,* 15 April 1987, p. 355.

THE FIRST DECLARATION: **God Creates**

1. Reinhold Niebuhr, *Discerning the Signs of the Times* (New York: Charles Scribner's Sons, 1946), ch. 8.

2. Harvey Cox, *The Secular City* (New York: Macmillan, 1965), pp. 24, 82.

3. Quoted by H. Richard Niebuhr in *Christian Ethics: Sources of the Living Tradition,* edited by Waldo Beach and Niebuhr, 2nd ed., p. 382 (New York: Ronald Press, 1973).

4. Dietrich Bonhoeffer, *Creation and Fall:* A Theological Interpretation of Genesis 1—3 (first German ed. 1937, New York: Macmillan, 1959), pp. 30–37.

THE SECOND DECLARATION: **God Seeks to Save**

1. Karl Menninger, *Whatever Became of Sin?* (New York: Hawthorne Books, 1973), p. 18.

THE FOURTH DECLARATION: **God Comes to Us in Christ**

1. Albert Schweitzer, *The Quest of the Historical Jesus,* 2nd English ed. (London: A. C. Black, 1911), p. 401.

2. Karl Barth, conversation with Tübingen students, reported by Eberhard Busch, *Karl Barth: His Life from Letters and Autobiographical Texts,* trans. from 2nd rev. ed., 1976 (Philadelphia: Fortress Press, 1976), p. 284.

3. Dietrich Bonhoeffer, *Letters and Papers from Prison,* enlarged ed. (New York: Macmillan, 1972), letter of 16 July 1944.

4. Augustine, *The City of God* 12. 14, trans. Henry Bettenson. Augustine is quoting from Paul, Romans 6:9, and using Paul's words for his own purposes.

THE FIFTH DECLARATION: **God Bestows the Holy Spirit**

1. James Forbes, *The Holy Spirit and Preaching* (Nashville: Abingdon Press, 1989), pp. 23–100.

2. Henry P. Van Dusen, "The Holy Spirit and the United Church."
   United Church Herald, September 17, 1959, pp. 8–9, 31–32. Van
   Dusen had written a much discussed article in *Life*, "The Third Force
   in Christendom" (June 9, 1958) and a book, *Spirit, Son and Father:
   Christian Faith in the Light of the Holy Spirit* (New York: Scribners Sons,
   1958).

THE SIXTH DECLARATION: **God Calls to Discipleship**

1. Isaiah 42:1–4, 49:1–6, 50:4–9, 52:13—53:12. See the Fourth Declaration above.
2. Hans Küng, "God's Free Spirit in the Church," in *Freedom and Man*,
   edited by John Courtney Murray (New York: J. P. Kenedy & Sons,
   1965), p. 24.

CPSIA information can be obtained at www.ICGtesting.com
Printed in the USA
269989BV00001B/1/P